Consequences of Pragmatism

Consequences of Pragmatism
(Essays: 1972-1980)

Richard Rorty

University of Minnesota Press Minneapolis

Published by the University of Minnesota Press,
2037 University Avenue Southeast, Minneapolis, MN 55414
Printed in the United States of America.

Library of Congress Cataloging in Publication Data

Rorty, Richard.
    Consequences of pragmatism.

    Includes index.
    Contents: The world well lost—Keeping philosophy pure—
Overcoming the tradition—[etc.]
    1. Philosophy—Addresses, essays, lectures. I. Title.
B29.R625   144'.3   82-2597
ISBN 0-8166-1063-0   AACR2
ISBN 0-8166-1064-9 (pbk.)

The University of Minnesota
is an equal-opportunity
educator and employer.

To

Jay

Contents

Preface

This volume contains essays written during the period 1972-1980. They are arranged roughly in order of composition. Except for the Introduction, all have been published previously and are reprinted with minor changes, ranging from a few words here and there in the earlier essays to a few paragraphs here and there in the later ones. I have updated footnote references in a few cases where it seemed particularly appropriate to do so. For the most part, however, I have made no attempt to refer to literature which has appeared since the essay was originally published (except for internal cross-references to other essays in this volume).

I no longer agree with everything said in these essays—particularly the ones written in the early seventies. Nor are they entirely consistent with one another. I reprint them nevertheless because, with one exception, the general drift of what they say still seems right. The exception is Essay 3—a piece comparing Heidegger and Dewey. I now think that my view of Heidegger in the concluding pages of that essay was unduly unsympathetic; but I reprint the essay in the hope that the earlier pages may be of interest. I hope to offer a more balanced and useful interpretation in a book on Heidegger which I am now writing.

Various other pieces which I wrote during this period have not been included—those which were largely polemical or technical in character. I have included only essays which might have some interest for readers outside of philosophy. I am grateful to readers of my *Philosophy and the Mirror of Nature* who have suggested that they would find it useful to have these essays more readily available. The essays treat in more detail various topics dealt with sketchily in that book.

Finally, I am grateful to Pearl Cavanaugh, Lee Ritins, Bunny Romano, Ann Getson, and Laura Bell for patient retyping, and to David Velleman for helpful editorial advice.

The provenance of the essays is as follows. I am most grateful to each of the editors and publishers of the journals and collections listed below for their permission to reprint.

Essay 1 ("The World Well Lost") was read to the Eastern Division of the American Philosophical Association in December of 1972, and commented upon by Bruce Aune and Milton Fisk. It appeared in *The Journal of Philosophy*, LXIX (1972): 649-665.

Essay 2 ("Keeping Philosophy Pure") appeared in *The Yale Review*, LXV (1976): 336-356.

Essay 3 ("Overcoming the Tradition: Heidegger and Dewey") was read to a conference on Heidegger held at the University of California at San Diego in 1974. It appeared in *The Review of Metaphysics*, XXX (1976): 280-305.

Essay 4 ("Professionalized Philosophy and Transcendentalist Culture") was read to the Bicentennial Symposium of Philosophy arranged by the City University of New York in 1976. It appeared first in *The Georgia Review*, XXX (1976): 757-769, and later (under the title "Genteel Syntheses, Professional Analyses, and Transcendentalist Culture") in the proceedings of the Bicentennial Symposium— *Two Centuries of Philosophy in America*, ed. Peter Caws (Oxford: Blackwell, 1980), pp. 228-239.

Essay 5 ("Dewey's Metaphysics") was one of a series of lectures on the philosophy of Dewey held at the University of Vermont in 1975, sponsored by the John Dewey Foundation. It appeared in *New Studies in the Philosophy of John Dewey*, ed. Steven M. Cahn (Hanover, N. H.: University Press of New England, 1977), pp. 45-74.

Essay 6 ("Philosophy as a Kind of Writing: An Essay on Derrida") appeared in *New Literary History*, X (1978-79): 141-160.

Essay 7 ("Is There a Problem about Fictional Discourse?") is a paper written for the tenth biannual gathering of the Arbeitsgruppe Poetik und Hermeneutik, held at Bad Homburg in 1979. It was published in *Funktionen des Fictiven: Poetik und Hermeneutik*, X (Munich: Fink Verlag, 1981).

Essay 8 ("Nineteenth-Century Idealism and Twentieth-Century Textualism") was written for a conference honoring Maurice Mandelbaum, held at the Johns Hopkins University in 1980, and sponsored by the Matchette Foundation. It appeared in *The Monist*, LXIV (1981): 155-174.

Essay 9 ("Pragmatism, Relativism, and Irrationalism") was delivered as the presidential address to the Eastern Division of the American Philosophical Association in 1979. It appeared in *Proceedings of the American Philosophical Association*, LIII (1980): 719-738.

Essay 10 ("Cavell on Skepticism") appeared in *The Review of Metaphysics*, XXXIV (1980-81): 759-774.

Essay 11 ("Method, Social Science, and Social Hope") is a revised version of a paper written for a conference on "Values and the Social Sciences" held at the University of California at Berkeley in 1980. The earlier version will appear in *Values and the Social Sciences*, ed. Norman Hahn, Robert Bellah, and Paul Rabinow, under the title "Method and Morality." The present version appeared in *The Canadian Journal of Philosophy*, XI (1981): 569-588.

Essay 12 ("Philosophy in America Today") was delivered to a symposium with Alasdair MacIntyre on "The Nature and Future of Philosophy" at the 1981 annual meeting of the Western Division of the American Philosophical Association. It was also one of a series of lectures on "The Humanities in the Eighties: Some Current Debates" arranged by the Humanities Center of Stanford University. It appeared (in German translation) in *Analyse und Kritik* for 1981, and in *The American Scholar* for 1982.

Introduction:
Pragmatism and Philosophy

1. Platonists, Positivists, and Pragmatists

The essays in this book are attempts to draw consequences from a pragmatist theory about truth. This theory says that truth is not the sort of thing one should expect to have a philosophically interesting theory about. For pragmatists, "truth" is just the name of a property which all true statements share. It is what is common to "Bacon did not write Shakespeare," "It rained yesterday," "E equals mc²," "Love is better than hate," "*The Allegory of Painting* was Vermeer's best work," "2 plus 2 is 4," and "There are nondenumerable infinities." Pragmatists doubt that there is much to be said about this common feature. They doubt this for the same reason they doubt that there is much to be said about the common feature shared by such morally praiseworthy actions as Susan leaving her husband, America joining the war against the Nazis, America pulling out of Vietnam, Socrates not escaping from jail, Roger picking up litter from the trail, and the suicide of the Jews at Masada. They see certain acts as good ones to perform, under the circumstances, but doubt that there is anything general and useful to say about what makes them all good. The assertion of a given sentence—or the adoption of a disposition to assert the sentence, the conscious acquisition of a belief—is a justifiable, praiseworthy act in certain circumstances. But, *a fortiori*, it is not likely that there is something general and useful to be said about what makes all such actions good—about the common feature of all the sentences which one should acquire a disposition to assert.

Pragmatists think that the history of attempts to isolate the True or the Good, or to define the word "true" or "good," supports their suspicion that there is no interesting work to be done in this area. It might, of course, have turned out otherwise. People have, oddly enough, found something interesting to say about the essence of Force and the definition of "number." They might have found something interesting to say about the essence of Truth. But in fact they haven't. The history of attempts to do so, and of criticisms of such attempts, is roughly coextensive with the history of that literary genre we call "philosophy"—a genre founded by Plato. So pragmatists see the Platonic tradition as having outlived its usefulness. This does not mean that they have a new, non-Platonic set of answers to Platonic questions to offer, but rather that they do not think we should ask those questions anymore. When they suggest that we not ask questions about the nature of Truth and Goodness, they do not invoke a theory about the nature of reality or knowledge or man which says that "there is no such thing" as Truth or Goodness. Nor do they have a "relativistic" or "subjectivist" theory of Truth or Goodness. They would simply like to change the subject. They are in a position analogous to that of secularists who urge that research concerning the Nature, or the Will, of God does not get us anywhere. Such secularists are not saying that God does not exist, exactly; they feel unclear about what it would mean to affirm His existence, and thus about the point of denying it. Nor do they have some special, funny, heretical view about God. They just doubt that the vocabulary of theology is one we ought to be using. Similarly, pragmatists keep trying to find ways of making antiphilosophical points in nonphilosophical language. For they face a dilemma: if their language is too unphilosophical, too "literary," they will be accused of changing the subject; if it is too philosophical it will embody Platonic assumptions which will make it impossible for the pragmatist to state the conclusion he wants to reach.

All this is complicated by the fact that "philosophy," like "truth" and "goodness," is ambiguous. Uncapitalized, "truth" and "goodness" name properties of sentences, or of actions and situations. Capitalized, they are the proper names of objects—goals or standards which can be loved with all one's heart and soul and mind, objects of ultimate concern. Similarly, "philosophy" can mean simply what Sellars calls "an attempt to see how things, in the broadest possible sense of the term, hang together, in the broadest possible sense of the term." Pericles, for example, was using this sense of the term when he praised the Athenians for "philosophizing without unmanliness" (*philosōphein aneu malakias*). In this sense, Blake is as much a philosopher as Fichte, Henry Adams more of a philosopher than Frege. No one would be dubious about philosophy, taken in this sense. But the word can also denote something more specialized, and very dubious indeed. In this second sense, it can mean following Plato's and Kant's lead, asking questions about the nature of certain normative notions (e.g., "truth," "rationality," "goodness") in the hope of better obeying such norms. The idea is to believe more truths or do more good or be more rational by knowing more about Truth or Goodness or Rationality. I shall capitalize the term "philosophy" when used in this second sense, in order to help make the point that Philosophy, Truth, Goodness, and Rationality are interlocked Platonic notions. Pragmatists are saying that the best hope for philosophy is not to practise Philosophy. They think it will not help to say something true to think about Truth, nor will it help to act well to think about Goodness, nor will it help to be rational to think about Rationality.

So far, however, my description of pragmatism has left an important distinction out of account. Within Philosophy, there has been a traditional difference of opinion about the Nature of Truth, a battle between (as Plato put it) the gods and the giants. On the one hand there have been Philosophers like Plato himself who were otherworldly, possessed of a larger hope. They urged that human beings were entitled to self-respect only because they had one foot beyond space and time. On the other hand—especially since Galileo showed how spatio-temporal events could be brought under the sort of elegant mathematical law which Plato suspected might hold only for another world—there have been Philosophers (e.g., Hobbes, Marx) who insisted that space and time make up the only Reality there is, and that Truth is Correspondence to *that* Reality. In the nineteenth century, this opposition crystallized into one between "the transcendental philosophy" and "the empirical philosophy," between the "Platonists" and the "positivists." Such terms were, even then, hopelessly vague, but every intellectual knew roughly where he stood in relation to the two movements. To be on the transcendental side was to think that natural science was not the last word—that there was more Truth to be found. To be on the empirical side was to think that natural science—facts about how spatio-temporal things worked—was all the Truth there was. To side with Hegel or Green was to think that some normative sentences about rationality and goodness corresponded to something real, but invisible to natural science. To side with Comte or Mach was to think that such sentences either "reduced" to sentences about spatio-temporal events or were not subjects for serious reflection.

It is important to realize that the empirical philosophers—the positivists—were still doing Philosophy. The Platonic presupposition which unites the gods and the giants, Plato with Democritus, Kant with Mill, Husserl with Russell, is that what the vulgar call "truth"— the assemblage of true statements—should be thought of as divided into a lower and an upper division, the division between (in Plato's terms) mere opinion and genuine knowledge. It is the work of the Philosopher to establish an invidious distinction between such statements as "It rained yesterday" and "Men should try to be just in their dealings." For Plato the former sort of statement was second-rate, mere *pistis* or *doxa*. The latter, if perhaps not yet *epistēmē*, was at least a plausible candidate. For the positivist tradition which runs from Hobbes to Carnap, the former sentence was a paradigm of what Truth looked like, but the latter was either a prediction about the causal effects of certain events or an "expression of emotion." What the transcendental philosophers saw as the spiritual, the empirical philosophers saw as the emotional. What the empirical philosophers saw as the achievements of natural science in discovering the nature of Reality, the transcendental philosophers saw as banausic, as true but irrelevant to Truth.

Pragmatism cuts across this transcendental/empirical distinction by questioning the common presupposition that there is an invidious distinction to be drawn between kinds of truths. For the pragmatist, true sentences are not true because they correspond to reality, and so there is no need to worry what sort of reality, if any, a given sentence corresponds to—no need to worry about what "makes" it true. (Just as there is no need to worry, once one has determined what one should do, whether there is something in Reality which makes that act the Right one to perform.) So the pragmatist sees no need to worry about whether Plato or Kant was right in thinking that something nonspatio-temporal made moral judgments true, nor about whether the absence of such a thing means that such judgments are "merely expressions of emotion" or "merely conventional" or "merely subjective."

This insouciance brings down the scorn of both kinds of Philosophers upon the pragmatist. The Platonist sees the pragmatist as merely a fuzzy-minded sort of positivist. The positivist sees him as lending aid and comfort to Platonism by leveling down the distinction between Objective Truth—the sort of true sentence attained by "the scientific method"—and sentences which lack the precious "correspondence to reality" which only that method can induce. Both join in thinking the pragmatist is not really a philosopher, on the ground that he is not a Philosopher. The pragmatist tries to defend himself by saying that one can be a philosopher precisely by being anti-Philosophical, that the best way to make things hang together is to step back from the issues between Platonists and positivists, and thereby give up the presuppositions of Philosophy.

One difficulty the pragmatist has in making his position clear, therefore, is that he must struggle with the positivist for the position of radical anti-Platonist. He wants to attack Plato with different weapons from those of the positivist, but at first glance he looks like just another variety of positivist. He shares with the positivist the Baconian and Hobbesian notion that knowledge is power, a tool for coping with reality. But he carries this Baconian point through to its extreme, as the positivist does not. He drops the notion of truth as correspondence with reality altogether, and says that modern science does not enable us to cope because it corresponds, it just plain enables us to cope. His argument for the view is that several hundred years of effort have failed to make interesting sense of the notion of "correspondence" (either of thoughts to things or of words to things). The pragmatist takes the moral of this discouraging history to be that "true sentences work because they correspond to the way things are" is no more illuminating than "it is right because it fulfills the Moral Law." Both remarks, in the pragmatist's eyes, are empty metaphysical compliments—harmless as rhetorical pats on the back to the successful inquirer or agent, but troublesome if taken seriously and "clarified" philosophically.

2. Pragmatism and Contemporary Philosophy

Among contemporary philosophers, pragmatism is usually regarded as an outdated philosophical movement—one which flourished in the early years of this century in a rather provincial atmosphere, and which has now been either refuted or *aufgehoben*. The great pragmatists—James and Dewey—are occasionally praised for their criticisms of Platonism (e.g., Dewey on traditional conceptions of education, James on metaphysical pseudo-problems). But their anti-Platonism is thought by analytic philosophers to have been insufficiently rigorous and by nonanalytic philosophers to have been insufficiently radical. For the tradition which originates in logical positivism the pragmatists' attacks on "transcendental," quasi-Platonist philosophy need to be sharpened by more careful and detailed analysis of such notions as "meaning" and truth."[1] For the anti-Philosophical tradition in contemporary French and German thought which takes its point of departure from Nietzsche's criticism of both strands in nineteenth-century Philosophical thought—positivistic as well as transcendental—the American pragmatists are thinkers who never really broke out of positivism, and thus never really broke with Philosophy.[2]

I do not think that either of these dismissive attitudes is justified. On the account of recent analytic philosophy which I offered in *Philosophy and the Mirror of Nature*,[3] the history of that movement has been marked by a gradual "pragmaticization" of the original tenets of logical positivism. On the account of recent "Continental" philosophy which I hope to offer in a book on Heidegger which I am writing,[4] James and Nietzsche make parallel criticisms of nineteenth-century thought. Further, James's version is preferable, for it avoids the "metaphysical" elements in Nietzsche which Heidegger criticizes, and, for that matter, the "metaphysical" elements in Heidegger which Derrida criticizes.[5] On my view, James and Dewey were not only waiting at the end of the dialectical road which analytic philosophy traveled, but are waiting at the end of the road which, for example, Foucault and Deleuze are currently traveling.[6]

I think that analytic philosophy culminates in Quine, the later Wittgenstein, Sellars, and Davidson—which is to say that it transcends and cancels itself. These thinkers successfully, and rightly, blur the positivist distinctions between the semantic and the pragmatic, the analytic and the synthetic, the linguistic and the empirical, theory and observation. Davidson's attack on the scheme/content distinction,[7] in particular, summarizes and synthesizes Wittgenstein's mockery of his own *Tractatus*, Quine's criticisms of Carnap, and Sellars's attack on the empiricist "Myth of the Given." Davidson's holism and coherentism shows how language looks once we get rid of the central presupposition of Philosophy: that true sentences divide into an upper and a lower division—the sentences which correspond to something and those which are "true" only by courtesy or convention.[8]

This Davidsonian way of looking at language lets us avoid hypostatizing Language in the way in which the Cartesian epistemological tradition, and particularly the idealist tradition which built upon Kant, hypostatized Thought. For it lets us see language not as a *tertium quid* between Subject and Object, nor as a medium in which we try to form pictures of reality, but as part of the behavior of human beings. On this view, the activity of uttering sentences is one of the things people do in order to cope with their environment. The

Deweyan notion of language as tool rather than picture is right as far as it goes. But we must be careful *not* to phrase this analogy so as to suggest that one can separate the tool, Language, from its users and inquire as to its "adequacy" to achieve our purposes. The latter suggestion presupposes that there is some way of breaking out of language in order to compare it with something else. But there is no way to think about either the world or our purposes except by using our language. One can use language to criticize and enlarge itself, as one can exercise one's body to develop and strengthen and enlarge it, but one cannot see language-as-a-whole in relation to something else to which it applies, or for which it is a means to an end. The arts and the sciences, and philosophy as their self-reflection and integration, constitute such a process of enlargement and strengthening. But Philosophy, the attempt to say "how language relates to the world" by saying what *makes* certain sentences true, or certain actions or attitudes good or rational, is, on this view, impossible.

It is the impossible attempt to step outside our skins—the traditions, linguistic and other, within which we do our thinking and self-criticism—and compare ourselves with something absolute. This Platonic urge to escape from the finitude of one's time and place, the "merely conventional" and contingent aspects of one's life, is responsible for the original Platonic distinction between two kinds of true sentence. By attacking this latter distinction, the holistic "pragmaticizing" strain in analytic philosophy has helped us see how the metaphysical urge—common to fuzzy Whiteheadians and razor-sharp "scientific realists"—works. It has helped us be skeptical about the idea that some particular science (say physics) or some particular literary genre (say Romantic poetry, or transcendental philosophy) gives us that species of true sentence which is not *just* a true sentence, but rather a piece of Truth itself. Such sentences may be very useful indeed, but there is not going to be a Philosophical explanation of this utility. That explanation, like the original justification of the assertion of the sentence, will be a parochial matter—a comparison of the sentence with alternative sentences formulated in the same or in other vocabularies. But such comparisons are the business of, for example, the physicist or the poet, or perhaps of the philosopher—not of the Philosopher, the outside expert on the utility, or function, or metaphysical status of Language or of Thought.

The Wittgenstein-Sellars-Quine-Davidson attack on distinctions between classes of sentences is the special contribution of analytic philosophy to the anti-Platonist insistence on the ubiquity of language. This insistence characterizes both pragmatism and recent "Continental" philosophizing. Here are some examples:

Man makes the word, and the word means nothing which the man has not made it mean, and that only to some other man. But since man can think only by means of words or other external symbols, these might turn around and say: You mean nothing which we have not taught you, and then only so far as you address some word as the interpretant of your thought. . . . . . . the word or sign which man uses is the man himself. . . . Thus my language is the sum-total of myself; for the man is the thought. (Peirce)[9]

Peirce goes very far in the direction that I have called the de-construction of the transcendental signified, which, at one time or another, would place a reassuring end to the reference from sign to sign. (Derrida)[10]

. . . *psychological nominalism*, according to which *all* awareness of sorts, resemblances, facts, etc., in short all awareness of abstract entities—indeed, all awareness even of particulars—is a linguistic affair. (Sellars)[11]

It is only in language that one can mean something by something. (Wittgenstein)[12]

Human experience is essentially linguistic. (Gadamer)[13]

. . . man is in the process of perishing as the being of language continues to shine ever brighter upon our horizon. (Foucault)[14]

Speaking about language turns language almost inevitably into an object . . . and then its reality vanishes. (Heidegger)[15]

This chorus should not, however, lead us to think that something new and exciting has recently been discovered about Language—e.g., that it is more prevalent than had previously been thought. The authors cited are making only *negative* points. They are saying that attempts to get back behind language to something which "grounds" it, or which it "expresses," or to which it might hope to be "adequate," have not worked. The ubiquity of language is a matter of language moving into the vacancies left by the failure of all the various candidates for the position of "natural starting-points" of thought, starting-points which are prior to and independent of the way some culture speaks or spoke. (Candidates for such starting-points include clear and distinct ideas, sense-data, categories of the pure understanding, structures of prelinguistic consciousness, and the like.) Peirce and Sellars and Wittgenstein are saying that the regress of interpretation cannot be cut off by the sort of "intuition" which Cartesian epistemology took for granted. Gadamer and Derrida are saying that our culture has been dominated by the notion of a "transcendental signified" which, by cutting off this regress, would bring us out from contingency and convention and into the Truth. Foucault is saying that we are gradually losing our grip on the "metaphysical comfort" which that Philosophical tradition provided—its picture of Man as having a "double" (the soul, the Noumenal Self) who uses Reality's own language rather than merely the vocabulary of a time and a place. Finally, Heidegger is cautioning that if we try to make Language into a new topic of Philosophical inquiry we shall simply recreate the hopeless old Philosophical puzzles which we used to raise about Being or Thought.

This last point amounts to saying that what Gustav Bergmann called "the linguistic turn" should not be seen as the logical positivists saw it—as enabling us to ask Kantian questions without having to trespass on the psychologists' turf by talking, with Kant, about "experience" or "consciousness." That was, indeed, the initial motive for the "turn,"[16] but (thanks to the holism and pragmatism of the authors I have cited) analytic philosophy of language was able to transcend this Kantian motive and adopt a naturalistic, behavioristic attitude toward language. This attitude has led it to the same outcome as the "Continental" reaction against the traditional Kantian problematic, the reaction found in Nietzsche and Heidegger. This convergence shows that the traditional association of analytic philosophy with tough-minded positivism and of "Continental" philosophy with tender-minded Platonism is *completely* misleading. The pragmaticization of analytic philosophy gratified the logical positivists' hopes, but not in the fashion which they had envisaged. It did not find a way for Philosophy to become "scientific," but rather found a way of setting Philosophy to one side. This postpositivistic kind of analytic philosophy thus comes to resemble the Nietzsche-Heidegger-Derrida tradition in beginning with criticism of Platonism and ending in criticism of Philosophy as such. Both traditions are now in a period of doubt about their own status. Both are living between a repudiated past and a dimly seen post-Philosophical future.

3. The Realist Reaction (I): Technical Realism

Before going on to speculate about what a post-Philosophical culture might look like, I should make clear that my description of the current Philosophical scene has been deliberately oversimplified. So far I have ignored the anti-pragmatist backlash. The picture I have been sketching shows how things looked about ten years ago—or, at least, how they looked to an optimistic pragmatist. In the subsequent decade there has been, on both sides of the Channel, a reaction in favor of "realism"—a term which has come to be synonymous with "anti-pragmatism." This reaction has had three distinct motives: (1) the view that recent, technical developments in the philosophy of language have raised doubt about traditional pragmatist criticisms of the "correspondence theory of truth," or, at least, have made it necessary for the pragmatist to answer some hard, technical questions before proceeding further; (2) the sense that the "depth," the human significance, of the traditional textbook "problems of philosophy" has been underestimated, that pragmatists have lumped real problems together with pseudo-problems in a feckless orgy of "dissolution"; (3) the sense that something important would be lost if Philosophy as an autonomous discipline, as a *Fach*, were to fade from the cultural scene (in the way in which theology has faded).

This third motive—the fear of what would happen if there were merely philosophy, but no Philosophy—is not simply the defensive reaction of specialists threatened with unemployment. It is a conviction that a culture without Philosophy would be "irrationalist"—that a precious human capacity would lie unused, or a central human virtue no longer be exemplified. This motive is shared by many philosophy professors in France and Germany and by many analytic philosophers in Britain and America. The former would like something to do that is not merely the endless, repetitive, literary-historical "deconstruction" of the "Western metaphysics of presence" which was Heidegger's legacy. The latter would like to recapture the spirit of the early logical positivists, the sense that philosophy is the accumulation of "results" by patient, rigorous, preferably cooperative work on precisely stated problems (the spirit characteristic of the younger, rather than of the older, Wittgenstein). So philosophy professors on the Continent are casting longing glances toward analytic philosophy—and particularly toward the "realist" analytic philosophers who take Philosophical problems seriously. Conversely, admirers of "Continental" philosophy (e.g., of Nietzsche, Heidegger, Derrida, Gadamer, Foucault) are more welcome in American and British departments of, e.g., comparative literature and political science, than in departments of philosophy. On both continents there is fear of Philosophy's losing its traditional claim to "scientific" status and of its relegation to "the merely literary."

I shall talk about this fear in some detail later, in connection with the prospects for a culture in which the science/literature distinction would no longer matter. But here I shall concentrate on the first and second motives I just listed. These are associated with two fairly distinct groups of people. The first motive is characteristic of philosophers of language such as Saul Kripke and Michael Dummett, the second with less specialized and more broadly ranging writers like Stanley

Cavell and Thomas Nagel. I shall call those who turn Kripke's views on reference to the purposes of a realistic epistemology (e.g., Hartry Field, Richard Boyd, and, sometimes, Hilary Putnam) "technical realists." I shall call Cavell, Nagel (and others, such as Thompson Clarke and Barry Stroud) "intuitive realists." The latter object that the pragmatists' dissolutions of traditional problems are "verificationist": that is, pragmatists think our inability to say what would count as confirming or disconfirming a given solution to a problem is a reason for setting the problem aside. To take this view is, Nagel tells us, to fail to recognize that "unsolvable problems are not for that reason unreal."[17] Intuitive realists judge verificationism by its fruits, and argue that the pragmatist belief in the ubiquity of language leads to the inability to recognize that philosophical problems arise precisely where language is inadequate to the facts. "My realism about the subjective domain in all its forms," Nagel says, "implies a belief in the existence of facts beyond the reach of human concepts."[18]

Technical realists, by contrast, judge pragmatism wrong not because it leads to superficial dismissals of deep problems, but because it is based on a false, "verificationist" philosophy of language. They dislike "verificationism" not because of its metaphilosophical fruits, but because they see it as a misunderstanding of the relation between language and the world. On their view, Quine and Wittgenstein wrongly followed Frege in thinking that meaning—something determined by the intentions of the user of a word—determines reference, what the word picks out in the world. On the basis of the "new theory of reference" originated by Saul Kripke, they say, we can now construct a better, non-Fregean picture of word-world relationships. Whereas Frege, like Kant, thought of our concepts as carving up an undifferentiated manifold in accordance with our interests (a view which leads fairly directly to Sellars's "psychological nominalism" and a Goodman-like insouciance about ontology), Kripke sees the world as already divided not only into particulars, but into natural kinds of particulars and even into essential and accidental features of those particulars and kinds. The question "Is 'X is ϕ' *true*?" is thus to be answered by discovering what—as a matter of physical fact, not of anybody's intentions—'X' refers to, and then discovering whether that particular or kind is ϕ. Only by such a "physicalistic" theory of reference, technical realists say, can the notion of "truth as correspondence to reality" be preserved. By contrast, the pragmatist answers this question by inquiring whether, all things (and especially our purposes in using the terms 'X' and 'ϕ') considered, 'X is ϕ' is a more useful belief to have than its contradictory, or than some belief expressed in different terms altogether. The pragmatist agrees that if one wants to preserve the notion of "correspondence with reality" then a physicalistic theory of reference is necessary[19] — but he sees no point in preserving that notion. The pragmatist has no notion of truth which would enable him to make sense of the claim that if we achieved everything we ever hoped to achieve by making assertions we might still be making *false* assertions, failing to "correspond" to something.[20] As Putnam says:

> The trouble is that for a strong antirealist [e.g., a pragmatist] *truth* makes no sense except as an intra-theoretic notion. The antirealist can use truth intra-theoretically in the sense of a "redundancy theory" [i.e., a theory according to which "S is true" means exactly, only, what "S" means] but he does not have the notion of truth and reference available extra-theoretically. But extension [reference] is tied to the notion of truth. The extension of a term is just what the term is *true of*. Rather than try to retain the notion of truth via an awkward operationalism, the antirealist should reject the notion of extension as he does the notion of truth (in any extra-theoretic sense). Like Dewey, he can fall back on a notion of 'warranted assertibility' instead of truth. . . .[21]

The question which technical realism raises, then, is: are there technical reasons, within the philosophy of language, for retaining or discarding this extra-theoretic notion? Are there nonintuitive ways of deciding whether, as the pragmatist thinks, the question of what 'X' refers to is a sociological matter, a question of how best to make sense of a community's linguistic behavior, or whether, as Hartry Field says,

> one aspect of the sociological role of a term is the role that term has in the psychologies of different members of a linguistic community; another aspect, *irreducible to the first* [italics added], is what physical objects or physical property the term stands for.[22]

It is not clear, however, what these technical, nonintuitive ways might be. For it is not clear what data the philosophy of language must explain. The most frequently cited datum is that science *works, succeeds* — enables us to cure diseases, blow up cities, and the like. How, realists ask, would this be possible if some scientific statements did not correspond to the way things are in themselves? How, pragmatists rejoin, does *that* count as an explanation? What further specification of the "correspondence" relation can be given which will enable this explanation to be better than "dormitive power" (Molière's doctor's explanation of why opium puts people to sleep)? What, so to speak, corresponds to the microstructure of opium in this case?

What is the microstructure of "corresponding"? The Tarskian apparatus of truth-conditions and satisfaction-relations does not fill the bill, because that apparatus is equally well adapted to physicalist "building-block" theories of reference like Field's and to coherentist, holistic, pragmatical theories like Davidson's. When realists like Field argue that Tarski's account of truth is merely a place-holder, like Mendel's account of "gene," which requires physicalistic "reduction to non-semantical terms,"[23] pragmatists reply (with Stephen Leeds) that "true" (like "good" and unlike "gene") is not an explanatory notion.[24] (Or that, if it is, the structure of the explanations in which it is used needs to be spelled out.)

The search for technical grounds on which to argue the pragmatist-realist issue is sometimes ended artificially by the realist assuming that the pragmatist not only (as Putnam says) follows Dewey in "falling back on a notion of 'warranted assertibility' *instead of* truth" but uses the latter notion to *analyze the meaning* of "true." Putnam is right that no such analysis will work. But the pragmatist, if he is wise, will not succumb to the temptation to fill the blank in

S is true if and only if S is assertible_____

with "at the end of inquiry" or "by the standards of our culture" or with anything else.[25] He will recognize the strength of Putnam's "naturalistic fallacy" argument: Just as nothing can fill the blank in

A is the best thing to do in circumstances C if and only if _____

so, *a fortiori*, nothing will fill the blank in

Asserting S is the best thing to do in C if and only if _____

If the pragmatist is advised that he must not confuse the *advisability of asserting* S with the *truth* of S, he will respond that the advice is question-begging. The question is precisely whether "the true" is more than what William James defined it as: "the name of whatever proves itself to be good in the way of belief, and good, too, for definite, assignable reasons."[26] On James's view, "true" resembles "good" or "rational" in being a normative notion, a compliment paid to sentences that seem to be paying their way and that fit in with other sentences which are doing so. To think that Truth is "out there" is, on their view, on all fours with the Platonic view that The Good is "out there." To think that we are "irrationalist" insofar as it does not "gratify our souls to know/That though we perish, truth is so" is like thinking that we are "irrationalist" just insofar as it does not gratify our moral sense to think that The Moral Law shines resplendent over the noumenal world, regardless of the vicissitudes of spatio-temporal

lives. For the pragmatist, the notion of "truth" as something "objective" is just a confusion between

(I)   Most of the world is as it is whatever we think about it (that
       is, our beliefs have very limited causal efficacy)

and

(II)   There is something out there in addition to the world called
       "the truth about the world" (what James sarcastically called
       "this tertium quid intermediate between the facts *per se*, on
       the one hand, and all knowledge of them, actual or potential,
       on the other").[27]

The pragmatist wholeheartedly assents to (I)—not as an article of
metaphysical faith but simply as a belief that we have never had any
reason to doubt—and cannot make sense of (II). When the realist tries
to explain (II) with

(III) The truth about the world consists in a relation of "corre-
       spondence" between certain sentences (many of which, no
       doubt, have yet to be formulated) and the world itself

the pragmatist can only fall back on saying, once again, that many
centuries of attempts to explain what "correspondence" is have failed,
especially when it comes to explaining how the final vocabulary of
future physics will somehow be Nature's Own—the one which, at long
last, lets us formulate sentences which lock on to Nature's own way
of thinking of Herself.

For these reasons, the pragmatist does not think that, whatever
else philosophy of language may do, it is going to come up with a
definition of "true" which gets beyond James. He happily grants that
it can do a lot of other things. For example, it can, following Tarski,
show what it would be like to define a truth-predicate for a given language. The pragmatist can agree with Davidson that to define such a
predicate—to develop a truth-theory for the sentences of English, e.g,
—would be a good way, perhaps the only way, to exhibit a natural
language as a learnable, recursive structure, and thus to give a systematic theory of meaning for the language.[28] But he agrees with
Davidson that such an exhibition is *all* that Tarski can give us, and all
that can be milked out of Philosophical reflection on Truth.

Just as the pragmatist should not succumb to the temptation to
"capture the intuitive content of our notion of truth" (including
whatever it is in that notion which makes realism tempting), so he
should not succumb to the temptation held out by Michael Dummett
to take sides on the issue of "bivalence." Dummett (who has his own

doubts about realism) has suggested that a lot of traditional issues in the area of the pragmatist-realist debate can be clarified by the technical apparatus of philosophy of language, along the following lines:

> In a variety of different areas there arises a philosophical dispute of the same general character: the dispute for or against realism concerning statements within a given type of subject-matter, or, better, statements of a certain general type. [Dummett elsewhere lists moral statements, mathematical statements, statements about the past, and modal statements as examples of such types.] Such a dispute consists in an opposition between two points of view concerning the kind of meaning possessed by statements of the kind in question, and hence about the application to them of the notions of truth and falsity. For the realist, we have assigned a meaning to these statements in such a way that we know, for each statement, what has to be the case for it to be true. . . . The condition for the truth of a statement is not, in general, a condition we are capable of recognizing as obtaining whenever it obtains, or even one for which we have an effective procedure for determining whether it obtains or not. We have therefore succeeded in ascribing to our statements a meaning of such a kind that their truth or falsity is, in general, independent of whether we know, or have any means of knowing, what truth-value they have. . . .
>
> Opposed to this realist account of statements in some given class is the anti-realist interpretation. According to this, the meanings of statements of the class in question are given to us, not in terms of the conditions under which these statements are true or false, conceived of as conditions which obtain or do not obtain independently of our knowledge or capacity for knowledge, but in terms of the conditions which we recognize as establishing the truth or falsity of statements of that class.[29]

"Bivalence" is the property of being either true or false, so Dummett thinks of a "realistic" view about a certain area (say, moral values, or possible worlds) as asserting bivalence for statements about such things. His way of formulating the realist-vs.-anti-realist issue thus suggests that the pragmatist denies bivalence for all statements, the "extreme" realist asserts it for all statements, while the level-headed majority sensibly discriminate between the bivalent statements of, e.g., physics and the nonbivalent statements of, e.g., morals. "Bivalence" thus joins "ontological commitment" as a way of expressing old-fashioned metaphysical views in up-to-date semantical language. If the pragmatist is viewed as a quasi-idealist metaphysician who is ontologically committed only to ideas or sentences, and does not believe that there is anything "out there" which makes any sort of statement true, then he will fit neatly into Dummett's scheme.

But, of course, this is not the pragmatist's picture of himself. He does not think of himself as *any* kind of a metaphysician, because he does not *understand* the notion of "there being _____ out there" (except in the literal sense of 'out there' in which it means "at a position in space"). He does not find it helpful to explicate the Platonist's conviction about The Good or The Numbers by saying that the Platonist believes that "There is truth-or-falsity about _____, regardless of the state of our knowledge or the availability of procedures for inquiry." The "is" in this sentence seems to him just as obscure as the "is" in "Truth is so." Confronted with the passage from Dummett cited above, the pragmatist wonders how one goes about telling one "kind of meaning" from another, and what it would be like to have "intuitions" about the bivalence or nonbivalence of kinds of statements. He is a pragmatist just because he doesn't have such intuitions (or wants to get rid of whatever such intuitions he may have). When he asks himself, about a given statement *S*, whether he "knows what has to be the case for it to be true" or merely knows "the conditions which we recognize as establishing the truth or falsity of statements of that class," he feels as helpless as when asked, "Are you really in love, or merely inflamed by passion?" He is inclined to suspect that it is not a very useful question, and that at any rate introspection is not the way to answer it. But in the case of bivalence it is not clear that there is another way. Dummett does not help us see what to count as a good argument for asserting bivalence of, e.g., moral or modal statements; he merely says that there are some people who do assert this and some who don't, presumably having been born with different metaphysical temperaments. If one is born without metaphysical views—or if, having become pessimistic about the utility of Philosophy, one is self-consciously attempting to eschew such views—then one will feel that Dummett's reconstruction of the traditional issues explicates the obscure with the equally obscure.

What I have said about Field and about Dummett is intended to cast doubt on the "technical realist's" view that the pragmatist-realist issue should be fought out on some narrow, clearly demarcated ground within the philosophy of language. There is no such ground. This is not, to be sure, the fault of philosophy of language, but of the pragmatist. He refuses to take a stand—to provide an "analysis" of "*S* is true," for example, or to either assert or deny bivalence. He refuses to make a move in *any* of the games in which he is invited to take part. The *only* point at which "referential semantics" or "bivalence" becomes of interest to him comes when somebody tries to treat these notions as explanatory, as not *just* expressing intuitions but as doing some work—explaining, for example, "why science is so successful."[30] At this point the pragmatist hauls out his bag of tried-and-true dialectical gambits.[31] He proceeds to argue that there is no pragmatic difference, no difference that makes a difference, between "it works because it's true" and "it's true because it works"—any more than between "it's pious because the gods love it" and "the gods love it because it's pious." Alternatively, he argues that there is no pragmatic difference between the nature of truth and the test of truth, and that the test of truth, of what statements to assert, is (except maybe for a few perceptual statements) not "comparison with reality." All these gambits will be felt by the realist to be question-begging, since the realist intuits that some differences can be real *without* making a difference, that sometimes the *ordo essendi* is *different* from the *ordo cognoscendi*, sometimes the nature of X is *not* our test for the presence of Xness. And so it goes.

What we should conclude, I think, is that technical realism collapses into intuitive realism—that the *only* debating point which the realist has is his conviction that the raising of the good old metaphysical problems (are there *really* universals? are there *really* causally efficacious physical objects, or did we just *posit* them?) served some good purpose, brought something to light, was important. What the pragmatist wants to debate is just this point. He does not want to discuss necessary and sufficient conditions for a sentence being true, but precisely *whether* the practice which hopes to find a Philosophical way of isolating the essence of Truth has, in fact, paid off. So the issue between him and the intuitive realist is a matter of what to make of the history of that practice—what to make of the history of Philosophy. The real issue is about the place of Philosophy in Western philosophy, the place within the intellectual history of the West of the particular series of texts which raise the "deep" Philosophical problems which the realist wants to preserve.

4. The Realist Reaction (II): Intuitive Realism

What really needs debate between the pragmatist and the intuitive realist is *not* whether we have intuitions to the effect that "truth is more than assertibility" or "there is more to pains than brain-states" or "there is a clash between modern physics and our sense of moral responsibility." *Of course* we have such intuitions. How could we escape having them? We have been educated within an intellectual tradition built around such claims—just as we used to be educated within an intellectual tradition built around such claims as "If God does not exist, everything is permitted," "Man's dignity consists in his link with a supernatural order," and "One must not mock holy things." But it begs the question between pragmatist and realist to say that we must find a philosophical view which "captures" such intuitions. The pragmatist is urging that we do our best to *stop having* such intuitions, that we develop a *new* intellectual tradition.

What strikes intuitive realists as offensive about this suggestion is that it seems as dishonest to suppress intuitions as it is to suppress experimental data. On their conception, philosophy (not merely Philosophy) requires one to do justice to *everybody's* intuitions. Just as social justice is what would be brought about by institutions whose existence could be justified to every citizen, so intellectual justice would be made possible by finding theses which everyone would, given sufficient time and dialectical ability, accept. This view of intellectual life presupposes either that, contrary to the prophets of the ubiquity of language cited above, language does *not* go all the way down, or that, contrary to the appearances, all vocabularies are commensurable. The first alternative amounts to saying that some intuitions, at least, are *not* a function of the way one has been brought up to talk, of the texts and people one has encountered. The second amounts to saying that the intuitions built into the vocabularies of Homeric warriors, Buddhist sages, Enlightenment scientists, and contemporary French literary critics, are not really as different as they seem—that there are common elements in each which Philosophy can isolate and use to formulate theses which it would be rational for all these people to accept, and problems which they all face.

The pragmatist, on the other hand, thinks that the quest for a universal human community will be self-defeating if it tries to preserve the elements of every intellectual tradition, all the "deep" intuitions everybody has ever had. It is not to be achieved by an attempt at commensuration, at a common vocabulary which isolates the common human essence of Achilles and the Buddha, Lavoisier and Derrida. Rather, it is to be reached, if at all, by acts of making rather than of finding—by poetic rather than Philosophical achievement. The culture which will transcend, and thus unite, East and West, or the Earthlings and the Galactics, is not likely to be one which does equal justice to each, but one which looks back on both with the amused condescension typical of later generations looking back at their ancestors. So the pragmatist's quarrel with the intuitive realist should be about the *status* of intuitions—about their *right* to be respected—as opposed to how particular intuitions might be "synthesized" or "explained away." To treat his opponent properly, the pragmatist must begin by admitting that the realistic intuitions in question are as deep and compelling as the realist says they are. But he should then try to change the subject by asking, "And what should we *do* about such intuitions—extirpate them, or find a vocabulary which does justice to them?"

From the pragmatist point of view the claim that the issues which the nineteenth century enshrined in its textbooks as "the central problems of philosophy" are "deep" is simply the claim that you will not understand a certain period in the history of Europe unless you can get some idea of what it was like to be preoccupied by such questions. (Consider parallel claims about the "depth" of the problems about Patripassianism, Arianism, etc., discussed by certain Fathers of the Church.) The pragmatist is even willing to expand his range and say, with Heidegger, that you won't understand the West unless you understand what it was like to be bothered by the kinds of issues which bothered Plato. Intuitive realists, rather than "stepping back" in the historicist manner of Heidegger and Dewey, or the quasi-anthropological manner of Foucault, devote themselves to safeguarding the tradition, to making us even more deeply Western. The way in which they do this is illustrated by Clarke's and Cavell's attempt to see "the legacy of skepticism" not as a question about whether we can be sure we're not dreaming but as a question about what sort of being could ask itself such a question.[32] They use the existence of figures like Descartes as indications of something important about *human beings*, not just about the modern West.

The best illustration of this strategy is Nagel's way of updating Kant by bringing a whole series of apparently disparate problems under the rubric "Subjective-Objective," just as Kant brought a partially overlapping set of problems under the rubric "Conditioned-Unconditioned." Nagel echoes Kant in saying:

> It may be true that some philosophical problems have no solution. I suspect that this is true of the deepest and oldest of them. They show us the limits of our understanding. In that case such insight as we can achieve depends on maintaining a strong grasp of the problem instead of abandoning it, and coming to understand the failure of each new attempt at a solution, and of earlier attempts. (That is why we study the works of philosophers like Plato and Berkeley, whose views are accepted by no one.) Unsolvable problems are not for that reason unreal.[33]

As an illustration of what Nagel has in mind, consider his example of the problem of "moral luck"—the fact that one can be morally praised or blamed only for what is under one's control, yet practically nothing is. As Nagel says:

> The area of genuine agency, and therefore of legitimate moral judgment, seems to shrink under this scrutiny to an extensionless point. Everything seems to result from the combined influence of factors, antecedent and posterior to action, that are not within the agent's control.[34]

Nagel thinks that a typically shallow, verificationist "solution" to this problem is available. We can get such a solution (Hume's) by going into detail about what sorts of external factors we do and don't count as diminishing the moral worth of an action:

> This compatibilist account of our moral judgments would leave room for the ordinary conditions of responsibility—the absence of coercion, ignorance, or involuntary movement—as part of the determination of what someone has done—but it is understood not to exclude the influence of a great deal that he has not done.[35]

But this relaxed, pragmatical, Humean attitude—the attitude which says that there is no deep truth about Freedom of the Will, and that people are morally responsible for whatever their peers tend to hold them morally responsible for—fails to explain why there has been *thought* to be a problem here:

> The only thing wrong with this solution is its failure to explain how skeptical problems arise. For they arise not from the imposition of an arbitrary external requirement, but from the nature of moral judgment itself. Something in the ordinary idea of what someone does must explain how it can seem necessary to subtract from it anything that merely happens—even though the ultimate consequence of such subtraction is that nothing remains.[36]

But this is not to say that we need a metaphysical account of the Nature of Freedom of the sort which Kant (at least in some passages) seems to give us. Rather,

> . . . in a sense the problem has no solution, because something in the idea of agency is incompatible with actions being events or people being things.[37]

Since there is, so to speak, nothing *else* for people to be but things, we are left with an intuition—one which shows us "the limits of our understanding," and thus of our language.

Contrast, now, Nagel's attitude toward "the nature of moral judgment" with Iris Murdoch's. The Kantian attempt to isolate an agent who is not a spatio-temporal thing is seen by Murdoch as an unfortunate and perverse turn which Western thought has taken. Within a certain post-Kantian tradition, she says:

> Immense care is taken to picture the will as isolated. It is isolated from belief, from reason, from feeling, and is yet the essential center of the self. . . . [38]

This existentialist conception of the agent as isolated will goes along, Murdoch says, with "a very powerful image" of man which she finds "alien and implausible" — one which is "a happy and fruitful marriage of Kantian liberalism with Wittgensteinian logic solemnized by Freud."[39] On Murdoch's view,

> Existentialism, in both its Continental and its Anglo-Saxon versions, is an attempt to solve the problem without really facing it: to solve it by attributing to the individual an empty lonely freedom. . . . What it pictures is indeed the fearful solitude of the individual marooned upon a tiny island in the middle of a sea of scientific facts, and morality escaping from science only by a wild leap of will.[40]

Instead of reinforcing this picture (as Nagel and Sartre do), Murdoch wants to get behind Kantian notions of will, behind the Kantian formulation of an antithesis between determinism and responsibility, behind the Kantian distinction between the moral self and the empirical self. She wants to recapture the vocabulary of moral reflection which a sixteenth-century Christian believer inclined toward Platonism would have used: one in which "perfection" is a central element, in which assignment of moral responsibility is a rather incidental element, and in which the discovery of a self (one's own or another's) is the endless task of love.[41]

In contrasting Nagel and Murdoch, I am not trying (misleadingly) to enlist Murdoch as a fellow-pragmatist, nor (falsely) to accuse Nagel of blindness to the variety of moral consciousness which Murdoch represents. Rather, I want to illustrate the difference between taking a standard philosophical problem (or cluster of interrelated problems such as free will, selfhood, agency, and responsibility) and asking, on the one hand, "What is its essence? To what ineffable depths, what limit of language, does it lead us? What does it show us about *being human*?" and asking, on the other hand, "What sort of people would see these problems? What vocabulary, what image of man, would produce such problems? Why, insofar as we are gripped by these problems, do we see them as deep rather than as *reductiones ad absurdum* of a vocabulary? What does the persistence of such problems show us about *being twentieth-century Europeans*?" Nagel is certainly right, and splendidly lucid, about the way in which a set of ideas, illustrated best by Kant, shoves us toward the notion of something called "the subjective"—the personal point of view, what science doesn't catch, what no "stepping back" could catch, what forms a limit to the understanding. But how do we know whether to say, "So much the worse for the solubility of philosophical problems, for the reach of language, for our 'verificationist' impulses," or whether to say, "So much the worse for the Philosophical ideas which have led us to such an impasse"?

The same question arises about the other philosophical problems which Nagel brings under his "Subjective-Objective" rubric. The clash between "verificationist" and "realist" intuitions is perhaps best illustrated by Nagel's celebrated paper "What Is It Like to Be a Bat?" Nagel here appeals to our intuition that "there is something which it is like" to be a bat or a dog but nothing which it is like to be an atom or a brick, and says that this intuition is what contemporary Wittgensteinian, Rylean, anti-Cartesian philosophy of mind "fails to capture." The culmination of the latter philosophical movement is the cavalier attitude toward "raw feels"—e.g., the sheer phenomenological qualitative ipseity of pain—suggested by Daniel Dennett:

> I recommend giving up incorrigibility with regard to pain altogether, in fact giving up *all* "essential" features of pain, and letting pain states be whatever "natural kind" states the brain scientists find (if they ever do find any) that normally produce all the normal effects. . . . One of our intuitions about pain is that whether or not one is in pain is a brute fact, not a matter of decision to serve the convenience of the theorist. I recommend against trying to preserve that intuition, but if you disagree, whatever theory I produce, however predictive and elegant, will not be in your lights a theory of pain, but only a theory of what I illicitly choose to *call* pain. But if, as I have claimed, the intuitions we would have to honor were we to honor them all do not form a consistent set, there can be no true theory of pain, and so no computer or robot could instantiate the true theory of pain, which it would have to do to feel real pain. . . . The inability of a robot model to satisfy all our intuitive demands may be due not to any irredeemable mysteriousness about the phenomenon of pain, but to irredeemable incoherence in our ordinary concept of pain.[42]

Nagel is one of those who disagrees with Dennett's recommendation. His anti-verificationism comes out most strongly in the following passage:

> . . . if things emerged from a spaceship which we could not be sure were machines or conscious beings, what we were wondering would have an answer even if the things were so different from anything we were familiar

with that we could never discover it. It would depend on whether there was something it was like to be them, not on whether behavioral similarities warranted our saying so. . . .

I therefore seem to be drawn to a position more 'realistic' than Wittgenstein's. This may be because I am drawn to positions more realistic than Wittgenstein's about everything, not just the mental. I believe that the question about whether the things coming out of the spaceship are conscious *must* have an answer. Wittgenstein would presumably say that this assumption reflects a groundless confidence that a certain picture unambiguously determines its own application. That is the picture of something going on in their heads (or whatever they have in place of heads) that cannot be observed by dissection.

Whatever picture I may use to represent the idea, it does seem to me that I know what it means to ask whether there is something it is like to be them, and that the answer to that question is what determines whether they are conscious—not the possibility of extending mental ascriptions on evidence analogous to the human case. Conscious mental states are real states of something, whether they are mine or those of an alien creature. Perhaps Wittgenstein's view can accommodate this intuition, but I do not at the moment see how.[43]

Wittgenstein certainly *cannot* accommodate this intuition. The question is whether he should be asked to: whether we should abandon the pragmatical "verificationist" intuition that "every difference must *make* a difference" (expressed by Wittgenstein in the remark "A wheel that can be turned though nothing else moves with it, is not part of the mechanism")[44] or instead abandon Nagel's intuition about consciousness. We certainly *have* both intuitions. For Nagel, their compresence shows that the limit of understanding has been reached, that an ultimate depth has been plumbed—just as the discovery of an antinomy indicated to Kant that something transcendental had been encountered. For Wittgenstein, it merely shows that the Cartesian tradition has sketched a compelling picture, a picture which "held us captive. And we could not get outside it, for it lay in our language and language seemed to repeat it to us inexorably."[45]

I said at the beginning of this section that there were two alternative ways in which the intuitive realist might respond to the pragmatist's suggestion that some intuitions should be deliberately repressed. He might say either that language does not go all the way down—that there is a kind of awareness of facts which is not expressible in language and which no argument could render dubious—or, more mildly, that there is a core language which is common to all traditions and which needs to be isolated. In a confrontation with

Murdoch one can imagine Nagel making the second claim—arguing that even the kind of moral discourse which Murdoch recommends must wind up with the same conception of "the isolated will" as Kantian moral discourse. But in a confrontation with Dennett's attempt to weed out our intuitions Nagel must make the first claim. He has to go all the way, and deny that our knowledge is limited by the language we speak. He says as much in the following passage:

> If anyone is inclined to deny that we can believe in the existence of facts like this whose exact nature we cannot possibly conceive, he should reflect that in contemplating the bats we are in much the same position that intelligent bats or Martians would occupy if they tried to form a conception of what it was like to be us. The structure of their own minds might make it impossible for them to succeed, but we know they would be wrong to conclude that there is not anything precise that it is like to be us. . . . We know they would be wrong to draw such a skeptical conclusion because we know what it is like to be us. And we know that while it includes an enormous amount of variation and complexity, and *while we do not possess the vocabulary to describe it adequately,* its subjective character is highly specific, and in some respects describable in terms that can be understood only by creatures like us [italics added].[46]

Here we hit a bedrock metaphilosophical issue: can one ever appeal to nonlinguistic knowledge in philosophical argument? This is the question of whether a dialectical impasse is the mark of philosophical depth or of a bad language, one which needs to be replaced with one which will not lead to such impasses. *That* is just the issue about the status of intuitions, which I said above was the real issue between the pragmatist and the realist. The hunch that, e.g., reflection upon anything worthy of the name "moral judgment" will eventually lead us to the problems Nagel describes is a discussable question—one upon which the history of ethics can shed light. But the intuition that there is something ineffable which it is like to be us—something which one cannot learn about by believing true propositions but only by *being* like that—is not something on which anything could throw further light. The claim is either deep or empty.

The pragmatist sees it as empty—indeed, he sees many of Nagel's discussions of "the subjective" as drawing a line around a vacant place in the middle of the web of words, and then claiming that there is something there rather than nothing. But this is not because he has independent arguments for a Philosophical theory to the effect that (in Sellars's words) "All awareness is a linguistic affair," or that "The meaning of a proposition is its method of verification." Such slogans as these are not the result of Philosophical inquiry into Awareness or Meaning, but merely ways of cautioning the public against the

Philosophical tradition. (As "No taxation without representation" was not a discovery about the nature of Taxation, but an expression of distrust in the British Parliament of the day.) There are no fast little arguments to show that there are no such things as intuitions—arguments which are themselves based on something stronger than intuitions. For the pragmatist, the *only* thing wrong with Nagel's intuitions is that they are being used to legitimize a vocabulary (the Kantian vocabulary in morals, the Cartesian vocabulary in philosophy of mind) which the pragmatist thinks should be eradicated rather than reinforced. But his *only* argument for thinking that these intuitions and vocabularies should be eradicated is that the intellectual tradition to which they belong has not paid off, is more trouble than it is worth, has become an incubus. Nagel's dogmatism of intuitions is no worse, or better, than the pragmatist's inability to give noncircular arguments.

This upshot of the confrontation between the pragmatist and the intuitive realist about the status of intuitions can be described either as a conflict of intuitions about the importance of intuitions, or as a preference for one vocabulary over another. The realist will favor the first description, and the pragmatist, the second. It does not matter which description one uses, as long as it is clear that *the issue is one about whether philosophy should try to find natural starting-points which are distinct from cultural traditions, or whether all philosophy should do is compare and contrast cultural traditions*. This is, once again, the issue of whether philosophy should be Philosophy. The intuitive realist thinks that there is such a thing as Philosophical truth because he thinks that, deep down beneath all the texts, there is something which is not just one more text but that to which various texts are trying to be "adequate." The pragmatist does not think that there is anything like that. He does not even think that there is anything isolable as "the purposes which we construct vocabularies and cultures to fulfill" against which to test vocabularies and cultures. But he does think that in the process of playing vocabularies and cultures off against each other, we produce new and better ways of talking and acting—not better by reference to a previously known standard, but just better in the sense that they come to *seem* clearly better than their predecessors.

5. A Post-Philosophical Culture

I began by saying that the pragmatist refused to accept the Philosophical distinction between first-rate truth-by-correspondence-to-reality and second-rate truth-as-what-it-is-good-to-believe. I said that this raised the question of whether a culture could get along without Philosophy, without the Platonic attempt to sift out the merely contingent and conventional truths from the Truths which were something more than that. The last two sections, in which I have been going over the latest round of "realist" objections to pragmatism, has brought us back to my initial distinction between philosophy and Philosophy. Pragmatism denies the possibility of getting beyond the Sellarsian notion of "seeing how things hang together"—which, for the bookish intellectual of recent times, means seeing how all the various vocabularies of all the various epochs and cultures hang together. "Intuition" is just the latest name for a device which will get us off the literary-historical-anthropological-political merry-go-round which such intellectuals ride, and onto something "progressive" and "scientific"—a device which will get us from philosophy to Philosophy.

I remarked earlier that a third motive for the recent anti-pragmatist backlash is simply the hope of getting off this merry-go-round. This hope is a correlate of the fear that if there is nothing quasi-scientific for philosophy as an academic discipline to do, if there is no properly professional *Fach* which distinguishes the philosophy professor from the historian or the literary critic, then something will have been lost which has been central to Western intellectual life. This fear is, to be sure, justified. If Philosophy disappears, something will have been lost which was central to Western intellectual life—just as something central was lost when religious intuitions were weeded out from among the intellectually respectable candidates for Philosophical articulation. But the Enlightenment thought, rightly, that what would succeed religion would be *better*. The pragmatist is betting that what succeeds the "scientific," positivist culture which the Enlightenment produced will be *better*.

The question of whether the pragmatist is right to be so sanguine is the question of whether a culture is imaginable, or desirable, in which no one—or at least no intellectual—believes that we have, deep down inside us, a criterion for telling whether we are in touch with reality or not, when we are in the Truth. This would be a culture in which neither the priests nor the physicists nor the poets nor the Party were thought of as more "rational," or more "scientific" or "deeper" than one another. No particular portion of culture would be singled out as exemplifying (or signally failing to exemplify) the condition to which the rest aspired. There would be no sense that, beyond the current intra-disciplinary criteria, which, for example, good priests or good physicists obeyed, there were other, transdisciplinary, transcultural, ahistorical criteria, which they also obeyed.

There would still be hero-worship in such a culture, but it would not be worship of heroes as children of the gods, as marked off from the rest of mankind by closeness to the immortal. It would simply be admiration of exceptional men and women who were very good at doing the quite diverse kinds of things they did. Such people would not be those who knew a Secret, who had won through to the Truth, but simply people who were good at being human.

A fortiori, such a culture would contain nobody called "the Philosopher" who could explain why and how certain areas of culture enjoyed a special relation to reality. Such a culture would, doubtless, contain specialists in seeing how things hung together. But these would be people who had no special "problems" to solve, nor any special "method" to apply, abided by no particular disciplinary standards, had no collective self-image as a "profession." They might resemble contemporary philosophy professors in being more interested in moral responsibility than in prosody, or more interested in the articulation of sentences than in that of the human body, but they might not. They would be all-purpose intellectuals who were ready to offer a view on pretty much anything, in the hope of making it hang together with everything else.

Such a hypothetical culture strikes both Platonists and positivists as "decadent." The Platonists see it has having no ruling principle, no center, no structure. The positivists see it as having no respect for hard fact, for that area of culture—science—in which the quest for objective truth takes precedence over emotion and opinion. The Platonists would like to see a culture guided by something eternal. The positivists would like to see one guided by something temporal —the brute impact of the way the world is. But both want it to be *guided*, constrained, not left to its own devices. For both, decadence is a matter of unwillingness to submit oneself to something "out there"—to recognize that beyond the languages of men and women there is something to which these languages, and the men and women themselves, must try to be "adequate." For both, therefore, Philosophy as the discipline which draws a line between such attempts at adequacy and everything else in culture, and so between first-rate and second-rate truth, is bound up with the struggle against decadence.

So the question of whether such a post-Philosophical culture is desirable can also be put as the question: can the ubiquity of language ever really be taken seriously? Can we see ourselves as never encountering reality *except under a chosen description*—as, in Nelson Goodman's phrase, making worlds rather than finding them?[47] This question has nothing to do with "idealism"—with the suggestion that we can or should draw metaphysical comfort from the fact that reality is "spiritual in nature." It is, rather, the question of whether we can give up what Stanley Cavell calls the "possibility that one among endless true descriptions of me tells who I am."[48] The hope that one of them will do just that is the impulse which, in our present culture, drives the youth to read their way through libraries, cranks to claim that they have found The Secret which makes all things plain, and sound scientists and scholars, toward the ends of their lives, to hope that their work has "philosophical implications" and "universal human significance." In a post-Philosophical culture, some other hope would drive us to read through the libraries, and to add new volumes to the ones we found. Presumably it would be the hope of offering our descendants a way of describing the ways of describing we had come across—a description of the descriptions which the race has come up with so far. If one takes "our time" to be "our view of previous times," so that, in Hegelian fashion, each age of the world recapitulates all the earlier ones, then a post-Philosophical culture would agree with Hegel that philosophy is "its own time apprehended in thoughts."[49]

In a post-Philosophical culture it would be clear that that is *all* that philosophy can be. It cannot answer questions about the relation of the thought of our time—the descriptions it is using, the vocabularies it employs—to something which is not just some alternative vocabulary. So it is a study of the comparative advantages and disadvantages of the various ways of talking which our race has invented. It looks, in short, much like what is sometimes called "culture criticism"—a term which has come to name the literary-historical-anthropological-political merry-go-round I spoke of earlier. The modern Western "culture critic" feels free to comment on anything at all. He is a prefiguration of the all-purpose intellectual of a post-Philosophical culture, the philosopher who has abandoned pretensions to Philosophy. He passes rapidly from Hemingway to Proust to Hitler to Marx to Foucault to Mary Douglas to the present situation in Southeast Asia to Ghandi to Sophocles. He is a name-dropper, who uses names such as these to refer to sets of descriptions, symbol-systems, ways of seeing. His specialty is seeing similarities and differences between great big pictures, between attempts to see how things hang together. He is the person who tells you how all the ways of making things hang together hang together. But, since he does not tell you about how all *possible* ways of making things hang together *must* hang together—since he has no extra-historical Archimedean point of this sort—he is doomed to become outdated. Nobody is so passé as the intellectual czar of the previous generation—the man who redescribed all those old descriptions, which, thanks in part to his redescription of them, nobody now wants to hear anything about.

The life of such inhabitants of Snow's "literary culture," whose highest hope is to grasp their time in thought, appears to the Platonist and the positivist as a life not worth living—because it is a life which leaves nothing permanent behind. In contrast, the positivist and the Platonist hope to leave behind true propositions, propositions which have been shown true once and for all—inheritances for the human race unto all generations. The fear and distrust inspired by "historicism"—the emphasis on the mortality of the vocabularies in which such supposedly immortal truths are expressed—is the reason why Hegel (and more recently Kuhn and Foucault) are *bêtes noires* for Philosophers, and especially for spokesmen for Snow's scientific culture."[50] (Hegel himself, to be sure, had his Philosophical moments, but the temporalization of rationality which he suggested was the single most important step in arriving at the pragmatist's distrust of Philosophy.)

The opposition between mortal vocabularies and immortal propositions is reflected in the opposition between the inconclusive comparison and contrast of vocabularies (with everybody trying to *aufheben* everybody else's way of putting everything) characteristic of the literary culture, and rigorous argumentation—the procedure characteristic of mathematics, what Kuhn calls "normal" science, and the law (at least in the lower courts). Comparisons and contrasts between vocabularies issue, usually, in new, synthetic vocabularies. Rigorous argumentation issues in agreement in propositions. The really exasperating thing about literary intellectuals, from the point of view of those inclined to science or to Philosophy, is their inability to engage in such argumentation—to agree on what would count as resolving disputes, on the criteria to which all sides must appeal. In a post-Philosophical culture, this exasperation would not be felt. In such a culture, criteria would be seen as the pragmatist sees them—as temporary resting-places constructed for specific utilitarian ends. On the pragmatist account, a criterion (what follows from the axioms, what the needle points to, what the statute says) *is* a criterion because some particular social practice needs to block the road of inquiry, halt the regress of interpretations, in order to get something done.[51] So rigorous argumentation—the practice which is made possible by agreement on criteria, on stopping-places—is no more *generally* desirable than blocking the road of inquiry is generally desirable.[52] It is something which it is convenient to have if you can get it. If the purposes you are engaged in fulfilling can be specified pretty clearly in advance (e.g., finding out how an enzyme functions, preventing violence in the streets, proving theorems), then you *can* get it. If they are not (as in the search for a just society, the resolution of a moral dilemma, the choice of a symbol of ultimate concern, the quest for a "postmodernist" sensibility), then you probably cannot, and you should not try for it. If what you are interested in is *philosophy*, you *certainly* will not get it—for one of the things which the various vocabularies for describing things differ about is the purpose of describing things. The philosopher will not want to beg the question between these various descriptions in advance. The urge to make philosophy into Philosophy is to make it the search for some final vocabulary, which can somehow be known in advance to be the common core, the truth of, all the other vocabularies which might be advanced in its place. This is the urge which the pragmatist thinks should be repressed, and which a post-Philosophical culture would have succeeded in repressing.

The most powerful reason for thinking that no such culture is possible is that seeing all criteria as no more than temporary resting-places, constructed by a community to facilitate its inquiries, seems morally humiliating. Suppose that Socrates was wrong, that we have *not* once seen the Truth, and so will not, intuitively, recognize it when we see it again. This means that when the secret police come, when the torturers violate the innocent, there is nothing to be said to them of the form "There is something within you which you are betraying. Though you embody the practices of a totalitarian society which will endure forever, there is something beyond those practices which condemns you." This thought is hard to live with, as is Sartre's remark:

> Tomorrow, after my death, certain people may decide to establish fascism, and the others may be cowardly or miserable enough to let them get away with it. At that moment, fascism will be the truth of man, and so much the worse for us. In reality, things will be as much as man has decided they are.[53]

This hard saying brings out what ties Dewey and Foucault, James and Nietzsche, together—the sense that there is nothing deep down inside us except what we have put there ourselves, no criterion that we have not created in the course of creating a practice, no standard of rationality that is not an appeal to such a criterion, no rigorous argumentation that is not obedience to our own conventions.

A post-Philosophical culture, then, would be one in which men and women felt themselves alone, merely finite, with no links to something Beyond. On the pragmatist's account, positivism was only a halfway stage in the development of such a culture—the progress toward, as Sartre puts it, doing without God. For positivism preserved a god in its notion of Science (and in its notion of "scientific philosophy"), the notion of a portion of culture where we touched something not ourselves, where we found Truth naked, relative to no description. The culture of positivism thus produced endless swings of the pendulum between the view that "values are merely 'relative' (or 'emotive,' or 'subjective')" and the view that bringing the "scientific method" to bear on questions of political and moral choice was the solution to all our problems. Pragmatism, by contrast, does not erect Science as an idol to fill the place once held by God. It views science as one genre of literature—or, put the other way around, literature and the arts as inquiries, on the same footing as scientific inquiries. Thus it sees ethics as neither more "relative" or "subjective" than scientific theory, nor as needing to be made "scientific." Physics is a way of trying to cope with various bits of the universe; ethics is a matter of trying to cope with other bits. Mathematics helps physics do its job; literature and the arts help ethics do its. Some of these inquiries come up with propositions, some with narratives, some with paintings. The question of what propositions to assert, which pictures to look at, what narratives to listen to and comment on and retell, are all questions about what will help us get what we want (or about what we *should* want).

The question of whether the pragmatist view of truth—that it is not a profitable topic—is itself *true* is thus a question about whether a post-Philosophical culture is a good thing to try for. It is not a question about what the word "true" means, nor about the requirements of an adequate philosophy of language, nor about whether the world "exists independently of our minds," nor about whether the intuitions of our culture are captured in the pragmatists' slogans. There is no way in which the issue between the pragmatist and his opponent can be tightened up and resolved according to criteria agreed to by both sides. This is one of those issues which puts everything up for grabs at once—where there is no point in trying to find agreement about "the data" or about what would count as deciding the question. But the messiness of the issue is not a reason for setting it aside. The issue between religion and secularism was no less messy, but it was important that it got decided as it did.

If the account of the contemporary philosophical scene which I offer in these essays is correct, then the issue about the truth of pragmatism is the issue which all the most important cultural developments since Hegel have conspired to put before us. But, like its predecessor, it is not going to be resolved by any sudden new discovery of how things really are. It will be decided, if history allows us the leisure to decide such issues, only by a slow and painful choice between alternative self-images.

Notes

1. A. J. Ayer, *The Origins of Pragmatism* (San Francisco: Freeman, Cooper, 1968) is a good example of the point of view.

2. For this attitude, see Habermas' criticism of Peirce in *Knowledge and Human Interests* (Boston: Beacon Press, 1968), chap. 6, esp. p. 135, and also the quotation from Heidegger at n. 66 of Essay 3, below.

3. Richard Rorty, *Philosophy and the Mirror of Nature* (Princeton: Princeton University Press, 1979).

4. To appear in the Cambridge University Press *Modern European Philosophy* series.

5. I develop this claim in Essays 6 and 8, below.

6. See the concluding section of Essay 11, below.

7. See Davidson, "On the Very Idea of a Conceptual Scheme," *Proceedings and Addresses of the American Philosophical Association*, 47 (1973-74): 5-20. See also my discussion of Davidson in Essay 1, below, in chap. 6 of *Philosophy and the Mirror of Nature*, and in "Transcendental Arguments, Self-Reference and Pragmatism" (*Transcendental Arguments and Science*, ed. P. Bieri, R.-P. Horstmann, and L. Krüger [Dordrecht: Reidel, 1979]), pp. 77-103.

8. For more on this distinction see sect. 6 of Essay 7, below.

9. *Collected Papers of Charles Sanders Peirce*, ed. Charles Hartshorne, Paul Weiss, and Arthur Burks (Cambridge, Mass.: Harvard University Press, 1933-58), 5.313-314.

10. Jacques Derrida, *Of Grammatology* (Baltimore: Johns Hopkins University Press, 1976), p. 49.

11. Wilfrid Sellars, *Science, Perception and Reality* (London: Routledge and Kegan Paul, 1967), p. 160.

12. Ludwig Wittgenstein, *Philosophical Investigations* (New York: Macmillan, 1953), p. 18.

13. Hans-Georg Gadamer, *Philosophical Hermeneutics* (Berkeley: University of California Press, 1976), p. 19.

14. Michel Foucault, *The Order of Things* (New York: Random House, 1973), p. 386.

15. Martin Heidegger, *On the Way to Language* (New York: Harper and Row, 1971), p. 50.

16. See Hans Sluga, *Frege* (London: Routledge and Kegan Paul, 1980), Introduction and chap. 1, for a discussion of Frege's neo-Kantian, anti-naturalistic motives.

17. Thomas Nagel, *Mortal Questions* (Cambridge: Cambridge University Press, 1979), p. xii.

18. *Ibid.*, p. 171.

19. See sect. 6 of Essay 7 on this point.

20. See Hilary Putnam's definition of "metaphysical realism" in these terms in his *Meaning and the Moral Sciences* (London: Routledge and Kegan Paul, 1978), p. 125.

21. Hilary Putnam, *Mind, Language and Reality* (Cambridge: Cambridge University Press, 1975), p. 236.

22. Hartry Field, "Meaning, Logic and Conceptual Role," *Journal of Philosophy*, LXXIV (1977): 398.

23. Field, "Tarski's Theory of Truth," *Journal of Philosophy*, LXIX (1972): 373.

24. Putnam attributes this point to Leeds in his *Meaning and the Moral Sciences*, p. 16. Field would presumably reply that it *is* explanatory because we use people's beliefs as indicators of how things are in the world. (See "Tarski's Theory of Truth," p. 371, and also Field, "Mental Representations," in *Readings in Philosophical Psychology*, ed. Ned Block, vol. 2 [Cambridge, Mass.: Harvard University Press, 1981], p. 103, for this argument.) The pragmatist should rejoin that what we do is not to say, "I shall take what Jones says as, *ceteris paribus*, a reliable indication of how the world is," but rather to say, "I shall, *ceteris paribus*, say what Jones says."

25. Many pragmatists (including myself) have not, in fact, always been wise enough to avoid this trap. Peirce's definition of truth as that to which inquiry will converge has often seemed a good way for the pragmatist to capture the realists' intuition that Truth is One. But he should not try to capture it. There is no more reason for the pragmatist to try to assimilate this intuition than for him to accept the intuition that there is always One Morally Best Thing To Do in every situation. Nor is there any reason for him to think that a science in which, as in poetry, new vocabularies proliferate without end, would be inferior to one in which all inquirers communicated in The Language of Unified Science. (I am grateful to discussions with Putnam for persuading me to reject the seductions of Peirce's definition—although, of course, Putnam's reasons for doing so are not mine. I am also grateful to a recent article by Simon Blackburn, "Truth, Realism, and the Regulation of Theory," *Midwest Studies in Philosophy*, V [1980]: 353-371, which makes the point that "It may be that the notion of improvement [in our theories] is sufficient to interpret remarks to the effect that my favorite theory may be wrong, but not itself sufficient to justify the notion of a limit of investigation" [p. 358].)

26. William James, *Pragmatism and the Meaning of Truth* (Cambridge, Mass.: Harvard University Press, 1978), p. 42.

27. *Ibid.*, p. 322.

28. Note that the question of whether there can be a "systematic theory of meaning for a language" is ambiguous between the question "Can we give a systematic account of what the user of a given natural language would have to know to be a competent speaker?" and "Can we get a philosophical semantics which will provide a foundation for the rest of philosophy?" Michael Dummett runs these two questions together in a confusing way when he says that Wittgenstein's metaphilosophical view that philosophy cannot be systematic presupposes that there can be no "systematic theory of meaning." (Dummett, *Truth and Other Enigmas* [Cambridge, Mass.: Harvard University Press, 1978], p. 453). Dummett says, rightly, that Wittgenstein has to admit that

> the fact that anyone who has a mastery of any given language is able to understand an infinity of sentences of that language . . . can hardly be explained otherwise than by supposing that each speaker has an implicit grasp of a number of general principles governing the use in sentences of words in the language. (*Ibid.*, p. 451)

and thus is committed to such a "systematic theory." But by granting that this is the only explanation of the fact in question, one is not committed to thinking, with Dummett, that "philosophy of language is the foundation for all the rest of philosophy" (*ibid.*, p. 454). One might, with Wittgenstein, *not* see philosophy as a matter of giving "analyses," and thus might deny the presupposition of Dummett's claim that "the correctness of any piece of analysis carried out in another part of philosophy cannot be fully determined until we know with reasonable certainty what form a correct theory of meaning for our language must take" (*ibid.*). This latter remark is Dummett's only explication of the sense in which philosophy of language is "foundational" for the rest of philosophy. As I tried to argue in chap. 6 of *Philosophy and the Mirror of Nature*, the fact that philosophical semantics grew up in the bosom of metaphilosophy does not mean that a mature and successful semantics — a successful "systematic theory of meaning for a language" — would necessarily have any metaphilosophical import. Children often disown their parentage. Dummett is certainly right that Wittgenstein's work does not "provide a solid foundation for future work in philosophy" in the sense in which the positivists hoped (and Dummett still hopes) that Frege's work does (*ibid.*, p. 452). But only someone antecedently convinced that semantics must give philosophers guidance about how to "analyze" would blame this lack of a foundation on the fact that Wittgenstein fails to "provide us with any outline of what a correct theory of meaning would look like" (*ibid.*, p. 453). Wittgenstein believed, on nonsemantical grounds, that philosophy was not the sort of thing that had foundations, semantical or otherwise.

29. Dummett, *Truth and Other Enigmas*, p. 358.

30. On the claim that pragmatism cannot explain why science works (elaborated most fully in a forthcoming book by Richard Boyd), see Simon Blackburn, "Truth, Realism, and the Regulation of Theory" (cited in n. 25 above), esp. pp. 356-360. I agree with Blackburn's final conclusion that ". . . realism, in the disputed cases of morals, conditionals, counterfactuals, mathematics, can only be worth defending in an interpretation which makes it noncontroversial" (p. 370).

31. This bag of tricks contains lots of valuable antiques, some bequeathed to the pragmatist by Berkeley *via* the British Idealists. This association of pragmatism with Berkeley's arguments for phenomenalism has led many realists (Lenin, Putnam) to suggest that pragmatism is (a) just a variant of idealism and (b) inherently "reductionist." But an argument for Berkeleian phenomenalism requires not only the pragmatic maxim that things are what they are known as, but the claim (deservedly criticized by Reid, Green, Wittgenstein, Sellars, Austin, *et al.*) that we can make sense of Berkeley's notion of "idea." Without this latter notion, we cannot proceed further in the direction of the British Idealist claim that "reality is spiritual in nature." Failure to distinguish among Berkeley's premises has led to a great deal of realist rhetoric about how pragmatists think reality is "malleable," do not appreciate the brutishness of the material world, and generally resemble idealists in not realizing that "physical things are externally related to minds." It must be confessed, however, that William James did sometimes say things which are susceptible to such charges. (See, e.g., the disastrously flighty passage at p. 125 of *Pragmatism*. In Essay 5, below, I criticize Dewey for occasionally having wandered down the same garden path.) As for reductionism, the pragmatist reply to this charge is that since he regards all vocabularies as tools for accomplishing purposes and none as representations of how things really are, he cannot possibly claim that "X's *really are* Y's," although he *can* say that it is more fruitful, for certain purposes, to use Y-talk than to use X-talk.

32. See Thompson Clarke, "The Legacy of Skepticism," *Journal of Philosophy*, LXIX (1972): 754-769, esp. the concluding paragraph. This essay is cited by both Cavell and Nagel as making clear the "depth" of the tradition of epistemological skepticism. See Essay 10, below, on Cavell.

33. Nagel, *Mortal Questions*, p. xii.

34. *Ibid.*, p. 35.

35. *Ibid.*, pp. 35-36.

36. *Ibid.*, p. 36.

37. *Ibid.*, p. 37.

38. Iris Murdoch, *The Sovereignty of Good* (New York: Schocken, 1971), p. 8.

39. *Ibid.*, p. 9.

40. *Ibid.*, p. 27.

41. *Ibid.*, pp. 28-30.

42. Daniel Dennett, *Brainstorms* (Montgomery, Vt.: Bradford Books, 1978), p. 228.

43. Nagel, *Mortal Questions*, pp. 192-193.

44. Wittgenstein, *Philosophical Investigations*, I, sect. 271.

45. *Ibid.*, I, sect. 115.

46. Nagel, *Mortal Questions*, p. 170.

47. See Nelson Goodman, *Ways of Worldmaking* (Indianapolis: Hackett, 1978). I think that Goodman's trope of "many worlds" is misleading and that we need not go beyond the more straightforward "many descriptions of the same world" (provided one does not ask, "And what world is *that*?"). But his point that there is no way to compare descriptions of the world in respect of adequacy seems to me crucial, and in the first two chapters of this book he makes it very vividly.

48. Stanley Cavell, *The Claim of Reason* (Oxford: Oxford University Press, 1979), p. 388.

49. Hegel, *Philosophy of Right*, trans. T. M. Knox (Oxford: Oxford University Press, 1952), p. 11. This passage, like the famous one which follows ("When philosophy paints its grey in grey, then has a shape of life grown old. By a philosophy's grey on grey it cannot be rejuvenated but only understood. The owl of Minerva spreads its wings only with the falling of the dusk.") is not typical of Hegel, and is hard to reconcile with much of the rest of what he says about philosophy. But it perfectly represents the side of Hegel which helped create the historicism of the nineteenth century and which is built into the thinking of the present-day literary intellectual. I say more about this point in Essay 8.

50. The opposition between the literary and the scientific cultures which C. P. Snow drew (in *The Two Cultures and the Scientific Revolution* [Cambridge: Cambridge University Press, 1959]) is, I think, even deeper and more important than Snow thought it. It is pretty well co-incident with the opposition between those who think of themselves as caught in time, as an evanescent moment in a continuing conversation, and those who hope to add a pebble from Newton's beach to an enduring structure. It is not an issue which is going to be resolved by literary critics learning physics or physicists reading the literary quarterlies. It was already drawn in Plato's time, when physics had not yet been invented, and when Poetry and Philosophy first squared off. (I think, incidentally, that those who criticize Snow along the lines of "not just *two* cultures, but many" miss his point. If one wants a neat dichotomy between the two cultures he was talking about, just ask any Eastern European censor which Western books are importable into his country. The line he draws will cut across fields like history and philosophy, but will almost always let physics in and keep highbrow novels out. The nonimportable books will be the ones which might suggest new vocabularies for self-description.)

51. There are, of course, lots of criteria which cut across all divisions between parts of culture — e.g., the laws of logic, the principle that a notorious liar's reports do not count as evidence, and the like. But these do not possess some special authority by virtue of their universality, any more than the set consisting of the fulcrum, the screw, and the lever is privileged by virtue of contributing to every other machine.

52. Peirce said that "the first rule of reason" was "Do not block the way of inquiry" (*Collected Papers*, 1.135). But he did not mean that one should always go down any road one saw — a point that comes out in his emphasis on "logical self-control" as a corollary of "ethical self-control." (See, e.g., *Collected Papers*, 1.606.) What he was getting at in his "rule of reason" was the same point as he makes about the ubiquity of language — that we should never think that the regress of interpretation can be stopped once and for all, but rather realize that there may always be a vocabulary, a set of descriptions, around the corner which will throw everything into question once again. To say that obedience to criteria is a good thing *in itself* would be like saying that self-control is a good in itself. It would be a species of Philosophical puritanism.

53. Jean-Paul Sartre, *L'Existentialisme est un Humanisme* (Paris: Nagel, 1946), pp. 53-54.

Consequences of Pragmatism

1

The World Well Lost

The notion of alternative conceptual frameworks has been a commonplace of our culture since Hegel. Hegel's historicism gave us a sense of how there might be genuine novelty in the development of thought and of society. Such a historicist conception of thought and morals was, we may see by hindsight, rendered possible by Kant, himself the least historicist of philosophers. For Kant perfected and codified the two distinctions that are necessary to develop the notion of an "alternative conceptual framework"—the distinction between spontaneity and receptivity and the distinction between necessary and contingent truth. Since Kant, we find it almost impossible not to think of the mind as divided into active and passive faculties, the former using concepts to "interpret" what "the world" imposes on the latter. We also find it difficult not to distinguish between those concepts which the mind could hardly get along without and those which it can take or leave alone—and we think of truths about the former concepts as "necessary" in the most proper and paradigmatic sense of the term. But as soon as we have this picture of the mind in focus, it occurs to us, as it did to Hegel, that those all-important a priori concepts, those which determine what our experience or our morals will be, might have been different. We cannot, of course, imagine what an experience or a practice *that* different would be like, but we can abstractly suggest that the men of the Golden Age, or the inhabitants of the Fortunate Isles, or the mad, might shape the intuitions that are our common property in different molds, and might thus be conscious of a different "world."

3

Various attacks on the contrast between the observed and the theoretical (in, e.g., Kuhn, Feyerabend, and Sellars) have led recently to a
new appreciation of Kant's point that to change one's concepts would
be to change what one experiences, to change one's "phenomenal
world." But this appreciation leads us to question the familiar distinction between spontaneity and receptivity. The possibility of different
conceptual schemes highlights the fact that a Kantian unsynthesized
intuition can exert no influence on how it is to be synthesized—or,
at best, can exert only an influence we shall have to describe in a way
as relative to a chosen conceptual scheme as our description of everything else. Insofar as a Kantian intuition is effable, it is just a perceptual judgment, and thus not *merely* "intuitive." Insofar as it is
ineffable, it is incapable of having an explanatory function. This dilemma—a parallel to that which Hegelians raised concerning the
thing-in-itself—casts doubt on the notion of a faculty of "receptivity."
There seems no need to postulate an intermediary between the physical thrust of the stimulus upon the organ and the full-fledged conscious judgment that the properly programmed organism forms in
consequence. Thus there is no need to split the organism up into a
receptive wax tablet on the one hand and an "active" interpreter of
what nature has there imprinted on the other. So the Kantian point
that different a priori concepts would, if there could be such things,
give a different phenomenal world gives place either to the straightforward but paradoxical claim that different concepts give us different worlds, or to dropping the notion of "conceptual framework"
altogether. 'Phenomenal' can no longer be given a sense, once Kantian
"intuitions" drop out. For the suggestion that our concepts shape
neutral material no longer makes sense once there is nothing to serve
as this material. The physical stimuli themselves are not a useful substitute, for the contrast between the "posits" which the inventive
mind constructs to predict and control stimuli, and the stimuli themselves, can be no more than a contrast between the effable world and
its ineffable cause.[1]

The notion of *alternative* conceptual frameworks thus contains the
seeds of doubt about the root notion of "conceptual framework," and
so of its own destruction. For once the faculty of receptivity and,
more generally, the notion of neutral material becomes dubious,
doubt spreads easily to the notion of conceptual thought as "shap-
ing" and thus to the notion of the World-Spirit moving from one set
of a priori concepts to the next.

But the doubts about the Hegelian picture produced by an attack
on the given/interpretation distinction are vague and diffuse by

comparison with those which result from attacking the necessary/ contingent distinction. Quine's suggestion that the difference between a priori and empirical truth is merely that between the relatively difficult to give up and the relatively easy brings in its train the notion that there is no clear distinction to be drawn between questions of meaning and questions of fact. This, in turn, leaves us (as Quine has pointed out in criticizing Carnap) with no distinction between questions about alternative "theories" and questions about alternative "frameworks."[2] The philosophical notion of "meaning," against which Quine is protesting is, as he says, the latest version of the "idea idea"—a philosophical tradition one of whose incarnations was the Kantian notion of "concept." The notion of a choice among "meaning postulates" is the latest version of the notion of a choice among alternative conceptual schemes. Once the necessary is identified with the analytic and the analytic is explicated in terms of meaning, an attack on the notion of what Harman has called the "philosophical" sense of 'meaning' becomes an attack on the notion of "conceptual framework" in any sense that assumes a distinction of kind between this notion and that of "empirical theory."[3]

So far we have seen how criticisms of givenness and of analyticity both serve to dismantle the Kantian notion of "conceptual framework"—the notion of "concepts necessary for the constitution of experience, as opposed to concepts whose application is necessary to control or predict experience." I have been arguing that without the notions of "the given" and of "the a priori" there can be no notion of "the constitution of experience." Thus there can be no notion of alternative experiences, or alternative worlds, to be constituted by the adoption of new a priori concepts. But there is a simpler and more direct objection to the notion of "alternative conceptual framework," to which I now wish to turn. This objection has recently been put forward, in connection with Quine's thesis of indeterminacy, by Davidson and Stroud.[4] The argument is verificationist, and turns on the unrecognizability of persons using a conceptual framework different from our own (or, to put it another way, the unrecognizability as a *language* of anything that is not translatable into English). The connection between Quine's attack on "conventionalist" notions of meaning and this verificationist argument is supposed to be as follows: if one thinks of "meaning" in terms of the discovery of the speech dispositions of foreigners rather than in terms of mental essences (ideas, concepts, chunks of the crystalline structure of thought), then one will not be able to draw a clear distinction between the foreigner's using words different in meaning from any words in our language and the foreigner's having many false beliefs. We can and must play off awkward translations against ascriptions of quaint beliefs, and vice versa, but we will never reach the limiting case of a foreigner all or most of whose beliefs must be viewed as false according to a translating scheme that pairs off all or most of his terms as identical in meaning with some terms of English. We will not reach this case (so the Davidsonian argument goes) because any such translation scheme would merely show that we had not succeeded in finding a translation at all.

But (to extend Davidson's argument a bit) if we can never find a translation, why should we think that we are faced with language users at all? It is, of course, possible to imagine humanoid organisms making sounds of great variety at one another in very various circumstances with what appear to be various effects upon the interlocutors' behavior. But suppose that repeated attempts systematically to correlate these sounds with the organisms' environment and behavior fail. What should we say? One suggestion might be that the analytic hypotheses we are using in our tentative translation schemes use concepts that we do not share with the natives—because the natives "carve up the world" differently, or have different "quality spaces" or something of the sort. But could there be a way of deciding between this suggestion and the possibility that the organisms' sounds are *just* sounds? Once we imagine different ways of carving up the world, nothing could stop us from attributing "untranslatable languages" to *anything* that emits a variety of signals. But, so this verificationist argument concludes, this degree of open-endedness shows us that the purported notion of an untranslatable language is as fanciful as that of an invisible color.

It is important to note that Quinean arguments against analyticity and for the indeterminacy of translation are not necessary for this argument. The argument stands on its own feet—Quine's only contribution to it being to disparage the possibility that 'meaning' can mean something more than what is contextually defined in the process of predicting the foreigner's behavior. To adopt this view of meaning is all that is required to suggest that the notion of "people who speak our language but believe nothing that we believe" is incoherent.[5] To *show* that it is incoherent, however—to complete the argument—one would have to show in detail that no amount of non-linguistic behavior by the foreigner could be sufficient to underwrite a translation that made all or most of his beliefs false.[6] For it might be the case, for example, that the way in which the foreigner dealt with trees while making certain sounds made it clear that we had to translate some of his utterances as "These are not trees," and so on for everything else with which he had dealings. Some of his utterances might be translated as: "I am not a person," "These are not words," "One should never use *modus ponens* if one wishes valid arguments," "Even if I were thinking, which I am not, that would not show that I exist." We might ratify these translations by showing that his nonlinguistic ways of handling himself and others showed that he actually did hold such paradoxical beliefs. The only way to show that this suggestion cannot work, would be actually to tell the whole story about this hypothetical foreigner. It might be that a story could be told to show the coherence of these false beliefs with each other and with his actions, or it might not. To show that Davidson and Stroud were right would be to show that, indeed, no such story was tellable.

There is, I think, no briefer way to decide on the soundness of this a priori argument against the possibility of alternative conceptual frameworks than to run over such possible stories. But this inconclusiveness is a feature this argument has in common with all interesting verificationist anti-skeptical arguments. It conforms to the following pattern: (1) the skeptic suggests that our own beliefs (about, e.g., other minds, tables and chairs, or how to translate French) have viable alternatives which unfortunately can never be known to hold but which justify the suspension of judgment; (2) the anti-skeptic replies that the very meaning of the terms used shows that the alternatives suggested are not merely dubious but in principle unverifiable, and thus not reasonable alternatives at all; (3) the skeptic rejoins that verificationism confuses the *ordo essendi* with the *ordo cognoscendi* and that it may well be that some alternative is true even though we shall never know that it is; (4) the anti-skeptic replies that the matter is not worth debating until the skeptic spells out the suggested alternative in full detail, and insinuates that this cannot be done; (5) the controversy degenerates into a dispute about assuming the burden of proof, with the skeptic claiming that it is not up to him to build up a coherent story around his suggested alternative but rather up to the anti-skeptic to show a priori that this cannot be done.

In the case at hand, the skeptic is the fan of "alternative conceptual frameworks," practicing his skepticism on a global scale by insinuating that our entire belief structure might dissolve, leaving not a wrack behind, to be replaced by a complete but utterly dissimilar alternative. The Davidsonian anti-skeptic is in the position of asking how one could come to call any pattern of behavior evidence for such an alternative. The skeptic replies that perhaps we could *never* come to do so, but this merely shows how complete our egocentric predicament is. And so it goes.[7]

In this case, however (unlike the case of limited skepticism about whether, e.g., 'pain' or 'red' means to me what it does to you) the skeptic's global approach gives him a significant dialectical advantage. For he can here sketch what might bring about the actualization of his suggested alternative without being caught up in disagreement about how to interpret concrete experimental results. He can simply refer us to ordinary scientific and cultural progress extrapolated just beyond the range of science fiction. Consider, he will say, the following view of man's history and prospects. Our views about matter and motion, the good life for man, and much else have changed in subtle and complicated ways since the days of the Greeks. Many of the planks in Neurath's boat have been torn up and relaid differently. But since (1) we can describe why it was "rational" for each such change to have occurred, and (2) *many* more of our beliefs are the same as Greek beliefs than are different (e.g., our belief that barley is better than nettles and freedom than slavery, that red is a color, and that lightning often precedes thunder), we should not yet wish to talk about "an alternative conceptual framework." And yet we must admit that even the relatively slight refurbishings of the boat which have occupied the past two thousand years are enough to give us considerable difficulty in knowing just *how* to translate some Greek sentences, and just *how* to explain the "rationality" of the changes that have intervened. Again, the various shifts that have taken place in our understanding of the subject matter of the beliefs we purportedly "share" with the Greeks (resulting from, e.g., the development of new strains of nettles, new forms of slavery, new ways of producing color perceptions, and new explanations of the sound of the thunder and the look of the lightning) make us a little dubious about the claim to shared belief. They create the feeling that here too we may be imposing on history rather than describing it. Let us now extrapolate from ourselves to the Galactic civilization of the future, which we may assume to have moved and reshaped 10^{50} planks in the boat we are in, whereas since Aristotle we have managed to shift only about 10^{20}. Here the suggestion that we interpret these changes as a sequence of rational changes in views about a common matter seems a bit forced, and the fear that even the most empathic Galactic historians of science "won't really understand us properly" quite appropriate. So, our skeptic concludes, the Davidson-Stroud point that to describe in detail the Galactic civilization's beliefs is automatically to make them merely alternative theories within a common framework is not enough. Granting this point, we can still see that it is rational to expect that the incommunicably and unintelligibly novel will occur, even though, *ex hypothesi*, we can neither write nor read a science-fiction story that describes Galactic civilization. Here, then, we have a case in which there really is a difference between the *ordo cognoscendi* and the *ordo essendi*, and no verificationist argument can apply.

To intensify the antinomy we confront here, let us agree for the sake of argument that it is a necessary condition for an entity to be a person that it have or once have had the potentiality for articulating beliefs and desires comparable in quantity and complexity to our own. The qualifications are required if we are to include infants and the insane while excluding dogs and the simpler sort of robots. But the same qualifications will, of course, give trouble when we come to cases where it is not clear whether we are educating a person by developing his latent potentialities (as by teaching a child a language) or transforming a thing into a person (as by clamping some additional memory units onto the robot). Bating this difficulty for the moment, however, let us simply note that this formulation has the consequence that ascribing personhood, ascribing a language, and ascribing beliefs and desires go hand in hand. So, if Davidson is right, ascribing personhood and ascribing mostly the *right* beliefs and mostly the *appropriate* desires go hand in hand. This means that we shall never be able to have evidence that there exist persons who speak languages in principle untranslatable into English or hold beliefs all or most of which are incompatible with our own.

Despite this, however, we can extrapolate to a story about how just such persons might come into existence. So it seems that the world may come to be full of persons whom we could never conceivably recognize as such. A Galactic time-traveler come among us, we now realize, would eventually be forced to abandon his original presumption that we were persons when he failed to correlate our utterances with our environment in any way that enabled him to construct an English-Galactic lexicon. Our initial assumption that the Galactic emissary was a person would be frustrated by the same sort of discovery. How sad that two cultures who have so much to offer each other should fail to recognize each other's existence! What pathos in the thought that we, time-traveling among our Neanderthal ancestors, might stand to them as the Galactic stands to us! But the situation is even worse than that, for reasons I hinted at earlier. We can now see that, for all we know, our *contemporary* world is filled with unrecognizable persons. Why should we ignore the possibility that the trees and the bats and the butterflies and the stars all have their various untranslatable languages in which they are busily expressing their beliefs and desires to one another? Since their organs suit them to receive such different stimuli and to respond in such different ways, it is hardly surprising that the syntax and the primitive predicates of their languages bear no relation to our own.

The inclusion of this last possibility may suggest that something has gone wrong. Perhaps we should not have been so ready to admit the possibility of extrapolation. Perhaps we were too hasty in thinking that attributions of personhood and of articulate belief went hand in hand—for surely we know in advance that butterflies are not persons and therefore know in advance that they will have no beliefs to express. For myself, however, I see nothing wrong with the proposed extrapolation, and I do not see what 'known in advance not to be a person' could mean when applied to the butterfly save that the butterfly doesn't seem human. But there is no particular reason to think that our remote ancestors or descendants would seem human right off the bat either. Let the notion of a person be as complex and multiply criterioned as you please, still I do not think that it will come unstuck from that of a complex interlocked set of beliefs and desires, nor that the latter notion can be separated from that of the potentiality for translatable speech. So I think that to rule the butterflies out is to rule out the Galactics and the Neanderthals, and that to allow extrapolation to the latter is to allow for the possibility that the very same beliefs and desires which our Galactic descendants will hold are being held even now by the butterflies. We can dig in our heels and say that terms like 'person', 'belief', 'desire', and 'language' are ultimately as token-reflexive as 'here' and 'now' or 'morally right', so that in each case essential reference is made to where *we* are. But that will be the *only* way of ruling out the Galactic, and thus the *only* way of ruling out the butterfly.

If this seems puzzling, I think it will seem less so if we consider some parallels. Suppose we say that there is no poetry among the Patagonians, no astronomy among the aborigines, and no morality among the inhabitants of the planet Mongo. And suppose a native of each locale, protesting against our parochial view, explains that what they have is a *different* sort of poetry, astronomy, or morals, as the case may be. For the Patagonian, neither Homer nor Shelley nor Mallarmé nor Dryden look in the least like poets. He admits, however, that Milton and Swinburne are both faintly reminiscent, in the same only vaguely describable respect, of the paradigms of Patagonian poesy. Those paradigms strike him as clearly fulfilling some of the roles in his culture which our poets fulfill in ours, though not all. The aborigine knows nothing of the equinoxes and the solstices, but he does distinguish planets from stars. However, he uses the same term to refer to planets, meteors, comets, and the sun. The stories he tells about the movements of these latter bodies are bound up with a complicated set of stories about divine providence and cure of diseases, whereas the stories told about the stars have to do exclusively with sex. The inhabitants of the planet Mongo appear shocked when people tell the truth to social equals, and surprised and amused when people refrain from torturing helpless wanderers. They seem to have no taboos at all about sex, but a great many about food. Their social organizations seem held together half by a sort of lottery, and half by brute force. The inhabitants of Mongo, however, profess to be revolted by the Earthlings' failure to grasp the moral point of view, and by our apparent confusion of morality with etiquette and with expedients for ensuring social order.

In the three cases just cited the question, Is it a different *sort* of poetry (or astronomy, or morality), or do they simply have *none?* is obviously not the sort of question it is very important to answer. I suggest that the question, Are the Galactics, or the butterflies, different sorts of persons than ourselves or not persons at all? is also not very important. In the three cases mentioned, one can extend the argument indefinitely by pressing for further details. In the global case, where *ex hypothesi* no translation scheme will work, we cannot. But in the global case (having beliefs *tout court*), as in the particular cases of having beliefs about astronomy or about right and wrong, what is in question is just the best way of predicting, controlling, and generally coping with the entities in question. In the course of figuring this out, we encounter some of the same hard questions I referred to above—the questions that arise when coping with such borderline cases as fetuses, prelinguistic infants, computers, and the insane—Do they have civil rights? Must we try to justify ourselves to them? Are they thinking or acting on instinct? Are they holding beliefs or merely responding to stimuli? Is that a word to which they assign a sense, or are they just sounding off on cue? I doubt that many philosophers believe any longer that procedures for answering such questions are built into "our language" waiting to be discovered by "conceptual analysis." But if we do not believe this, perhaps we can be content to say, in the global case, that the question, Might there be alternative conceptual frameworks to our own, held by persons whom we could never recognize as persons? is the same case. I doubt that we can ever adumbrate general ways of answering questions like, Is it a conceptual framework very different from our own, or is it a mistake to think of it as a language at all? Is it a person with utterly different organs, responses, and beliefs, with whom communication is thus forever impossible, or rather just a complexly behaving thing?

This "don't-care" conclusion is all I have to offer concerning the antinomy created by the Davidson-Stroud argument on the one hand and the skeptic's extrapolation on the other. But this should not be thought of as denigrating the importance of what Davidson and Stroud are saying. On the contrary, I think that, having seen through this antinomy and having noticed the relevance of the original argument to our application of the notion of "person," we are now in a better position to see the importance that it has. This importance can be brought out by (a) looking at the standard objection to the coherence theory of truth ("it cuts truth off from the world") and (b) recurring to our previous discussion of the Kantian roots of the notion of "conceptual framework."

Consider first the traditional objection to coherence theories of truth which says that, although our only *test* of truth must be the coherence of our beliefs with one another, still the *nature* of truth must be "correspondence to reality." It is thought a sufficient argument for this view that Truth is One, whereas alternative equally coherent sets of beliefs are Many.[8] In reply to this argument, defenders of coherence and pragmatic theories of truth have argued that our so-called "intuition" that Truth is One is simply the expectation that, if all perceptual reports were in, there would be one optimal way of selecting among them and all other possible statements so as to have one ideally proportioned system of true beliefs. To this reply, the standard rebuttal is that there would clearly be many such possible systems, among which we could choose only on aesthetic grounds. A further, and more deeply felt, rebuttal is that it is the *world* that determines the truth. The accident of which glimpses of the world our sense organs have vouchsafed us, and the further accidents of the predicates we have entrenched or the theories whose proportions please us, may determine what we have a right to believe. But how could they determine the *truth?*[9]

Now the Davidson-Stroud argument supplies a simple, if temporizing, answer to this standard objection to the coherence theory. Since most of our beliefs (though not any particular one) simply *must* be true—for what could count as evidence that the vast majority of them were not?—the specter of alternative conceptual frameworks shrinks to the possibility that there might be a number of equally good ways to modify slightly our present set of beliefs in the interest of greater predictive power, charm, or what have you. The Davidson-Stroud point makes us remember, among other things, what a very small proportion of our beliefs are changed when our paradigms of physics, or poetry, or morals, change—and makes us realize how few of them *could* change. It makes us realize that the number of beliefs that changed among the educated classes of Europe between the thirteenth and the nineteenth centuries is ridiculously small compared to the number that survived intact. So this argument permits us to say: it is just not the case that there are "alternative" coherent global sets of beliefs. It is perfectly true that there will always be areas of inquiry in which alternative incompatible sets of beliefs are "tied." But the fact that we shall *always* be holding mostly true beliefs and, thus, presumably be "in touch with the world" the vast majority of the time makes this point seem philosophically innocuous. In particular, the claim that, since Truth is One and, therefore, is "correspondence," we must resurrect a foundationalist epistemology to explain "how knowledge is possible" becomes otiose.[10] We shall automatically be "in touch with the world" (most of the time) whether or not we have any incorrigible, or basic, or otherwise privileged or foundational statements to make.

But this way of dealing with the claim that "it is the *world* that determines what is true" may easily seem a fraud. For, as I have been using it, the Davidson-Stroud view seems to perform the conjuring trick of substituting the notion of "the unquestioned vast majority of our beliefs" for the notion of "the world." It reminds us of such coherence theorists as Royce, who claim that our notion of "the world" is just the notion of the ideally coherent contents of an ideally large mind, or of the pragmatists' notion of "funded experience"—those beliefs which are not at the moment being challenged, because they present no problems and no one has bothered to think of alternatives to them. In all these cases—Davidson and Stroud, Royce, Dewey—it may well seem that the issue about truth is just being ducked. For our notion of the world—it will be said—is not a notion of unquestioned beliefs, or unquestionable beliefs, or ideally coherent beliefs, but rather of a hard, unyielding, rigid *être-en-soi* which stands aloof, sublimely indifferent to the attentions we lavish upon it. The true realistic believer will view idealisms and pragmatisms with the same suspicion with which the true believer in the God of our Fathers will view, for example, Tillich's talk of an "object of ultimate concern."[11]

Now, to put my cards on the table, I think that the realistic true believer's notion of the world is an obsession rather than an intuition. I also think that Dewey was right in thinking that the only intuition we have of the world as determining truth is just the intuition that we must make our new beliefs conform to a vast body of platitudes, unquestioned perceptual reports, and the like. So I am happy to interpret the upshot of the Davidson-Stroud argument in a Deweyan way.

But I have no arguments against the true believer's description of our so-called "intuitions." All that can be done with the claim that "only the *world* determines truth" is to point out the equivocation in the realists' own use of 'world'. In the sense in which "the world" is just whatever that vast majority of our beliefs not currently in question are currently thought to be about, there is of course no argument.[12] If one accepts the Davidson-Stroud position, then "the world" will just be the stars, the people, the tables, and the grass — all those things which nobody except the occasional "scientific realist" philosopher thinks might not exist. The fact that the vast majority of our beliefs must be true will, on this view, guarantee the existence of the vast majority of the things we now think we are talking about. So in one sense of 'world' — the sense in which (except for a few fringe cases like gods, neutrinos, and natural rights) we now know perfectly well what the world is like and could not possibly be wrong about it — there is no argument about the point that it is the world that determines truth. All that "determination" comes to is that our belief that snow is white is true because snow is white, that our beliefs about the stars are true because of the way the stars are laid out, and so on.

But this trivial sense in which "truth" is "correspondence to reality" and "depends upon a reality independent of our knowledge" is, of course, not enough for the realist.[13] What he wants is precisely what the Davidson-Stroud argument prevents him from having — the notion of a world *so* "independent of our knowledge" that it might, for all we know, prove to contain none of the things we have always thought we were talking about. He wants to go from, say, "we might be wrong about what the stars are" to "none of the things we talk about might be anything like what we think they are." Given this projection from, as Kant would say, the "conditioned" to the "unconditioned," it is no wonder that antinomies are easily generated.

The notion of "the world" as used in a phrase like 'different conceptual schemes carve up the world differently' must be the notion of something *completely* unspecified and unspecifiable — the thing-in-itself, in fact. As soon as we start thinking of "the world" as atoms and the void, or sense data and awareness of them, or "stimuli" of a certain sort brought to bear upon organs of a certain sort, we have changed the name of the game. For we are now well within some particular theory about how the world is. But for purposes of developing a controversial and nontrivial doctrine of truth as correspondence, only an utterly vague characterization in some such terms as 'cause of the impacts upon our receptivity and goal of our faculty of spontaneity' will do. "Truth" in the sense of "truth taken apart from any theory" and "world" taken as "what determines such truth" are notions that were (like the terms 'subject' and 'object', 'given' and 'consciousness') made for each other. Neither can survive apart from the other.

To sum up this point, I want to claim that "the world" is either the purely vacuous notion of the ineffable cause of sense and goal of intellect, or else a name for the objects that inquiry at the moment is leaving alone: those planks in the boat which are at the moment not being moved about. It seems to me that epistemology since Kant has shuttled back and forth between these two meanings of the term 'world', just as moral philosophy since Plato has shuttled back and forth between 'the Good' as a name for an ineffable touchstone of inquiry which might lead to the rejection of *all* our present moral views, and as a name for the ideally coherent synthesis of as many of those views as possible. This equivocation seems to me essential to the position of those philosophers who see "realism" or "the correspondence theory of truth" as controversial or exciting theses.

To remove altogether the "realistic" temptation to use the word 'world' in the former vacuous sense, we should need to eschew once and for all a whole galaxy of philosophical notions that have encouraged this use—in particular, the Kantian distinctions I discussed at the outset. For suppose we have a simple theory of the eye of the mind either getting, or failing to get, a clear view of the natures of kinds of things—the sort of theory we get, say, in parts of Aristotle's *Posterior Analytics*. Then the notion of alternative sets of concepts will make no clear sense. *Noûs* cannot err. It is only when we have some form of the notion that the mind is split between "simple ideas" or "passively received intuitions" on the one hand and a range of complex ideas (some signifying real, and some only nominal, essences) on the other, that *either* the coherence theory of truth *or* the standard objections to it can begin to look plausible. Only then is the notion plausible that inquiry consists in getting our "representations" into shape, rather than simply describing the world. If we no longer have a view about knowledge as the result of manipulating *Vorstellungen*, then I think we can return to the simple Aristotelian notion of truth as correspondence with reality with a clear conscience—for it will now appear as the uncontroversial triviality that it is.

To develop this claim about the way in which Kantian epistemology is linked with the notion of a nontrivial correspondence theory of truth and thus with the "realist's" notion of "the world" would require another paper, and I shall not try to press it further. Instead I should like to conclude by recalling some of the historical allusions I have made along the way, in order (as Sellars says) to place my conclusions in philosophical space. I said at the outset that the notion of "conceptual framework" and, thus, that of "alternative conceptual framework" depend upon presupposing some standard Kantian distinctions. These distinctions have been the common target of Wittgenstein, Quine, Dewey, and Sellars. I can now express the same point by saying that the notion of "the world" that is correlative with the notion of "conceptual framework" is simply the Kantian notion of a thing-in-itself, and that Dewey's dissolution of the Kantian distinctions between receptivity and spontaneity and between necessity and contingency thus leads naturally to the dissolution of the true realistic believer's notion of "the world." If you start out with Kant's epistemology, in short, you will wind up with Kant's transcendental metaphysics. Hegel, as I suggested earlier, kept the epistemology, but tried to drop the thing-in-itself, thus making himself, and idealism generally, a patsy for realistic reaction. But Hegel's historical sense—the sense that nothing, including an a priori concept, is immune from cultural development—provided the key to Dewey's attack on the epistemology that Hegel shared with Kant. This attack was blunted by Dewey's use of the term 'experience' as an incantatory device for blurring every possible distinction, and so it was not until more sharply focused criticisms were formulated by Wittgenstein, Quine, and Sellars that the force of Dewey's point about "funded experience" as the "cash-value" of the notion of "the world" could be seen. But now that these criticisms have taken hold, the time may have come to try to recapture Dewey's "naturalized" version of Hegelian historicism. In this historicist vision, the arts, the sciences, the sense of right and wrong, and the institutions of society are not attempts to embody or formulate truth or goodness or beauty. They are attempts to solve problems—to modify our beliefs and desires and activities in ways that will bring us greater happiness than we have now. I want to suggest that this shift in perspective is the natural consequence of dropping the receptivity/spontaneity and intuition/concept distinctions, and more generally of dropping the notion of "representation" and the view of man that Dewey has called "the spectator theory" and Heidegger, the "identification of *physis* and *idea*." Because the idealists kept this general picture and occupied themselves with redefining the "object of knowledge," they gave the idealism and the "coherence theory" a bad name—and realism and the "correspondence theory" a good one. But if we can come to see both the coherence and correspondence theories as noncompeting trivialities, then we may finally move beyond realism and idealism. We may reach a point at which, in Wittgenstein's words, we are capable of stopping doing philosophy when we want to.

Notes

1. T. S. Kuhn, "Reflections on My Critics," in I. Lakatos and A. Musgrave, eds., *Criticism and the Growth of Knowledge* (New York: Cambridge, 1970), p. 276, says that "the stimuli to which the participants in a communication breakdown respond are, under pain of solipsism, the same" and then continues by saying that their "programming" must be so also, since men "share a history . . . a language, an every day world, and most of a scientific one." On the view I should like to support, the *whole* anti-solipsist burden is borne by the "programming," and the "stimuli" (like the noumenal unsynthesized intuitions) drop out. If a stimulus is thought of as somehow "neutral" in respect to different conceptual schemes, it can be so only, I would argue, by becoming "a wheel that can be turned though nothing else moves with it." (Cf. Ludwig Wittgenstein, *Philosophical Investigations* [New York: Macmillan, 1958], I, 271.)

2. See W. V. Quine, "On Carnap's View on Ontology," in *The Ways of Paradox* (New York: Random House, 1966), pp. 126-134.

3. See Gilbert Harman, "Quine on Meaning and Existence, I," *Review of Metaphysics*, XXI, 1 (September 1967): 124-151, p. 142.

4. I first became aware of this argument, and of the importance of the issues I am here discussing, on reading the sixth of the Locke Lectures which Davidson gave at Oxford in 1970. These lectures are at present still unpublished, and I am most grateful to Davidson for permission to see the manuscript, and also the manuscript of his 1971 University of London Lectures on "Conceptual Relativism"—the more especially as I want to turn Davidson's argument to purposes for which he would have slim sympathy. After reading Davidson's unpublished material, I read Barry Stroud's presentation of a partially similar argument in "Conventionalism and the Indeterminacy of Translation," in *Words and Objections: Essays on the Work of W. V. Quine*, ed. Davidson and J. Hintikka (Doredrecht: Reidel, 1969), esp. pp. 89-96. Stroud and Davidson concur in rejecting the notion of "alternative conceptual frameworks," but Davidson goes on to draw explicitly the radical conclusion that "most of our beliefs must be true." It is this latter conclusion on which I shall be focusing in this paper. (Addendum, 1981: Although Davidson has not yet published his Locke Lectures in full, the material most relevant to this paper has appeared in his "On the Very Idea of a Conceptual Scheme," *Proceedings of the American Philosophical Association*, 17 (1973-74), pp. 5-20.)

5. I have argued elsewhere ("Indeterminacy of Translation and of Truth," *Synthese*, 23 [1972]: 443-462) that Quine's doctrine that there is no "matter of fact" for translations to be right or wrong about, is philosophical overkill, and that the "idea idea" is adequately discredited by attacks on the Kantian distinctions discussed above.

6. The importance of this point was shown me by Michael Friedman. I am grateful also to Michael Williams for criticisms of my general line of argument.

7. I have tried to develop this view of the course of the argument between verification-

ists and skeptics in "Verificationism and Transcendental Arguments, *Noûs*, V, 1 (February 1971): 3-14, and in "Criteria and Necessity," *Noûs*, VIII, 4 (November 1973): 313-329.

8. For a recent formulation of this objection, see John L. Pollock, "Perceptual Knowledge," *Philosophical Review*, LXXX, 3 (July 1971): 290-292.

9. This sort of question is at the root of the attempt to distinguish between a "theory of truth" and a "theory of evidence" in reply to such truth-as-assertibility theorists as Sellars — see Harman's criticism of Sellars on this point in "Sellars' Semantics," *Philosophical Review*, LXXIX, 3 (July 1970): 404-419, pp. 409ff., 417ff.

10. See Pollock, *op. cit.*, for a defense of the claim that, once we reject a coherence theory of justification, such an explanation in foundationalist terms becomes necessary.

11. For examples of the programmatic passion that realism can inspire, see the "Platform of the Association for Realistic Philosophy" in *The Return to Reason*, ed. John Wild (Chicago: Henry Regnery, 1953); and the "Program and First Platform of Six Realists," in Edwin B. Holt *et al.*, *The New Realism* (New York: Macmillan, 1912), pp. 471ff.

12. I say "are currently thought to be about" rather than "are about" in order to skirt an issue that might be raised by proponents of a "causal theory of reference." Such a theory might suggest that we are in fact now talking about (referring to) what the Galactics will be referring to, but that the Galactics might know what this was and we might not. (The relevance of such theories of reference was pointed out to me by Michael Friedman and by Fred Dretske.) My own view, which I cannot develop here, is that an attempt to clarify epistemological questions by reference to "reference" will always be explaining the obscure by the more obscure — explicating notions ("knowledge," "truth") which have some basis in common speech in terms of a contrived and perpetually controversial philosophical notion. See Essay 7, below.

13. I do not wish to be taken as suggesting the triviality of Tarski's semantic theory, which seems to me not a theory relevant to epistemology (except perhaps, as Davidson has suggested, to the epistemology of language learning). I should regard Tarski as founding a new subject, not as solving an old problem. I think that Davidson is right in saying that, in the sense in which Tarski's theory is a correspondence theory, "it may be the case that no battle is won, or even joined between correspondence theories and others" ("True to the Facts," *Journal of Philosophy*, LXVI, 21 [Nov. 6, 1969]: 748-764, p. 761). The philosophically controversial "correspondence theory of truth" to which coherence and pragmatic theories were supposed alternatives is not the theory Strawson (quoted by Davidson, *op. cit.*, p. 763) identifies as "to say that a statement is true is to say that a certain speech-episode is related in a certain conventional way to something in the world exclusive of itself." For this latter view would, as far as it goes, be perfectly acceptable to, e.g., Blanshard or Dewey.

2

Keeping Philosophy Pure:
An Essay on Wittgenstein

Ever since philosophy became a self-conscious and professionalized discipline, around the time of Kant, philosophers have enjoyed explaining how different their subject is from such merely "first-intentional" matters as science, art, and religion. Philosophers are forever claiming to have discovered methods which are presuppositionless, or perfectly rigorous, or transcendental, or at any rate *purer* than those of nonphilosophers. (Or, indeed, of any philosophers save themselves and their friends and disciples.) Philosophers who betray this gnostic ideal (Kierkegaard and Dewey, for example) are often discovered not to have been "real philosophers."

Ludwig Wittgenstein began by thinking that he had made philosophy so pure that its problems had only to be stated to be solved or dissolved, and so he thought that philosophy had been brought to an end. The propositions of his *Tractatus Logico-Philosophicus* were supposed to be as remote from the world and its works as those of logic itself—propositions which showed what could not be said. Mere fact can be said, but philosophy, Wittgenstein thought, is a matter of showing the form of all possible facts. Once showing took the place of saying, philosophical disputes, and so philosophy itself, would be over. Yet Wittgenstein came in the end to mock his own creation, and especially its pretense of purity. But while mocking the *Tractatus*'s attempt to "show" the form of all possible facts by showing the form of all possible languages, he still wished to "show" something else which could not be said: the source of philosophy itself, the ineffable shift of focus which can make the jejune textbook

19

"problems of philosophy" genuine and compelling. The *Tractatus*
had said: there can be no genuine discursive discipline which deals
with those matters called "the problems of philosophy" for *here* are
the limits of language, and thus of discursive inquiry. The *Philosophical Investigations* said: there can be as much of a discipline as you
care to develop, but do you really wish to do so? Supplanting the
hermetic but still indicative sentences of the *Tractatus* by the rhetorical questions of the *Investigations* was a move away from precision,
away from argument, away from the Kantian attempt to "place philosophy on the secure path of science" by abjuring the empirical. But
in another way it was still Kantian. If, with Richard Kroner, one sees
the whole sweep of Kant's work in the light of his project of "denying reason to make room for faith," and if one thinks of Kant the
pietist rather than Kant the professor, of the "primacy of the practical" rather than of the "transcendental standpoint," then one can
see both Kant and Wittgenstein as yearning for that purity of heart
which replaces the need to explain, justify, and expound. This purity
is possible only for the twice-born—for those who once abandoned
themselves to the satisfaction of this need, but who are now redeemed.

Academic philosophy in our day stands to Wittgenstein as intellectual life in Germany in the first decades of the last century stood
to Kant. Kant had changed everything, but no one was sure just what
Kant had said—no one was sure what in Kant to take seriously and
what to put aside. To think seriously, in Germany in those days, was
either to pick and choose from Kant or to find some way of turning
one's back on him altogether. Philosophers are in an analogous situation now, twenty years after the publication of the *Investigations*.
One must either reject Wittgenstein's characterization of what philosophy has been or find something new for philosophy to be. In this
situation, philosophers are torn between the traditional Kantian ideal
of purity—*Philosophie als strenge Wissenschaft*—and the sort of post-
professional, redemptive, private purity of heart which Wittgenstein
seemed to suggest might be possible. They are torn between the need
to profess a pure subject, to rejoice in the possession of a distinctive
Fach, and the need to come to terms with Wittgenstein's account of
the nature of their discipline. (I use *Fach*, instead of "subject" or
"area," because the word happens to have been given an elegant and
precise contextual definition by William James, in his description of
Wilhelm Wundt: "He isn't a genius, he is a *professor*—a being whose
duty is to know everything and have his own opinion about everything connected with his *Fach* . . . He says of each possible subject,
'Here I must have an opinion. Let's see! What shall it be? How many

possible opinions are there? three? four? Yes! Just four! Shall I take one of these? It will seem more original to take a higher position, a sort of *Vermittelungsansicht* between them all. That I will do, etc., etc."[1])

In this situation, a split has come about between, as David Pears puts it, "systematic linguistic philosophy" on the one hand and "Wittgensteinian philosophy" on the other.[2] The former, which includes such growing points in contemporary philosophy as the work of Donald Davidson, Richard Montague, and Gilbert Harman, contrasts in both form and provenance with the work of such "Wittgensteinian" writers as T. S. Kuhn and Stanley Cavell.[3] For the first sort of philosopher, the structure of our language, our ability to learn it, and its ties with the world form a set of problems which are traditionally "philosophical" (dating, perhaps, from Parmenides), but which nevertheless lend themselves to discursive argument and possibly to precise solution. These philosophers take part of their inspiration from the early Wittgenstein — the author of the *Tractatus*. They see logic as the key to philosophy as a quasi-scientific discipline, a discipline which might solve real problems about language at the same time as it avoids the pseudo-problematic created by the Cartesian distinctions between subject and object, mind and matter. Insofar as such philosophers put forward a view of Wittgenstein, they tend to view him as rightly critical of the Cartesian tradition, but as having little to say (in the *Investigations*, at any rate) which is relevant to philosophy of language — a subject they see as now coextensive with metaphysics, and perhaps with philosophy itself. Philosophers who think of themselves as explaining where Wittgenstein has left us, on the other hand, tend to see the destruction of the Cartesian problematic not simply as the debunking of a few pseudo-problems, but as transforming philosophy, and perhaps thought and life itself. For these writers, the destruction of the frame of reference common to Descartes and Kant is much more than the occasion for dismissing a few textbook conundrums. It is something to be thought through over generations, as deeply and fully as men thought out the destruction of the Christian frame of reference common to Augustine and Newman. The split which occurred in the Enlightenment between writers who shrugged off religion and went on to serious matters, and those to whom religion was so important that religious skepticism had to be pressed unceasingly and uncompromisingly, is presently paralleled among philosophers reacting to Wittgenstein's skepticism about the post-Renaissance philosophical tradition.

It is obvious that "systematic linguistic philosophy" runs the risk of scholasticism and insignificance, and that "Wittgensteinian" philosophy runs the risk of vapid imitation of an aphoristic writer of genius. I shall not, however, be discussing these dangers, nor any of the post-Wittgensteinian movements in philosophy. I have described the split simply in order to provide a background against which to discuss the problem which engendered it: does it make sense to speak of a new philosophical view as bringing an end to philosophy? In particular, does it make sense to say that philosophy as a subject is somehow overcome, or outmoded, or ready to wither away, as the result of some discovery which Wittgenstein made about something called "linguistic facts"? Can one wriggle out of the dilemma that Wittgenstein either proposed one more dubious philosophical theory, or else was not "doing philosophy" at all?

Pears, in his book on Wittgenstein, struggles with these questions, and works out an account of what he calls Wittgenstein's "anthropocentrism" which is, I think, the most fully thought out and most perceptive treatment of the method and aim of the *Investigations* which has appeared. Still, I think that Pears takes the wrong tack, and that he does so because he interprets Wittgenstein within the framework of a set of distinctions ("linguistic facts" versus other facts, convention versus nature, conditional versus unconditional necessity, philosophy versus science, sense versus nonsense, "factual knowledge" versus other realms of discourse) which themselves are left over from the *Tractatus* and which cannot be used without perpetuating the notion of philosophy as a distinct *Fach*. One cannot have a *Fach*, after all, if one has no distinctions to use in setting it off from those alongside, or below, it. But if one accepts these distinctions, then one will face the question Pears poses: how on earth is one to tell whether Wittgenstein was right in being anthropocentric? What touchstone of philosophical truth will decide between Wittgenstein's anthropocentrism and "realism" or "objectivism"? If one accepts the various Tractarian distinctions Pears uses, these will be questions which it is part of the philosopher's *Fach* to answer. If one rejects them, it is hard to see that Wittgenstein has anything that could be called a philosophical view. For what would such a view be *about*?

Pears is well aware of this dilemma. He summarizes Wittgenstein's "extreme anthropocentrism" by saying that

> It is Wittgenstein's later doctrine that outside human thought and speech there are no independent, objective points of support, and meaning and necessity are preserved only in the linguistic processes which embody them. They are safe only because the practices gain a certain stability from

the rules. But even the rules do not provide a fixed point of reference, because they always allow divergent interpretations. What really gives the practices their stability is that we agree in our interpretations of the rules. We could say that this is fortunate, except that this would be like saying that it is fortunate that life on earth tolerates the earth's natural atmosphere. What we ought to say is that there is as much stability as there is.[4]

Two pages later, Pears introduces this *caveat*:

It is difficult to describe the move to anthropocentrism in an accurate and neutral way. Any description of it has to mention the point of departure, which was objectivism, and so there will be the suggestion that things are less secure than we had supposed. This suggestion must be canceled, if Wittgenstein's position is to be understood. He is not rejecting objectivism and offering a rival theory. The very use of the word "anthropocentrism" is likely to give the wrong impression, not because it is an inaccurate label, and some other word would be better, but because it instantly places Wittgenstein's view in the arena with its apparent rival, and so it is taken for granted that there will be a philosophical conflict according to the old rules. It is, therefore, essential to remember how different Wittgenstein's intention was. *He believed that the correct method was to fix the limit of language* by oscillation between two points. In this case the outer point was the kind of objectivism which tries to offer an independent support for our linguistic practises, and the inner point is a description of the linguistic practises themselves, a description which would be completely flat, if it were not given against the background of that kind of objectivism. His idea is that the outer point is an illusion, and that the inner point is the whole truth, which must, however, be apprehended through its contrast with the outer point. *It is quite correct to apply the word "anthropocentrism" to the inner point, provided that there is no implication that it is an alternative to objectivism.* Wittgenstein's idea is that objectivism, in its only tenable form, collapses into anthropocentrism. It would, therefore, be better to say that there is only one possible theory here, *the theory that there is nothing but the facts about the relevant linguistic practises* [italics added].[5]

Here Pears ties himself up in paradoxes. Some of these are the same paradoxes elaborated by Wittgenstein himself (who cheerfully tosses out half-a-dozen incompatible metaphilosophical views in the course of the *Investigations*). In Pears's treatment, however, they are less easy to laugh off, because more baldly and resolutely stated. Three such paradoxes are illustrated by the three sentences I have italicized. The notion of "fixing the limits of language," a relic of the *Tractatus*, is still as susceptible as ever to the standard rejoinder used against logical positivism: "when you say that something is beyond the limits of language, you don't mean literally that it can't be said, you must mean that it doesn't make sense. But you must understand it well enough to see that it 'doesn't make sense,' and it must have had sense if you understood it that well." The "objectivist's" notion that our language shapes itself around universals, or meanings, or necessities "out there"—the claim that there is something, not ourselves, which makes for rigor—is as intelligible (and as dubious) as the notion that the moral law expresses the will of God. No positivistic critique of religion has ever justified calling statements which have been the subject of intelligent discussion over centuries "nonsense." Nothing in the *Investigations* gives this term any greater force or reach.

A second paradox is offered in the second sentence I italicized, for if there is no "alternative to objectivism" contained in the definition of "anthropocentrism," then there is no force left in the term at all. If "nature" is an illusion, so is "convention" and so is "man." Contrastive terms of this sort stand or fall together. To have a view about where necessity comes from *is* to have a view which allows "a philosophical conflict according to the old rules." For this is a view about necessity in the sense in which an Arian or a pantheist might have a view about God (as opposed to the way in which the man who thinks religion too childish to be discussed seriously has a view about God).

The third paradox is really the same as the second. Pears is fond of the formulation that "there is nothing but the facts about the relevant linguistic practises" and the claim that "the only possible theory is the theory that there are only the linguistic facts." But, once again, either "language" contrasts with "the world" (and "linguistic fact" with "nonlinguistic fact") or the term has no force. If there are only linguistic facts, then we are just renaming all the old facts "linguistic." Pears is clearly torn between using the sort of resolute tautology he has used earlier ("There is as much stability as there is")—simply saying that "The only possible theory is that there are only the facts" —and making the thesis nontrivial by including the term "linguistic." But even apart from the paradox created by the lack of contrast between "language" and something else, there is paradox in any sentence that begins "The only possible theory is . . . ," for theories are things that come two (or many) at a time. When there is just one theory about the gods or the seasons, there is no *theory*—there are just the well-known facts about the gods or the seasons. Theory starts, as Dewey remarked, when somebody has doubts about what everyone has always believed, and suggests that there is another way of looking at the matter. The possibility of alternative theories ends only when interest in the subject has lapsed so far that no one cares what anyone else might say about it.

One important reason why anyone who tries to describe the upshot of the *Investigations* will become involved in such paradoxes comes from the notion that Wittgenstein (with the help of Gottlob Frege, Bertrand Russell, Rudolf Carnap, *et al.*) made philosophy *linguistic* —that he helped us see "the importance of language." It would be nice to think that philosophy has been making progress lately, and the handiest way of describing the difference between what up-to-date English-speaking philosophers do and what their ancestors did (and backward contemporaries still do) has been to talk about the "Linguistic Turn" and the "New Way of Words." But no one has been able to explain what it is that can be said in terms of words but cannot be as well said in terms of things, or how Carnap's "formal mode" carries more philosophical punch than his "material mode." When one believed, as Wittgenstein did in the *Tractatus*, that there was something called "the form of any possible language," then one might attempt to derive ontology from logic. But even then, Wittgenstein would have been hard put to it to say what the difference was between his familiar slogan "The limits of my language are the limits of my world" and its converse "The limits of my world are the limits of my language." Once the whole notion of "ontology" is abandoned, as it is in the *Investigations*, the paradox created by the lack of contrastive force in the notion of "language" is redoubled. Attempts to supply some force have resulted in an immense amount of talk about the need to distinguish "conceptual" (or "grammatical" or "semantic") from "empirical" questions. It has even been claimed, and is sometimes suggested by Pears, that part of the contribution of the *Investigations* is to show that certain suggestions made by traditional philosophers (e.g., Hume's suggestion that two people might have numerically the same sensation) confuse possibilities left open by "our language" and possibilities closed off by "our language."[6] Indeed, Pears holds that in the *Investigations*

[he] maintained that the right method in philosophy is to collect facts about language, but not because of their own intrinsic interest, nor in order to construct some scientific theory about them, such as a theory about the common grammatical structure of all languages. The facts are to be collected because they point beyond themselves. They point back in the direction from which critical philosophy has traveled in the last two centuries.[7]

I shall argue in a moment that any criticism of the tradition which can be done by collecting facts about language could be done as well by collecting facts about things, and that anyway there is no clear way of distinguishing the two activities. But I want to prepare the way for this argument by a remark about the split in post-Wittgensteinian philosophy I mentioned earlier. This split is encouraged if one thinks of Wittgenstein as "collecting facts about language." For it is natural to ask: If this is the right method of philosophy, why not practice it scientifically? Why not replace Wittgenstein's flair for apposite analogies (or J. L. Austin's ear for cute distinctions) with, for example, a computer program which would accept slices of everyday banality as input and produce statements about the meanings of words as output? This urge to put philosophy back on the secure path of a science has ramified into a whole series of programs in recent philosophy of language, few of which any longer have much connection with Wittgenstein's own interests. Pears worries about this, and his worry takes the form of wondering "whether philosophy can avoid being a science" and whether it should. Pears sympathizes with Wittgenstein's "resistance to science," but he is not sure that he has any right to. On the one hand, it is difficult to have a *Fach* if you do not have a science—artists, for example, have no *Fach*, but merely skills, or perhaps genius. On the other hand, philosophy has always prided itself on being deeper, or higher, or purer, than empirical science, and what sort of science could there be of "facts about language" if not an empirical one? So Wittgenstein's discovery of "the right method in philosophy" seems to lead either to linguistics getting above itself, or to a claim that we can discover "facts about language" nonempirically. Either philosophy "will be absorbed into the science of linguistics"[8] or it will be a sort of art. But "if philosophy really is like art, the impression made by a linguistic example would be something which could not be caught in any general formula."[9] Can one call something which has no such formula "philosophy"?

This art-vs.-science distinction is central to Pears's treatment of Wittgenstein, and it connects up with the dissolution of the *Tractatus* program of finding "unconditional necessities"—the program which Wittgenstein once shared with Plato, Descartes, and Hegel. For if one has to depend upon "conditional necessities which depend on contingent facts about language"[10] then one is in the sphere of the mutable, the practical, the unpredictable—just where, in fact, philosophy has always made it a point not to be. If such remarks as "No person can have numerically the same sensation as another" gets its "necessity" from the way in which people talk, why should not philosophers who dislike that way of talking suggest changes, and why may they not have a point? The specter of philosophy as merely "linguistic recommendation" enters, only to be pushed aside by the still more terrifying specter of "philosophy as a matter of taste." (For who cares whether other people accept my recommendations, if I, for myself, have found a new and better way of speaking?) It begins to seem as if anthropocentrism about necessity (the claim that all necessity rests on the contingencies of social practice) must necessarily be the death of philosophy as we have known it. Either Wittgenstein is showing how empirical means can be used to discover "the limits of language" (in which case philosophical error will be, of all things, a failure to gather enough facts) or he is somehow playing on our mixed feelings about the philosophical tradition (now in the manner of a satirist, now in that of a parlor psychoanalyst).

Notice that all these dilemmas turn on the notion of "necessity." Pears does not question that there is something out there to be found —the limits of language—which, once found, will tell us where Descartes, Hume, Kant, etc., went wrong. Nor does he question that finding a limit to language is finding something "necessary." The point about the so-called "linguistic turn" in recent philosophy is supposed to be that whereas once we thought, with Aristotle, that necessity came from things, and later thought with Kant that it came from the structure of our minds, we now know that it comes from language. And since philosophy must seek the necessary, philosophy must become linguistic. All this Pears is reasonably happy with—his only problem is whether language (as one more social practice) is strong enough to stand the strain. If language is not constrained by things, or the transcendental ego, or *something*, then when one finds its limits is one really finding anything that counts as *necessary*? And if one isn't, is one doing *philosophy*?

So, it would seem, we are in the following position. If we got rid of the concept of necessity we might see our way out of the dilemmas. But to drop this concept would seem to be to drop the concept of philosophy itself. If we stop thinking of Wittgenstein as the anthropocentric theorist who said that necessity comes from man, and start thinking of him as the satirist who suggested that we get along without the concept of necessity, then we might have fewer dilemmas about what sort of a discipline philosophy was, but only at the cost of being dubious about its very existence.

There are two questions here. First, can Wittgenstein actually be interpreted as talking against "necessity" rather than about it? Second, would it be a good idea to stop using this notion? The answer to the first question is, I think, "Yes, about half the time." Wittgenstein can be interpreted either way; texts can be cited as definitive refutations of either sort of exegesis. But it is only the second question which I want to discuss, and here I think the answer is simply "yes." I want to argue that the later Wittgenstein belongs with Dewey as much as the earlier Wittgenstein belongs with Kant—that Dewey's debunking of traditional notions of philosophy, and his attempt to break down the distinctions between art and science, philosophy and science, art and religion, morality and science, are a natural outcome of Wittgenstein's critique of the Cartesian tradition. On Dewey's view, "philosophy" as what is common to Plato, Kant, and the *Tractatus* is, indeed, a distinctive cultural tradition—but it is not a *Fach* (though its study is). Philosophy in a broader sense—roughly, the sort of writing which generalizes so sweepingly that one has no other compartment for it—is something else, but it is not a *Fach* either. No *Fach*, no metaphilosophical problems about its subject and method—so no dilemmas of the sort I have been running through. To stop using the concept of necessity would be to cease to try to keep philosophy pure, but that attempt, I think, has cost us too much waste motion already.

At bottom, the argument about whether the notion of "necessity" is of any use is an argument between the sort of holism which Pears says is characteristic of the *Investigations* and the sort of atomism characteristic of the *Tractatus*. Holism, as in Duhem, Quine, and Kuhn, focuses on the fact that there is an indefinitely large variety of ways in which one can readjust what one has been in the habit of saying to conform to a surprising scientific discovery (or a philosophical perplexity, or a religious experience). Given this variety, one will have doubts (of the sort which have become especially identified with Quine) about how to tell which of one's changes in conversation express changes "in belief" and which are changes "in the meaning one assigns to certain terms." *Ad hoc* and for a given audience, one may wish to say "I still mean by 'X' what I always did, but I no longer think that all X's are Y's," or instead say "I now have a different concept of 'X'—I no longer mean the same thing by the word." But which one says is a rhetorical matter, not a mark of the line between "factual knowledge" on the one hand and "philosophy" on the other. Thus holism brings (as it did to Dewey and Hegel) doubts about necessity-vs.-contingency, about language-vs.-fact, and about philosophy-vs.-science.

Pears thinks of the later Wittgenstein as "anthropocentrist" because Pears himself retains notions which make sense in the light of the atomistic program of the *Tractatus* but which no longer seem of interest when one adopts the holistic outlook of the *Investigations*. But he does no more than Wittgenstein himself had done. In the *Investigations*, Tractarian notions keep turning up in contexts where Wittgenstein himself seems puzzled about whether to cherish or to make fun of them. My hunch, for which I do not know how to argue, is that both Pears and Wittgenstein hang on to Tractarian distinctions which the *Investigations* transcends because both of them cherish the purity of philosophy. Both would like "philosophy" to be the name of something distinctive and extraordinary—not a *Fach*, perhaps, but, in Pears's words, "something outside ordinary life and ideas." Neither would relish philosophy's becoming what Dewey thought it was: critical thought at a level of generality which differs only in degree from all the rest of inquiry. It is not that they worry about the nature of philosophy because there are difficulties with the notions of "necessity" and of "linguistic fact," but that they worry about the latter notions because there are difficulties in the notion of "philosophy."

Even if one accepts this last point, however, the notion that Wittgenstein might somehow have brought philosophy to an end will remain just as perplexing. Even if I am right in saying that Wittgenstein leads himself and Pears into needless puzzles by the suggestion that philosophy can be brought to an end by a recognition of the anthropocentric character of necessity, what would "an end" mean? Suppose that the "necessity" of a philosophically interesting categorical proposition is, as I have been arguing, just a rhetorical compliment to the so-called "distinctively philosophical" character of the proposition. Is there then *nothing* that makes a proposition, or an issue, distinctively (or "purely") philosophical? If not, what is it that might be brought to an end? So far, all I have been trying to show is that we can avoid the self-contradictory claim that philosophy has been brought to an end by a new philosophical theory about a distinctively philosophical topic (e.g., necessity). But the more general paradox remains. Philosophy resembles space and time: it is hard to imagine what an "end" to any of the three would look like.

To discuss this larger paradox, I need to distinguish three sorts of things to which the term "philosophy" is applied: (1) discussion of (in Wilfrid Sellars's phrase) "how things, in the largest sense of the term, hang together, in the largest sense of the term"; (2) a collection of the principal topics discussed by most of the "great philosophers" —subject and object, mind and matter, utilitarian and deontological ethics, free will and determinism, language and thought, God and the world, universals and particulars, meaning and reference, etc., etc.; (3) an academic subject—that is, whatever batch of issues the people who teach in one's favorite philosophy departments are talking about at the moment.

Different things have to be said about the purity of philosophy, and about the possibility of ending philosophy, for each of these three senses. In the first sense, philosophy is obviously not a distinct *Fach*, and nobody would ever claim "purity" for it. Nor would anybody think it could or should be ended. But in this sense "philosopher" is almost synonymous with "intellectual." Philosophy as synoptic vision is obviously not the province of a single academic discipline. If one lists all the various people who usually count as "philosophers" (e.g., those whose names might turn up on examinations for the Ph.D. in philosophy), a random sample might include Heraclitus, Abelard, Spinoza, Marx, Kierkegaard, Frege, Gödel, Dewey, and Austin. Nobody would claim that there was a common subject, the study of which set these men apart from (say) Euripides, the pseudo-Dionysius, Montaigne, Newton, Samuel Johnson, Leopold von Ranke, Stendhal, Thomas Huxley, Edmund Wilson, and Yeats. The topics and authors which fall under the care of philosophy departments form a largely accidental, and quite temporary, hodgepodge—determined mostly by the accidents of power struggles within universities and by current fashions. (Compare a contemporary Ph.D. exam in philosophy with one given in 1900, and imagine what one might be like in 2050.) This is not a matter for regret; curricular arrangements are not that important. But it helps to bear in mind that having large views about things in general does not entail that one will be studied by teachers of philosophy, nor does being so studied entail that one has such views.

Skipping for a moment over the second sense—philosophy as "the traditional problems"—notice that in the third sense also there is no problem about the purity of philosophy. The issues being discussed at any given moment by any given philosophy department or philosophical school have that routine sort of purity which any technical subject has. They will automatically be "purely philosophical" issues simply because there will be a body of literature which provides the contextual definition of what these issues are, and which only professors of philosophy have read. This sort of purity is the sort which any topic develops after a lot of people have worked on it for a while —they will be the only people who know what is relevant, and they will justifiably resent intrusions from nonspecialists who know the name of the issue but not its substance. This purity is not distinctively "philosophical"—it is possessed also by the study of fluorides and the study of Chaucer's prosody. Nor is there a problem about bringing philosophy in *this* sense to an end. A technical problem—no matter how scholastic or silly it may appear to outsiders—has a natural life-span of its own, and nothing can kill it off save its successful resolution or an agreement among those who were once attracted by it that it was indeed a dead end.

So to see what is meant by the possibility of an end to philosophy, and to appreciate the poignancy of the need for philosophical purity, we have to turn away from both philosophy-as-vision and philosophy-as-academic-specialty. One has to think of philosophy as a name for the study of certain definite and permanent problems—deep-lying problems which any attempt at vision must confront: problems which professors of philosophy have a moral obligation to continue working on, whatever their current preoccupations. The Nature of Being, the Nature of Man, the Relation of Subject and Object, Language and Thought, Necessary Truth, the Freedom of the Will—this is the sort of thing which philosophers are supposed to have views about but which novelists and critics, historians and scientists, may be excused from discussing. It is such textbook problems which Wittgensteinians think the *Investigations* may let us dismiss. Among these problems it is especially those created by Cartesian dualism which they have in mind: the problems created by thinking of man as somehow categorically distinct from the rest of nature, of knowing as a process unlike anything else, of the mind as something which is aware only of representations of the world (and thus perhaps "cut off" from the world), of volition as a mental act which mysteriously has physical effects, of language and thought as systems of representations which have somehow to "correspond" to the world. As to the study of *these* problems, it is true that, as Pears says, "Philosophy, unlike religion, is not a part of ordinary life, but a kind of excursion from it." If one grants that these problems are indeed based on "confusions," then Pears is right in saying that "human thought has a natural and almost irresistible temptation to make these confusions, and we feel that there really are hidden depths in the direction indicated by them" (though perhaps "human thought" should read "human thought since 1600").

Now to say that these typically Cartesian problems are "purely philosophical" has a fairly definite meaning: it is just to say that nothing that the sciences (or the arts, for that matter) do is going to be of any help in solving them. No facts about evolution or the DNA molecule, or the brain as computer, or child development, or primitive tribes, or quantum physics, will be of any use—because the

problems are constructed in such a way as to remain equally problematic no matter how many details are added. Work by philosophers
on the Cartesian problems has spun off plenty of new disciplines
(formal logic, psychology, the history of ideas) but the problems stand
as they stood—any respect in which they seem to have changed is
easily dismissed as a confusion of "purely philosophical" problems
with some "merely factual" question. In every generation, brilliant
and feckless philosophical naifs (Herbert Spencer, Thomas Huxley,
Aldous Huxley, Jean Piaget, B. F. Skinner, Noam Chomsky) turn from
their own specialties to expose the barrenness of academic philosophy
and to explain how some or all of the old philosophical problems will
yield to insights gained outside of philosophy—only to have the philosophy professors wearily explain that nothing has changed at all. Philosophy in the second sense—the solution of the traditional problems—
must necessarily be thought of as having a pure, distinctively philosophical, method. Questions as distinct from "fact" as these must be
approached by a method whose purity is adequate to the "hidden
depths" from which these problems spring, just as the priests of Apollo
purified themselves at Castalia before descending into the crypt.

So to say that the *Investigations* might bring philosophy to an end
can only mean that this book might somehow rid us of "the picture
which held us captive"—the picture of man which generates the
traditional problems. To say that philosophy might end is not to say
that holding large views might become unfashionable, or that philosophy departments might be plowed under, but rather to say that a
certain cultural tradition might die out. If this change occurred, one
would no longer think of the standard list of Cartesian problems as a
Fach: rather, one would think of study of the concern that once was
felt about these problems as a *Fach*. The best analogy available is the
shift from "theology" to "the study of religion." Once grace, salva-
tion, and the Divine Nature were subjects of study; now the fact that
they were so is a subject of study. Once theology was a pure and
autonomous subject; now religion lies at the mercy of psychology,
history, anthropology, and whatever other discipline cares to jump
in. Once we had a picture of man as held in the hand of God, and a
discipline which discussed alternative ways of describing the fact.
Later (when, as Comte said, the "metaphysical" succeeded the "theological" state) we had a picture of man as mind, or spirit, or source
of the transcendental constitution of objects in the world, or assemblage of sense-contents. We had a discipline which discussed these
various alternatives—never questioning that there was *something* of

central importance which needed to be said about the relation between man and nature: some bridge to be built, some dualism to be
transcended, some gap to be closed. If philosophy comes to an end,
it will be because this picture is as remote from us as the picture of
man as a child of God. If that day comes, it will seem as quaint to
treat a man's knowledge as a special relation between his mind and
its object as it now does to treat his goodness as a special relation between his soul and God.

If one thinks of the end of philosophy in these terms, it is quite
clear that it is not the sort of thing which might be brought about by
exposing some confusions, or marking the boundaries of areas of discourse, or pointing out some "facts about language." Logical positivism got a bad name by calling religion and metaphysics "nonsense"
and by seeming to dismiss the Age of Faith as a matter of incautious
use of language. It would give the *Investigations* an equally bad name
to think of it as saying that Cartesian philosophy is a similar "confusion." Any such term suggests that there is something called "our
language" sitting about waiting for theologians and philosophers (but
not, presumably, scientists or poets) to come along and become confused about it, ignore its complexities, and otherwise misuse it. But
nobody really believes this; our language is the creation of theologians
and philosophers as much as it is anybody's, and when Cartesian philosophers took over from theologians they did not do so because
their use of language was less (or less obviously) confused but because
the kinds of things they were saying captured the audience's attention. "Our language" is as hopeless an explanation of truth or necessity as God or the structure of reality, or as any of the wholesale explanations of the acquisition of knowledge which the Cartesian
tradition has offered. It is not, as Pears suggests, that our language
may not stand up to the demands imposed by philosophy because it
offers only "conditional" necessities (as opposed to the "unconditional" ones purportedly offered by "logic" and by "realistic" philosophies)—but rather that "our language" is just one more name for
the device which is supposed to let us jump the Cartesian gap between
mind and its object.

Even if one grants all this, one still has to explain why the *Investigations* has the importance it does. If it does not offer a new and
purer and more powerful philosophical method, and if it does not
offer a new account of necessity, where does its impact come from?
I think that part of the answer is that it is the first great work of polemic against the Cartesian tradition which does *not* take the form of

saying "philosophers from Descartes onward have thought that the relation between man and the world is so-and-so, but I now show you that it is such-and-such." Typically, attempts to overthrow the traditional problems of modern philosophy have come in the form of proposals about how we ought to think so as to avoid those problems. When Wittgenstein is at his best, he resolutely avoids such constructive criticism and sticks to pure satire. He just shows, by examples, how hopeless the traditional problems are — how they are based on a terminology which is as if designed expressly for the purpose of making solution impossible, how the questions which generate the traditional problems cannot be posed except in this terminology, how pathetic it is to think that the old gaps will be closed by constructing new gimmicks. (The gaps have been designed to widen automatically, just far enough to make each new device useless.) Wittgenstein does *not* say: cease thinking of man as cut off from the object by a veil of perceptions, and instead think of him as . . . (e.g., as constituting a world [Kant, Husserl], or divided into *en-soi* and *pour-soi* rather than into mind and body [Sartre], or having adopted *in-der-Welt-sein* as a basic *Existential* [Heidegger], or inducing from sense-contents to the properties of logical constructions of sense-contents [logical positivism]). He does not say: the tradition has pictured the world with gaps in it, but here is how the world looks with the gaps closed. Instead he just makes fun of the whole idea that there is something here to be explained.

Can a few volumes of satire overthrow a tradition of three hundred years? Certainly not. Getting rid of theology as part of the intellectual life of the West was not the achievement of one book, nor one man, nor one generation, nor one century. The end of philosophy-as-successor-of-theology, a "pure" subject in which deep problems are attacked by appropriately pure methods, will not occur in our time. No one knows, indeed, whether it will ever occur — whether what Comte called "the positivistic stage" will ever be reached. If it is reached, however, it will not be as Comte conceived it; it will not be an age in which everything has become "scientific." Science as the source of "truth" — a value which outranks the mere goodness of moral virtue and the mere beauty of art — is one of the Cartesian notions which vanish when the ideal of "philosophy as strict science" vanishes. If the Cartesian picture of man should ever dissolve, the notion that one has said something interesting about morality and religion when one has said that their claims are "unverifiable" would go with it. So would the contrast which Wittgenstein himself drew, even in his later work, between propositions which "purport to represent factual possibilities" and those "whose meaning is gathered from their place in human life." Wittgenstein's "resistance to science" is, I believe, best interpreted as a resistance to the entire cultural tradition which made truth—the successful crossing of the void which divides man from the world—a central virtue. In an age in which the Cartesian picture no longer held us captive, it would not seem necessary to try to shelter morality and religion by putting them in their own separate compartment.

The contrast between Wittgenstein's satire and constructive criticism may best be seen, I think, by comparing Wittgenstein with Dewey. Dewey pressed holism to its extreme, criticized customary paradigms of "truth" and "necessity," showed how remote from actual life the Cartesian distinctions were, did his best to debunk the purity of philosophy and traditional notions of necessity, broke down distinctions between disciplines and cultural forms, and tried to elaborate a vision of life in which the consummating value was aesthetic rather than cognitive. As much as any philosopher has, he suggested what a post-Cartesian culture might be like. Yet his work took the form of elaborate explanations that "experience" or "nature" or "logic" were not what the tradition had thought them to be, but rather thus-and-so. He produced, in short, a new philosophical theory, built along traditional lines. He thus engendered, in Pears's phrase, "philosophical conflict according to the old rules"—and solemn discussions of whether he was right or wrong in his "definition" of "experience." If Wittgenstein's later work is interpreted in terms of the distinctions Pears uses, I think the same thing may happen. We shall have solemn debates about conditional versus unconditional necessity, various modified forms of conventionalism, the distinction between "rule" and "interpretation," and the like.

Such debates are perhaps inevitable, and indeed intellectual responsibility may require them. But it would be a pity if the impulse to keep philosophy pure were so strong as to distract us altogether from Wittgenstein's satire, and from the attempt to sketch new ways in which parts of our life can be seen without wearing Cartesian spectacles. Such books as Iris Murdoch's *The Sovereignty of Good* and Nelson Goodman's *Languages of Art* seem to me to show the possibility of a kind of philosophical writing which keeps an appropriate distance from the Cartesian tradition—benefiting from Wittgenstein's satire without trying to repeat or explain it. Murdoch's remark that "it is an attachment to what lies outside the fantasy mechanism, and not a scrutiny of the mechanism itself, which liberates"[11] is in point here. What gives Wittgenstein's work its power is, I think, the vision of a point where "we can cease doing philosophy when we want to." Similarly, Murdoch's and Goodman's books direct us toward moral virtue, and art, as they can be seen once we no longer ask ourselves which questions about them are "purely philosophical" and which not. In these books, as in the *Investigations*, we move from the sort of purity which characterizes a *Fach* to the sort one feels when no longer oppressed by a need to answer unanswerable questions.

Notes

1. James to Karl Stumpf, Feb. 6, 1887, in Henry James, ed., *Letters of William James* (Boston: Norton, 1920), pp. 263-264.
2. David Pears, *Ludwig Wittgenstein* (New York: Viking, 1969), p. 34.
3. But see Essay 10, below ("Cavell on Skepticism"), where I complain that Cavell himself has too much respect for what I am calling "textbook problems." (Note added in 1981.)
4. Pears, *op. cit.*, p. 179.
5. *Ibid.*, pp. 181-182.
6. Cf. *ibid.*, p. 121.
7. *Ibid.*, p. 112.
8. *Ibid.*, p. 110.
9. *Ibid.*, p. 196.
10. *Ibid.*, p. 111.
11. Iris Murdoch, *The Sovereignty of Good* (New York: Schocken, 1971), p. 67.

3

Overcoming the Tradition: Heidegger and Dewey

I

Philosophers who envy scientists think that philosophy should deal only with problems formulated in neutral terms—terms satisfactory to all those who argue for competing solutions. Without common problems and without argument, it would seem, we have no professional discipline, nor even a method for disciplining our own thoughts. Without discipline, we presumably have mysticism, or poetry, or inspiration—at any rate, something which permits an escape from our intellectual responsibilities. Heidegger is frequently criticized for having avoided these responsibilities. His defenders reply that what he has avoided is not the responsibility of the thinker, but simply the tradition of "metaphysics" or "ontology." Consider the following typical passage:

> "Ontology" itself, however, whether transcendental or precritical, is subject to criticism not because it thinks the Being of beings and thereby reduces Being to a concept, but because it does not think the truth of Being and so fails to recognize that there is a thinking more rigorous than the conceptual (. . . *und so verkennt dass es ein Denken gibt das strenger ist als das Begriffliche*).[1]

Contemplating this distinction, one may suspect that Heidegger wants to have it both ways. On the one hand, we usually distinguish "thought" from its purportedly "irresponsible" alternatives—mysticism, art, myth-making—by identifying "thought" with argumentative rigor. But whatever *strenger* means in this passage it is hardly what

37

Kant or Carnap or Husserl meant by it; it has nothing to do with argument, nor with *"Philosophie als strenge Wissenschaft."* So presumably *strenger* means something like "more difficult." From this Heideggerian angle, ontology is the easy way out; anybody can produce a new opinion on an old ontological question. Even working out whole new systems or "research programs" in ontology is not really very hard. But Heraclitus, for example, did neither of these, and what he did was much harder to do. So Heidegger wants not to have to argue with his fellow-philosophers and wants also to say that he is doing something much more difficult than they try to do.

We might now be inclined to say that it would be well for Heidegger to call whatever he wants to do something other than "Thought." For surely "thinking" ought to be opposed to something else—not "emotion," perhaps, but surely to something that has more to do with the arts than the sciences, more to do with religion than with philosophy. Surely what Heidegger is doing has more to do with *that.* But Heidegger thinks that these various distinctions are themselves products of metaphysical system-building. Since all the usual divisions between disciplines, and all the usual ways of dividing man's life into stages or modes, are the products of the various writers who constitute "the tradition of Western ontology," we can hardly use these divisions to "place" the work of a man whose aim is to overcome that tradition. But one may still feel exasperated. There ought, one feels, to be *some* standard by which to judge Heidegger, some competitor running in the same race.

Tediously enough, however, Heidegger suggests that our sense of exasperation is just one more product of the notion that philosophy is supposed to be a competition between arguments, a notion which we get from Plato and whose consequences, two thousand years later, were positivism and nihilism. To free ourselves from the notion that there ought to be competition here would be to free ourselves from what he calls "the technical interpretation of thought." About this interpretation, he says:

> The beginnings of that interpretation reach back to Plato and Aristotle. They take thinking itself to be a τέχνη, a process of reflection in service to doing and making. But here reflection is already seen from the perspective of πρᾶξις and ποίησις. For this reason thinking, when taken for itself, is not "practical." The characterization of thinking as θεωρία and the determination of knowing as "theoretical" behavior occur already within the "technical" interpretation of thinking. Such characterization is a reactive attempt to rescue thinking and preserve its autonomy over against acting and doing. Since then "philosophy" has been in the constant predicament

of having to justify its existence before the "sciences." It believes it can do that most effectively by elevating itself to the rank of a science. But such an effort is the abandonment of the essence of thinking . . . . Can then the effort to return thinking to its element be called "irrationalism"?[2]

So we cannot accuse Heidegger of irrationalism, it seems, without begging the question in favor of Plato and Aristotle. Nor can we even ask, "Who then is right about thought: Plato or Heidegger?" For the question supposes there to be a topic called "thought" on which there might be different views. But Heidegger claims no view about such a thing. He thinks that to attempt to offer views of this sort is to neglect the "essentially historical character of Being."[3] Since Thought is of Being,[4] and since Being is essentially historical, it is not as if Plato and Aristotle might have been wrong about what Thought was. It is not as if Thought had, so to speak, been waiting patiently for Heidegger to come along and put us right about it. Heidegger says that when, e.g., Plato or Aristotle represented Being as ἰδέα or as ἐνέργεια, "these were not doctrines advanced by chance, but rather words of Being."[5] There is no way of getting closer to Being by getting back behind Plato and starting off on the right foot. Heidegger tells us that his own definition of Being (as *"das* transcendens *schlechthin"*) in *Sein und Zeit* was not an attempt "to start over again and expose the falsity of all previous philosophy."[6] He regards the notion of "the unchanging unity of the underlying determinations of Being" as "only an illusion under whose protection metaphysics occurs as history of Being."[7] So it is not as if we might compare metaphysics-from-Plato-to-Nietzsche on the one hand and Heidegger on the other with their common topic—Thought, or Being—and then decide which offered the better account.

To sum up, we may conclude that Heidegger has done as good a job of putting potential critics on the defensive as any philosopher in history. There is no standard by which one can measure him without begging the question against him. His remarks about the tradition, and his remarks about the limitations the tradition has imposed on the vocabulary and imagination of his contemporaries, are beautifully designed to make one feel foolish when one tries to find a bit of common ground on which to start an argument.

II

One may feel tempted at this point to decide that "Heidegger is not really a *philosopher* at all." This too would be foolish. Heidegger brilliantly carries to extremes a tactic used by every original philosopher.

Heidegger is not the first to have invented a vocabulary whose purpose is to dissolve the problems considered by his predecessors, rather than to propose new solutions to them. Consider Hobbes and Locke on the problems of the scholastics, and Carnap and Ayer on "pseudo-problems." He is not the first to have said that the whole mode of argument used in philosophy up until his day was misguided. Consider Descartes on method, and Hegel on the need for dialectical thinking. His seemingly arrogant claim that the tradition has exhausted its potentialities[8] simply carries to its limit the sort of impatience sometimes manifested by quite mild-mannered philosophers in such remarks as "All the arguments for and against utilitarianism were canvassed well before 1900" or "All the worry about the external world is a result of confusing having a sensation with observing an object."[9] In urging new vocabularies for the statement of philosophical issues, or new paradigms of argumentation, a philosopher cannot appeal to antecedent criteria of judgment, but he may have spectacular success. The scholastics' vocabulary never recovered from the sarcasm of the seventeenth century. Half the philosophy written since Hegel attempted the sort of triumphant dialectical syntheses offered in the *Phenomenology*. Descartes and Hegel may have seemed "not real philosophers" to many of their contemporaries, but they created new problems in place of the old, kept philosophy going by the sheer brilliance of their example, and appear retrospectively as stages in a progressive development.

If it seems difficult to think of Heidegger coming to occupy the same position, it is because he does not, like Descartes and Hegel and Husserl and Carnap, say, "This is how philosophy has been; let philosophy henceforth be like *this*." Rather, like Nietzsche and Wittgenstein and Dewey, he asks, "Given that this is how philosophy has been, what, if anything, can philosophy now be?" Suggesting, as they did, that philosophy may have exhausted its potentialities, he asks whether the motives which led to philosophy's existence still exist and whether they should. Many philosophers—practically all those whom we think of as founding movements—saw the entire previous history of philosophy as the working out of a certain set of false assumptions, or conceptual confusions, or unconscious distortions of reality. But only a few of these have suggested that the notion of philosophy itself—a discipline distinct from science, yet not to be confused with art or religion—was one of the results of these false starts. And fewer still have suggested that we are not, even now, in a position to state alternatives to those false assumptions or confused concepts—to see reality plain. These few writers are often treated dismissively by philosophers who do claim to know where the future of philosophy lies. Heidegger's later style makes it easy to dismiss him as someone who has simply become tired of arguing, and who, taking refuge in the mystical, abandons the attempt to defend his almost-respectable earlier work. But even philosophers like Dewey and Santayana, who resemble Heidegger in seeing no interesting future for a distinct discipline called "philosophy," have been dismissed as "not really philosophical" on just this ground—that they neither held out hope of the successful completion of old "research programs" nor suggested new ones. It is as if to be a philosopher one had to have a certain minimal loyalty to the profession—as if one were not permitted to dissolve an old philosophical problem without being ready to put a new one in its place.[10]

There is, however, an obvious way of distinguishing critics of the tradition like Dewey and Heidegger from the amateur, the philistine, the mystic, or the belletrist. This is the depth and extent of their commentary on the details of the tradition. Any freshman can dismiss "Western thought" as merely "conceptual" and have done with it. It is not so easy to explain just what being "conceptual" amounts to, and what is common to the various paradigms of "conceptual thought." Dewey and Heidegger know exactly what their predecessors were worried about, and they each offer us an account of the dialectical course of the tradition. The self-image of a philosopher—his identification of himself as such (rather than as, perhaps, an historian or a mathematician or a poet)—depends almost entirely upon how he sees the history of philosophy. It depends upon which figures he imitates, and which episodes and movements he disregards. So a new account of the history of philosophy is a challenge which cannot be ignored. This suggests that insofar as there is any sensible question of the form "Who is right, Heidegger or the others?" it is going to be a question about historiography.[11] It is not as if historiography were less controversial than, say, epistemology or philosophy of language. It is rather that the adoption of a vocabulary—one's semiconscious decision about which questions one is content to dissolve or ignore and which one must set oneself to answer—is motivated almost entirely by a perception of one's relation to the history of philosophy. This may be a perception of one's place in a progressive sequence of discoveries (as in the sciences), or of the new-found needs and hopes of one's society, or simply of the relevance of certain figures in the history of philosophy to one's private needs and hopes. If we have Dewey's picture of what has happened in the intellectual history of the West, we shall have a certain quite specific account of Heidegger's role in this history; he will appear as a final decadent echo of Platonic and Christian otherworldliness. If we have Heidegger's perception, conversely, we shall have a quite specific picture of Dewey; he will appear as an exceptionally naive and provincial nihilist.

III

In what follows, I propose to offer sketches of Dewey as he would presumably look to Heidegger and of Heidegger as he would presumably look to Dewey. This exercise will show how an extraordinary amount of agreement on the need for a "destruction of the history of Western ontology" can be combined with an utterly different notion of what might succeed "ontology." It will, I hope, give us some ground on which to stand when trying to "place" Heidegger, by giving us a sense of how much room is left for maneuver even after one comes to see the philosophical tradition as having exhausted its potentialities. The frequent charges of arrogance brought against Heidegger result, in part, from the fact that he mentions few other "thinkers" of the day; he leaves one with the impression that if there are other mountain tops, they are now inhabited only by poets. Yet the vision of a culture in which philosophy was not a profession, nor art, a business,[12] and in which technology was something other than "a dreary frenzy,"[13] is hardly Heidegger's discovery. It is what Dewey offered us throughout his later life. Dewey can join Heidegger in saying that

> No metaphysics, whether idealist, materialistic, or Christian, can in accord with its own essence, and surely not in its attempts to explicate itself, "get a hold on" this [Europe's] destiny. . . .[14]

But for Dewey, Heidegger's succeeding gloss on "getting a hold on" ("thoughtfully to reach and gather together what in the fullest sense of Being now is") would seem, like all his talk of Being, just one more Christian metaphysics in disguise. Dewey's *Experience and Nature*, in turn, can easily be taken as just one more variant on materialist metaphysics: a bland restatement of the triumph of nihilism.

To guard against such superficial reciprocal dismissals, let me consider some obvious points of agreement between the two men. I shall cite their parallel views on four topics: (1) the distinction, in ancient philosophy, between contemplation and action; (2) the traditional Cartesian problems which center around epistemological skepticism; (3) the distinction between philosophy and science; and (4) the distinction between both and "the aesthetic."

Dewey begins a discussion of the distinction between theory and practice with a distinction between the "holy" and the "lucky."[15] He thinks of religion, and its heir philosophy, as attending to the former. Workmanship, and its heir technology, look to the latter. Because philosophy "inherited the realm with which religion had been concerned"[16] it naturally adopted "the notion, which has ruled philosophy ever since the time of the Greeks, that the office of knowledge is to uncover the antecedently real."[17] Given the further inheritance from religion of the premise that "only the completely fixed and unchanging can be real," it is natural that "the quest for certitude has determined our basic metaphysics."[18] "Metaphysics is a substitute for custom as the source and guarantor of higher moral and social values"[19] and will remain so until we recognize that "the distinctive office, problems and subject-matter of philosophy grow out of stresses and strains in the community life in which a given form of philosophy arises"[20] and until philosophy as criticism of morals and institutions takes the place of "the whole brood and nest of dualisms which have . . . formed the 'problems' of philosophy termed 'modern'."[21] The little dualisms of subject-object, mind-matter, experience-nature are seen by Dewey as dialectical diminutions of the great dualism between the holy and the lucky—the enduring and the day-to-day. Should we overcome all these dualisms, then philosophy might be, "instead of impossible attempts to transcend experience . . . the significant record of the efforts of men to formulate the things of experience to which they are most deeply and passionately attached."[22]

For Heidegger the confusion of Being with what endures unchangingly, can be known with certainty, and can be treated mathematically, was also the crucial first step in making philosophy what it is today. Because Greek philosophers preferred nouns to verbs,[23] and verbal substantives to infinitives[24] when they spoke of Being—because Plato left behind Heraclitus' union of πόλεμος and λόγος and coalesced φύσις with ἰδέα—we were put upon the path of ontology.

> Where the struggle ceases, beings do not vanish, but the world turns away. Beings are no longer asserted (i.e., preserved as such). Now they are merely found ready-made, are data. . . . The being becomes an object, either to be beheld (view, image) or to be acted upon (product and calculation). The original world-making power, φύσις, degenerates into a prototype to be copied and imitated. Nature becomes a special field, differentiated from art and everything that can be fashioned according to plan.[25]

Here Heidegger sees the distinction between action and contemplation not as Dewey does, as reflecting the gap between the freeman and the slave,[26] but rather as arising out of an initial diremption of an original united consciousness—a diremption which is presumably to be viewed as a fatality, one of the words of Being, rather than explained causally as a product of some natural environment or social arrangement. But Dewey and Heidegger agree that this initial adoption of a spectatorial notion of knowledge and its object has determined the subsequent history of philosophy. Heidegger's claim, in *Being and Time*, that the neglect of *Zuhandensein* lies behind the Cartesian problem of the existence of the external world[27] parallels Dewey's reiterated claim that "the brood and nest of dualisms" which appeared in the seventeenth century was due to the initial split between the enduring object of contemplation and the malleable objects of the artisan.[28] For both Dewey and Heidegger, the notion of the object as something to be viewed and represented led to subjectivism:

> When objects are isolated from the experience through which they are reached and in which they function, experience itself becomes reduced to the mere process of experiencing, and experiencing is therefore treated as if it were also complete in itself. . . . Since the seventeenth century this conception of experience as the equivalent of subjective private experience set over against nature, which consists wholly of physical objects, has wrought havoc in philosophy.[29]

Dewey's description fits in nicely with Heidegger's account of the sequence which leads from Plato through Descartes to Kant, e.g.:

> Subiectity says finally: beings are *subiectum* in the sense of the ὑποκείμενον which has the distinction of being πρώτη οὐσία in the presencing of what is actual. In its history as metaphysics, Being is through and through subiectity. But where subiectity becomes subjectivity, the *subiectum* preeminent since Descartes, the ego, has a multiple precedence.[30]

Dewey sees the epistemological problems of modern philosophy as the adjustment of old metaphysical assumptions to new conditions. Heidegger sees them as the internal dialectical working-out of those assumptions. Heidegger comments scornfully on the notion that the modern age "discovered" that epistemology was the true foundation of philosophy[31] and on the easy retreat to the question "subjective or objective?" which characterizes thought during this period.[32] Dewey sees the quest for certainty and fixity which the ancients satisfied by non-natural objects of knowledge as, in the modern period, transferred to show that "the conditions of the possibility of knowledge" are "of an ideal and rational character."[33] He thinks of the distinction between objective facts and subjective emotions, problems,

and doubts as another "product of the habit of isolating man and experience from nature,"[34] and remarks that modern science has joined
with traditional theology in perpetuating this isolation. Dewey thereby echoes Heidegger's insistence on the underlying identity of the
stance towards Being found in Aquinas' notion of an *ens a se* and
modern epistemologists' notions of "objectivity."[35] Both men say
things which reduce to despair the eager and sincere epistemologist,
anxious to classify them as idealists or realists, subjectivists or objec-
tivists. Consider Heidegger's exasperating remark: "Evidently truth's
independence *from* man is nonetheless manifestly a relation *to* human nature."[36] Consider also Dewey's coy refusal to treat meaning
and truth as relations between something "experiential" and something "in nature."[37]

When they discuss the relation between philosophy and science,
both men see Cartesian, Husserlian, and positivistic attempts to
"make philosophy scientific" as a disastrous abandonment of philosophy's proper function. Dewey says that "Philosophy has assumed
for its function a knowledge of reality. This fact makes it a rival instead of a complement of the sciences." He proceeds to endorse James'
description of philosophy as "vision."[38] Heidegger's remark that philosophy's attempt to "elevate itself to the rank of a 'science'" abandons the essence of Thought has already been cited. Both see philosophy, at its best, as clearing away what impedes our delight, not as
the discovery of a correct representation of reality. Both men insist
on the goal of philosophy as the reattainment of innocence and the
divestiture of the culture of our time.[39] Both stress the ties between
philosophy and poetry. For Dewey, when "philosophy shall have co-
operated with the course of events and made clear and coherent the
meaning of the daily detail, science and emotion will interpenetrate,
practice and imagination will embrace. Poetry and religious feeling
will be the unforced flowers of life."[40] He hopes that philosophy will
join with poetry as Arnold's "criticism of life."[41] For Heidegger,
"only poetry stands in the same order as philosophy"—because only
in these two are beings not related to other beings, but to Being.[42]

On the other hand, both abhor the notion that poetry is supposed
to offer us "values" as opposed to something else—"fact"—which
we are to find in science. Both regard the fact-value distinction as
springing from, and as dangerous as, the subject-object distinction.
Heidegger thinks that the whole notion of "values" is an awkward
attempt by the metaphysician to supply an additional *Vorhanden* in
order to make good the deficiency left by thinking of Being as
ἰδέα or as *Vorstellung*—an afterthought "necessary to round out the

ontology of the world."[43] Heidegger thinks that the very notion of a "subject" called "aesthetics" is one more disastrous result of our distinctions between the sensuous and the supersensuous, the subject and the object, and the other distinctions which flow from Plato's original treatment of φύσις and ἰδέα.[44] Dewey would entirely agree, as he would about every attempt to keep either the "aesthetic" or the "religious" apart from the "scientific" or the "empirical," and he would trace the notion of "objective value" and "purely aesthetic judgment" to the same historical roots as does Heidegger. Both of them see both poetry and philosophy as taking place where the distinction between contemplation and action does not arise, and as diminished and made pointless when this distinction is drawn.[45]

Citing all these similarities between Dewey and Heidegger may seem a *tour de force*. It is the differences which are interesting. But I think that it is important to note the similarities first. Doing so shows how both men are trying to encapsulate the whole sequence which runs from Plato and Aristotle to Nietzsche and Carnap, set it aside, and offer something new—or at least a hope of something new. Further, they are almost alone in this century in doing so. They are unique, unclassifiable, original philosophers, and both are historicist to the core. Both have been misleadingly assimilated to nonhistoricist philosophical schools. To lump Dewey with Peirce, James, and Quine is to forget that he was swept off his feet, and into a new intellectual world, by Hegel's and Comte's visions of our past.[46] To call Heidegger a phenomenologist and lump him with Husserl, or an existentialist and lump him with (the early) Sartre, is, as Heidegger himself has pointed out, to ignore precisely the historical perspective which he prides himself on sharing with Marx, and which both derived from Hegel.[47] Both men see what Heidegger calls "the unified history of Being, beginning with the essential character of Being as ἰδέα up to the completion of the modern essence of Being as the will to power"[48] as a single, long-drawn-out event. He sees Nietzsche as where we must end if, with Plato, we take Being as presence or as representation.[49] Deweyans are inclined to see Nietzsche as an over-reaction to the realization that we shall never fulfill Plato's demand for certainty and "rationality" in morals. The realization that we shall never achieve such certainty makes us alternate between despair at there being nothing but power in the world, and intoxication at our own possession of power. No other philosophers of this century, save perhaps Wittgenstein, have so distanced themselves from the assumptions and the problems common to Plato and Nietzsche.

If Hegel is their common ground, however, their notions of what to do with Hegel are the beginnings of their differences. Dewey, like

Marx, wants Hegel without the Absolute Spirit. He wants man and history to stand on their own feet, and man's history to be just that, neither Spirit's self-realization nor the fateful elephantine movements of Matter or of social classes. He does not think of "history" with a capital letter, and he is quite content, as Heidegger is not, to let his remarks on past philosophers be "one-sided and sporadic conceptual historiography." When he tells us about the consequences of the Greek separation of contemplation and action he does not think he is recollecting the words of Being—but rather, in Wittgenstein's phrase, "assembling reminders for a particular purpose." He thinks that German idealism was at bottom, and despite its achievements, a last desperate gesture in the direction of the old Platonic project of offering an ontological guarantee for the preconceptions of a leisure class.[50]

Heidegger, on the other hand, tells us that the so-called "collapse of German idealism" was not the fault of idealism but of "the age," which "was no longer strong enough to stand up to the greatness, breadth and originality of that spiritual world."[51] One of Heidegger's strongest feelings, and one which places him very far from Dewey indeed, is that ages, cultures, nations, and people are supposed to live up to the demands of philosophers, rather than the other way around. It is not Athens, Rome, Renaissance Florence, the Paris of the Revolution, and the Germany of Hitler which form the history of Being. Nor is it Sophocles, Horace, Dante, Goethe, Proust, and Nabokov. It is the sequence from Plato to Nietzsche. It is not just that Thought is always Thought of Being, but that Thought is the *only* thing which is *of* Being in this sense (in both the subjective and objective genitive, as Heidegger says).[52] Only poetry is of the same order, but there is no indication that Heidegger thinks that poetry has a history. Less crudely put, there is no indication that Heidegger thinks that the historicity of Being can be seen in poetry, any more than it can be seen where Macauley and Acton tended to see it—in a gradually widening access to literacy, voting booths, and nourishing foodstuffs.

All this emphasis on *philosophers* would look, to Dewey, like academic parochialism. Who but a philosophy professor, after all, would think that the drama of twentieth-century Europe had some essential relation to the *Vollendung der Metaphysik*? Consider the following passage, in which Heidegger wants to explain why the "inherently historical asking of the question about being is actually an integral part of history on earth":

> We have said that the world is darkening. The essential episodes of this darkening are: the flight of the gods, the destruction of the earth, the standardization of man, the pre-eminence of the mediocre.

> What do we mean by world when we speak of a darkening of the world?
> World is always world of the *spirit*. The animal has no world nor any en-
> vironment (*Umwelt*). Darkening of the world means emasculation of the
> spirit, the disintegration, wasting away, repression, and misinterpretation
> of the spirit. . . . What makes the situation of Europe all the more cata-
> strophic is that this enfeeblement of the spirit originated in Europe itself
> and—though prepared by earlier factors—was definitively determined by
> its own spiritual situation in the first half of the nineteenth century.[53]

That spiritual situation was, of all things, the inability of the age to
live up to the "greatness, breadth and originality" of German idealism. One might think that the destruction of the earth and the stan-
dardization of man were bad enough—that the strip-mines of Montana,
the assembly-lines of Detroit, and the Red Guards of Shanghai were
enough to show the world was darkening, without bringing in the
world of the spirit at all. But this would be to treat "forgetfulness of
being"[54] as just a handy label for whatever it is that has been going
wrong lately. Heidegger takes it much more seriously. He is not saying, like Tillich, that it is getting hard to find a good symbol of our
ultimate concern. He is saying, like Kierkegaard, that symbol-hunting
is sin.

This way of putting things may suggest that I am, like a good modern, neglecting the "ontological difference" between Being and beings.
But in such passages as the one I just cited, Heidegger neglects it too
—and it is well for him that he does. If he did not, he would no longer
have anything to differentiate his talk of Being from Kierkegaard's
talk of God and of Grace. Unless Heidegger connected the history of
Being with that of men and nations through such phrases as "a nation's (*eines Volkes*) relation to Being,"[55] and thus connected the
history of philosophy with just plain history, he would be able to say
only what Kierkegaard said: that when all the advances of modern
civilization are utilized, all the dog-tricks of the Hegelian dialectic
practiced and perfected, and all the aspects of life and culture related
by all the concepts one could imagine ever being evolved, we shall
still be as far as ever from that which is *strenger als das Begriffliche*.
Without the reference to the history of nations, we should obviously
have only what Versényi suggests is all we get anyway: "an all too
empty and formal, though often emotionally charged and mystically-
religious, thinking of absolute unity."[56] With this reference, we at
least seem to have an analogue of an eschatological and Augustinian
sort of Christianity, rather than an analogue of Kierkegaard's private
and Protestant hope that Grace may make him a New Being, able to
believe the self-contradictory doctrine of the Incarnation.

I can sum up this quasi-Deweyan view of Heidegger as follows. All we are told about Being, Thought, and the ontological difference is by negation. To grasp what these are is to grasp that they have nothing to do with metaphysics. Metaphysics encompasses any conceptual thought, any causal thought, any thought of ourselves as one among a plurality of causally related beings, which is not scientific or technological thinking about a concrete issue. Metaphysics can only be explained by showing its history, by showing how people have thought to speak Being and wound up speaking of beings. So far Dewey and Heidegger can agree. Dewey thinks that the moral of the story is that metaphysics, having exhausted its potentialities, leaves us with nothing except an increased appreciation for our concrete problems—for beings. But Heidegger thinks that the historical picture which has been sketched offers a glimpse of something else. Yet nothing further can be said about this something else, and so the negative way to Being, through the destruction of ontology, leaves us facing beings-without-Being, with no hint about what Thought might be of. The vacant place that remains when all metaphysical thinking has been destroyed is all that we have. So whether the history of philosophy is viewed as Dewey views it (as a working out of various causal processes in an intellectual "superstructure") or as Heidegger views it (as the words of Being) does not seem to matter. For the vacant place remains for both. For Dewey, it is to be filled in with concrete attention to beings—to the strip-mines, for example. For Heidegger, it is a clearing for Being. What is there to disagree about here? Once the history of philosophy is seen in the way in which Dewey and Heidegger agree on seeing it, what can be said about what remains? For Dewey, to go on talking about "Thought" is to insist that the end of metaphysics should not be the end of philosophy—without saying why it should not. For Heidegger, to say that philosophy has become obsolete is to succumb to a vulgarized version of the Nietzschean Being-as-will-to-power. It may be that any concrete phenomenon—a poem, a revolution, a person—can be viewed as just that, or as an opening for Being. Perhaps how one views it is a matter of which philosophers one has been reading lately, and of which jargon one fancies.

To take this aestheticist, relativist, quasi-Tillichian attitude is to align oneself with Dewey and against Heidegger. It is, as will by now have become obvious, the attitude and the alignment I prefer. But, before adopting it, I want to try to look at the matter through Heidegger's eyes once again. It is important, I think, to see that for Heidegger Dewey's ultimate sin is not his emphasis on the practical

but precisely the adoption of the aesthetic attitude.[57] Heidegger sees
the outcome of a technological age as "the world as View," and the
aesthetic attitude towards philosophical systems which Dewey shares
with Santayana as the ultimate expression of this attitude. "The fundamental event of the modern age is the conquest of the world as
picture."[58] When Dewey praises our modern manner of seeing nature
as something to be used rather than contemplated he is simply falling
in with modern technology's insistence on seeing "the earth's crust as
a coal mine, the soil as a source of minerals."[59] This is just being realistic, and not, even on Heidegger's account, an occasion for criticism.
It is when Dewey proceeds to view *philosophies*—the thought of
Plato, of Thomas, of Hegel—in the same way as an engineer views
ore-bearing regions of the earth that Heidegger would recoil. To treat
the thought of Hegel as a *Weltanschauung* is to view him as an object
of exploitation rather than a possible occasion of revelation. It is to
treat philosophies as if they were means to the enhancement of human life.[60] Dewey's humanism is, for Heidegger, simply the modern
consciousness incarnate, against which there is no point in protesting
—save perhaps when the very possibility of Thought is denied, as it is
when these philosophers who exemplify Thought are treated as mere
means for the mutual adjustment of beings to beings. Heidegger's
sense of the vulgarity of the age—its trivialization of everything holy
—is strongest when what is trivialized is the history of metaphysics.
For this history is the history of Being, and to make that history into
a useful lesson for modern man is to make Being itself an instrument
for our employment and an object of exploitation. To treat "the
world as a view and man as a *subiectum*"[61] is simply to be in tune
with the times, but to treat the great philosophers as stepping stones,
or to choose among them as we choose our favorite pictures, is to
make a mockery of Being itself. For Heidegger, Dewey's sketches of
the history of philosophy are, at best, pathetic examples of the futility of attempting to overcome metaphysics by using the vocabulary
of metaphysics (e.g., "experience" and "nature").[62] Heidegger sees
even his own early attempt at overcoming—his redescription of
Dasein in order to prepare the way for a reopening of the question of
Being—as self-defeating.[63] Sometimes he suggests that *any* overcoming
of metaphysics, indeed any *mention* of the history of metaphysics,
may be equally self-defeating: "A regard for metaphysics still prevails
even in the intention to overcome metaphysics. Therefore, our task is
to cease all overcoming, and leave metaphysics to itself."[64]

   Still, Heidegger insists that in *Being and Time* he at least had the
question of Being in mind when he offered us *Existentiale* in place of

the "categories" of the tradition, and he still thinks that something of the sort is a necessary first step.[65] Dewey, despite the fact that he too wants to offer us a new jargon to replace the notions of the "subject" and "substance" which are common to Aristotle and Descartes, will appear to Heidegger as self-deceptive and self-defeating. If one reads Dewey through Heidegger's eyes, one sees his thought as so thoroughly infected by these traditional conceptions that he has no notion of Thought as an alternative to metaphysics. Thus Dewey forgets his own Peircian subordination of truth to beauty, sees "science" as somehow replacing philosophy, or philosophy as becoming somehow "scientific." Dewey's version of the history of philosophy is designed to purify our self-image of all the remnants of the previous epochs in the history of metaphysics—all reminders of an age before technology had become supreme. He is thus a good illustration of the latest and most degenerate stage of "humanistic" philosophy, the stage which Heidegger describes as follows:

> Philosophy in the age of completed metaphysics is anthropology. Whether or not one says "philosophical" anthropology makes no difference. In the meantime philosophy has become anthropology and in this way a prey to the derivatives of metaphysics, that is, of physics in the broadest sense, which includes the physics of life and man, biology and psychology. Having become anthropology, philosophy itself perishes of metaphysics.[66]

V

So much for Dewey's view of Heidegger and Heidegger's of Dewey. It would be pleasant to conclude with an impartially sympathetic synthesis. But I have no broader perspective to offer. The two men seem to me, together with Wittgenstein, the richest and most original philosophers of our time, and I have no notions about how to transcend them. The best I can do is sharpen the conflict by recurring to the questions about "the end of philosophy" with which I began and, in that context, restating Dewey's case.

I think that even if the differences in the way the two men tell the story of our tradition were somehow ironed out, there would remain this impasse: Dewey wants the tradition overcome by blurring all the distinctions it has drawn, whereas Heidegger hopes Being will overcome it for us by granting us a sense of the ontological difference. In particular, Dewey wants the distinctions between art, science, and philosophy to be rubbed out, and replaced with the vague and uncontroversial notion of intelligence trying to solve problems and provide meaning. Heidegger is equally contemptuous of the traditional distinctions, save one: he does not want *philosophy* to be lost in this shuffle, and would view Dewey's attempt to mislay it as resulting from the assumption that Thought is co-extensive with ontology. One way of bringing the difference to a point is to say that Dewey thinks of philosophy, as a discipline or even as a distinct human activity, as obsolete. Heidegger, on the other hand, thinks of philosophy—of Thought as opposed to ontology—as something which might be recaptured, even though the form it might take is, in our darkened world, still invisible.

Is there anything which Dewey should oppose in such a faint, modest, and inarticulate hope? Yes, there is indeed. Heidegger's hope is just what was worst in the tradition—the quest for the holy which turns us away from the relations between beings and beings (the relations, for example, between the ghastly apparatus of modern technology and the people whose children will die of hunger unless that apparatus spreads over the rest of the planet).[67] *Tout commence en mystique et finit en politique.*[68] The politics which one can imagine stemming from Heidegger's notion of technology's relation to man are more awful than the apparatus of technology itself, and for neither Dewey nor Heidegger is there a way to separate that sort of relation to politics from "philosophical truth." Heidegger's attachment to the notion of "philosophy"—the pathetic notion that even after metaphysics goes, something called "Thought" might remain—is simply the sign of Heidegger's own fatal attachment to the tradition: the last infirmity of the greatest of the German professors. It amounts to saying that even though everybody who has previously counted as a paradigm of philosophy—Plato, Thomas, Descartes, Nietzsche— turned out to be a step on a path toward chaos, we must still try to be philosophers. For "philosophy" is a name for that activity which is essential to our humanity. No matter how much Heidegger seems to have overcome our professional urge to compete with the great dead philosophers on their own ground, no matter how much he may try to distance himself from the tradition (not to mention his fellow-professors), he is still insistent that the tradition offered us "words of Being." He still thinks that the place where philosophy was is the place to be. He thinks that to cease thinking about what Plato and Kant were thinking about is to be diminished, to lose hold of what is most important, to sink into darkness. If he were true to his own dictum that we should "cease all overcoming, and leave metaphysics to itself," he would have nothing to say, nowhere to point. *The whole force of Heidegger's thought lies in his account of the history of philosophy.*

That vision demands that he place himself in a sequence which begins with the Greeks. But the only thing which links him with the tradition is his claim that the tradition, though persistently sidetracked onto beings, was really concerned with Being all the time—and, indeed, constituted the history of Being. This is like saying, "*Every* previous notion of how to come unto Christ, starting with the Apostles and St. Paul and continuing on through Augustine and Luther to Tillich and Barth, has been a further step away from Him. But His Grace may still bring us to Him, if we can only overcome the tradition of theology, or even just leave it alone." Someone who said this would be trying to make an *ad hoc* distinction between "theology" and "Christianity" of the sort which Heidegger wants to make between "ontology" and "Thought." But Heidegger wants to have it both ways, as did Kierkegaard in his day. Both need to invoke the tradition to identify what it is that has been wrongly approached, or has veiled itself. But both need to repudiate the tradition utterly in order to say what they want to say. When Kierkegaard reaches beyond Hegel and history for that which thought cannot think—the intersection of the temporal and the eternal—he has no business hinting that we should call it "Christ." Christ, after all, is what Christians think He is.[69] Being is what Nietzsche, as spokesman for the concluding moment of the dialectic of the last two thousand years, said it was: a "vapor and a fallacy."[70] Heidegger says that "*the* question" is "is 'being' a mere word and its meaning a vapor or is it the spiritual destiny of the Western world?"[71] But this suggested alternative is simply an attempt to renew our interest in Being by suggesting that our present troubles are somehow due to the Plato-Nietzsche tradition. All Heidegger can do to explain why that tradition is of more than parochial academic interest is to say that it was where the question of Being got asked. All he can do to explain why we shouldn't shrug off Being as a vapor and a fallacy is to say that our fate is somehow linked to that tradition.

To conclude: what Dewey and Heidegger both wanted was a way of seeing things which would take us as far beyond the world of historicist philosophizing which succeeded Hegel, as Hegel had taken us beyond the epistemologically oriented philosophy of the eighteenth century. Dewey found what he wanted in turning away from philosophy as a distinctive activity altogether, and towards the ordinary world—the problems of men, freshly seen by discarding the distinctions which the philosophical tradition had developed. Heidegger hoped that a new path would open. But he thought we shall only see it open if we detach ourselves from the problems of men and are still;

in that silence we may perhaps hear the word of Being. Which of these attitudes one adopts depends on how devoted one is to the notion of "philosophy." Heidegger's weakness was that he could not escape the notion that philosophers' difficulties are more than *just* philosophers' difficulties—the notion that if philosophy goes down, so will the West.

Heidegger should not be criticized for wanting something *strenger als das Begriffliche*. Few of us do not. If he is to be criticized, it is for helping keep us under the spell of Plato's notion that there is something special called "philosophy" which it is our duty to undertake. One may say of Heidegger what he himself says of Nietzsche: misled by a superficial understanding of the Platonic ideas, he tried to replace them, but instead only translated Platonism into a newer jargon.[72] By offering us "openness to Being" to replace "philosophical argument," Heidegger helps preserve all that was worst in the tradition which he hoped to overcome.[73]

Notes

1. *"Brief über den 'Humanismus'"* in M. Heidegger, *Wegmarken (WM)* (Frankfurt: Klostermann, 1967), p. 187; trans. in *Basic Writings of Heidegger (BW)*, ed. David Krell (New York: Harper and Row, 1977), p. 235.

I shall use the following abbreviations for other works by, and translations of, Heidegger: *VA = Vorträge und Aufsätze* (Pfullingen: Neske, 1954); *HW = Holzwege* (Frankfurt: Klostermann, 1952); *SZ = Sein und Zeit* (7th ed.; Tübingen: Niemeyer, 1953), and *BT* = the translation of this work by McQuarrie and Robinson (*Being and Time*; London: SCM Press, 1962); *US = Unterwegs zur Sprache* (Pfullingen: Neske, 1960), and *OWL* = its translation by Peter D. Hertz and Joan Stambaugh, *On the Way to Language* (New York: Harper and Row, 1971); *N = Nietzsche* (2 vols.; Pfullingen: Neske, 1961), and *EP = The End of Philosophy*, trans. Stambaugh (New York: Harper and Row, 1973)—a selection of passages from *N* together with a translation of *"Überwindung der Metaphysik"* from *VA*; *IM = Introduction to Metaphysics*, trans. Mannhein (New Haven: Yale University Press, 1959), and *EM* = the original, *Einführung in der Metaphysik* (Tübingen: Niemeyer, 1953); *BR* = the *"Brief an Richardson"* published in German and English on facing pages in W. J. Richardson, *Heidegger: Through Phenomenology to Thought* (The Hague: Nijhoff, 1963), pp. viii-xxiii; *QT = The Question Concerning Technology and Other Essays*, trans. William Lovitt (New York: Harper and Row, 1977); *ZSD = Zur Sache des Denkens* (Tübingen: Niemeyer, 1969), and *TB = Of Time and Being*, trans. Stambaugh (New York: Harper and Row, 1972)—a partial translation of *ZSD*.

2. *BW*, pp. 194-195 (*WM*, pp. 146-147).

3. Cf. *BW*, p. 220 (*WM*, p. 170) on Husserl's and Sartre's failure to grasp this and on why "the Marxist view of history excels all other accounts of the past." See also *BR*, p. xiv.

4. *BW*, p. 196 (*WM*, pp. 147-148).

5. *TB*, p. 9 (*ZSD*, p. 9).

6. *BW*, p. 217 (*WM*, p. 168); cf. *OWL*, pp. 38ff. (*US*, pp. 133ff.).

7. *EP*, p. 11 (*N*, II, p. 411). The notion that "even though the linguistic formulations of the essential constituents of Being change, the constituents . . . remain the same"

which Heidegger discusses in this passage is well illustrated by the tendency of recent historians of philosophy to see the problems of analytic philosophy as turning up throughout the
history of thought.

8. *N*, II, p. 201.

9. When such remarks are offered wholesale (as by Wisdom, Bouwsma, and the Ryle of
Dilemmas) they tend to be dismissed as facile and self-indulgent—as lacking the patience
and the labor of the negative. But even his worst enemies would hesitate to use such terms
of Heidegger; what he tries to do may be impossible or perverse, but it is not easy.

10. This defensive reaction is especially common in discussions of Wittgenstein's later
work. I consider this reaction to Wittgenstein in "Keeping Philosophy Pure" (Essay 2,
above).

11. To be sure, Heidegger warns us against taking him to offer just a new version of intellectual history—as he warns us against taking him to be doing anything which anybody
else has ever done. Cf. *EP*, p. 77 (*N*, II, pp. 483-484): "Because we only know, and only
want to know, history in the context of historiography which explores and exposes elements of the past for the purpose of using them in the present, recollection in the history
of Being also falls prey to the illusion that makes it appear to be conceptual historiography,
and a one-sided and sporadic one at that. But when recollection of the history of Being
names thinkers and pursues their thoughts, this thinking is the listening response which
belongs to the claim of Being, as determination attuned by the voice of that claim." I would
only remark that Dewey's remarks about the history of philosophy are, equally, a listening
response which belongs to the claim of Being.

12. Cf. *OWL*, p. 43 (*US*, p. 139).

13. Cf. *IM*, p. 37 (*EM*, p. 28).

14. *BW*, p. 221 (*WM*, pp. 171-172). Heidegger distinguishes Europe's destiny from
Russia's or America's, regions of the earth which have presumably passed beyond recall (as
of 1936). See *IM*, p. 45 (*EM*, p. 34): "Europe lies in a pincers between Russia and America
which are, metaphysically speaking, the same." The vulgarity of the remark should not lead
one to underestimate its importance. Heidegger's intense political consciousness, which led
him to make the remarks reprinted by Guido Schneeberger in *Nachlese zu Heidegger* (Bern,
1962), needs to be recognized when trying to see what he thinks "Thought" might do, just
as Dewey's must be remembered in understanding why he urged "reconstruction in philosophy." For more on Heidegger's mixed feelings on philosophy's influence on the lives of
nations and states, see *IM*, p. 10 (*EM*, p. 8).

15. See Dewey's *The Quest for Certainty (QC)* (New York: Capricorn Books, 1960),
p. 11. Other books by Dewey whose titles I shall abbreviate are *Reconstruction in Philosophy (RP)* (New York: Dover, 1958); *Art as Experience (AE)* (New York: Capricorn Books,
1958); *Experience and Nature (EN)* (New York: Dover, 1958).

16. *QC*, p. 14; compare Heidegger, *IM*, p. 106 (*EM*, p. 80): "Nietzsche was right in saying that Christianity was Platonism for the people"; cf. also *EP*, p. 24. (*N*, II, p. 427).

17. *QC*, p. 17.

18. *QC*, pp. 21-22.

19. *RP*, p. 17.

20. *RP*, p. v.

21. *RP*, p. xxxi.

22. *RP*, p. 25.

23. Cf. *EP*, pp. 55-56 (*N*, II, pp. 458-459). See Werner Marx, *Heidegger and the Traditions* (Evanston, Ill.: Northwestern University Press, 1971), p. 126.

24. Cf. *IM*, p. 69 (*EM*, pp. 52-53) and compare pp. 57ff. (*EM*, pp. 43ff.).

25. *IM*, pp. 62-63 (*EM*, p. 48). I have substituted "beings" for Mannheim's "essents" as

a translation of *Seienden* in order to bring this passage into harmony with other texts I cite in translation.

26. Cf. *RP*, p. ix.

27. Cf. *BT*, sects. 15-21, especially the introduction of the notion of *Zuhandensein* at pp. 98-99 (*SZ*, p. 69), and the claim at p. 130 (*SZ*, p. 97): "Thus Descartes' discussion of possible kinds of *access* to entities within the world is dominated by an idea of Being which has been gathered from a definite realm of these entities themselves." The latter realm is that of *Vorhandensein*. For the connection between the latter notion and Platonic and Aristotelian notions of ἰδέα ἐνέργεια, and οὐσία see Werner Marx, *op. cit.*, part II, chap. 1

28. Cf. *QC*, p. 22, on the common assumption of idealism and realism that "the operation of inquiry excludes any element of practical activity that enters into the construction of the object known."

29. *EN*, p. 11.

30. *EP*, p. 47 (*N*, II, p. 451).

31. See the discussion of the dominance of "epistemology" in the modern era at *EP*, p. 88 (*VA*, p. 67).

32. See *What Is a Thing?*, trans. Barton and Deutsch (Chicago: H. Regnery Co., 1967), p. 27 (*Die Frage nach dem Ding* [Tübingen: Niemeyer, 1962], p. 20).

33. *QC*, p. 41; cf. *RP*, pp. 49-51.

34. *QC*, p. 233.

35. See, e.g., *TB*, p. 7, and the discussion at *EP*, p. 22 (*N*, II, p. 424) of the relation between Christianity, truth-as-certainty, and "the modern period."

36. Heidegger, *Discourse on Thinking*, trans. Anderson and Freund (New York: Harper and Row, 1966), p. 84 (*Gelassenheit* [Pfullingen: Neske, 1960], p. 66).

37. Cf., e.g., *EN*, pp. 321ff. and *RP*, pp. 156ff.

38. *QC*, p. 309. There is, however, another side of Dewey in which philosophy is not vision but something much more specific—a criticism of society following "the method of science" in the hope of bringing morals and institutions into line with the spirit of science and technology. See *RP*, p. xxiii. This notion contrasts with the sort of thing Dewey says when he thinks of philosophers as "recording the efforts of men to formulate the things of experience to which they are most deeply and passionately attached" (*RP*, p. 25). This other side of Dewey is discussed briefly below, in the context of a polemically Heideggerian interpretation of his thought. I think that Dewey was at his best when he emphasized the similarities between philosophy and poetry, rather than when he emphasized those between philosophy and engineering, but I cannot debate the matter in this paper.

39. Cf. *EN*, pp. 37-38: "An empirical philosophy is in any case a kind of intellectual disrobing. . . . If the chapters that follow contribute to an artful innocence and simplicity they will have served their purpose." Like Heidegger he thinks, however, that "a cultivated naivete . . . can be acquired only through the discipline of severe thought." See J. Glenn Gray's essay "The Splendor of the Simple" in his *On Understanding Violence Philosophically, and Other Essays* (New York: Harper and Row, 1970), esp. pp. 50ff.

40. *RP*, pp. 212-213.

41. *EM*, p. 204.

42. Cf. *IM*, p. 26 (*EM*, p. 20).

43. *BT*, p. 133 (*SZ*, p. 100); see also p. 132, and sect. 59. At *IM*, pp. 47-48 (*EM*, p. 36), Heidegger says that when "the spirit is degraded into intelligence, into a tool," then "the energies of the spiritual process, poetry and art, statesmanship and religion, become subject to *conscious* cultivation and planning. They are split into branches. . . . These branches become fields of free endeavor, which sets its own standards and barely manages to live up to them. These standards of production and consumption are called values. The cultural values preserve their meaning only by restricting themselves to an autonomous field; poetry

for the sake of poetry, art for the sake of art, science for the sake of science." Compare Dewey's polemics in *AE* against the notion of "fine art" (chap. 1) and against Kant's isolation of the aesthetic from both experience and knowledge (pp. 252ff.), as well as his ubiquitous attempts to break down every dualism of disciplines or of faculties (art/science, reason/imagination, etc.). In moral philosophy one should compare Dewey's insistence that values are made by practice, rather than found and contemplated, with Heidegger's reply to Beaufret on the relation between ontology and ethics. Cf. *BW*, pp. 231 ff. (*WM*, pp. 183ff.). Heidegger's protest in the latter passage against the traditional ethics/logic/physics distinction should be compared with Dewey's insistence (e.g., *RP*, chap. 7) that there is no such thing as "moral philosophy" which seeks out "universal values" or "moral laws." Dewey would heartily agree with Heidegger's remark (*BW*, p. 232; *WM*, p. 184) that Sophocles' tragedies "preserve ἦθος more primordially than Aristotle's *Ethics.*

44. Cf. *OWL*, p. 43, with pp. 14ff. (*US*, pp. 140-141, with pp. 101ff.).

45. Cf. *BW*, p. 239 (*WM*, p. 191) on thought and the theory/practice distinction, and also *IM*, p. 26 (*EM*, p. 20) on poetry. Compare Dewey, *AE*, p. 40: "The enemies of the aesthetic are neither the practical nor the intellectual. They are the humdrum; slackness of loose ends; submission to convention in practice and intellectual procedure."

46. Cf. Dewey's autobiographical "From Absolutism to Experimentalism" (1930), reprinted in *On Experience, Nature and Freedom*, ed. R. J. Bernstein (Indianapolis: Bobbs-Merrill, 1960), pp. 3-18, esp. pp. 10-11.

47. Cf. n. 3 above. For a good discussion of Heidegger's historicism and his relation to Hegel, see Stanley Rosen, *Nihilism* (New Haven: Yale University Press, 1969), chaps. 3-4. Commentators on Heidegger's development differ about whether the "destruction of the tradition of Western ontology" is a project which continues after the "turn," but the following remarks by Stambaugh seem to sum up accurately Heidegger's feelings about the earlier version of the project: "The originally planned 'destruction' was to be phenomenological in terms of a transcendental hermeneutic. These elements—phenomenology, hermeneutics, and transcendental philosophy—Heidegger linked indissolubly together in *Being and Time*, and it is precisely all three which he wishes to relinquish in his later thinking. Thus the destruction to be carried out can no longer have the character of these three elements, because they themselves constitute the history of ontology and are thus by no means capable of 'destroying' or undoing that history. A destruction of the history of ontology must be undertaken in terms of the history of Being and must be "thought from the Appropriation" ("Introduction" to *EP*, p. ix). However, though I think Stambaugh rightly represents Heidegger's intentions, I suspect that "thinking from the Appropriation (*Ereignis*)" is too chaste, delicate, and private an activity to accomplish any destructive work, and that the work is actually done by what Heidegger dismissively calls "conceptual historiography"—the sort illustrated by the texts from *N* which Stambaugh translates in *EP*. (Cf. n. 11 above.)

48. *EP*, p. 48 (*N*, II, pp. 452-453).

49. Cf. "Plato's Doctrine of Truth" (*WM*, pp. 139ff.).

50. Cf. *RP*, pp. 49-51.

51. *IM*, p. 45 (*EM*, p. 34).

52. *BW*, p. 194 (*WM*, pp. 147-148).

53. *IM*, p. 45 (*EM*, p. 34).

54. Cf. *IM*, p. 19, with p. 50 (*EM*, p. 15, with p. 38).

55. *IM*, p. 51 (*EM*, p. 39). See also *EP*, p. 103 (*VA*, p. 84).

56. Laszlo Versényi, *Heidegger, Being and Truth* (New Haven: Yale University Press, 1965), pp. 167-168.

57. See Versényi, *op. cit.*, pp. 72ff., on Heidegger's discussion of Nietzsche's inversion of Plato's ranking of art and mathematics.

58. *QT*, p. 134 (*HW*, p. 87).

59. *VA*, p. 14.

60. *QT*, pp. 133-134 (*HW*, pp. 85-86).

61. *Loc. cit.*

62. Cf. *The Question of Being*, trans. Kluback and Wilde (New York: Twayne, 1958; original text of *Zur Seinsfrage* [p. 25 in original] facing), p. 71: "What if even the language of metaphysics and metaphysics itself, whether it be of the living or of the dead God, as metaphysics, formed that barrier which forbids a crossing over of the line, that is, the overcoming of nihilism?" On the futility of Dewey's "metaphysics," see the exchange between Santayana and Dewey in *The Philosophy of John Dewey*, ed. Schilpp (Evanston, Ill.: Northwestern University Press, 1939). I have tried to develop Santayana's point in "Dewey's Metaphysics," Essay 5, below.

63. Some commentaries on *SZ* have noted the similarities between Heidegger's non-Cartesian redescriptions of man and Ryle's. See, for example, Richard Schmitt's remark (*Martin Heidegger on Being Human* [Gloucester, Me: Peter Smith, 1969], p. 16n.) that "what English-speaking philosophers call conceptual analysis of the revisionary variety is very close to what Heidegger [in *SZ*] calls 'ontology'." On Ryle's possible debt to Heidegger, see Michael Murray, "Heidegger and Ryle: Two Versions of Phenomenology," *Review of Metaphysics*, XXVII (1973): 88-111. Presumably Heidegger would say that the similarities are real, but that they just show how misleading and futile *SZ*, taken by itself, was.

64. *TB*, p. 24 (*ZSD*, p. 25).

65. "Only by way of what Heidegger I has thought does one gain access to what-is-to-be-thought by Heidegger II. But the thought of Heidegger I becomes possible only if it is contained in Heidegger II" (*BR*, p. xxii). I take this to mean that unless one sees that man, as a being who asks about Being, has to be thought of differently than the tradition thought of him, then one will think positivism justified in insisting that questions about Being have no sense. So if you approach later Heidegger without seeing that there is a conception of man (e.g., the one offered in *SZ*) which is radically different from the one positivism inherited from the tradition, you will find no sense in the later work. On the other hand, if you do not grasp the point of the later Heidegger, you will tend to treat the new jargon — the *Existentiale* — of *SZ* in the way in which Dewey would presumably treat it, as simply a new way of enhancing human life (or as Ryle would treat it, as a way of showing how silly Descartes was). Worse yet, Heidegger might have added, if you have not been pointed in the right direction by *SZ* you may treat "Heidegger II" as simply offering still fresher and more interesting bits of jargon, and so you will remain as mindless of Being as ever. Cf. *OWL*, p. 47 (*US*, p. 145) for Heidegger's nervousness about his terminology being "corrupted to signify a concept."

66. *EP*, p. 99 (*VA*, pp. 78-79). Cf. *QT*, p. 153 (*HW*, pp. 103-104) for Heidegger's dismissal of pragmatism: "Americanism is something European. It is an as-yet-uncomprehended species of the gigantic, the gigantic that is itself still inchoate and does not as yet originate at all out of the complete and gathered metaphysical essence of the modern age. The American interpretation of Americanism by means of pragmatism still remains outside the metaphysical realm."

67. Cf. J. Glenn Gray, *op. cit.*, pp. 65-66.

68. Charles Péguy, *Basic Verities: Prose and Poetry* (French with facing translation by A. and J. Green [New York: Pantheon, 1943]), p. 108.

69. As the comparison would suggest, I think that Versényi is on the right track in picking out the Kierkegaardian phrase *"das ganz Andere"* as a give-away (*US*, p. 128; cf. Versényi, *op. cit.*, pp. 135 ff. and p. 163). Mehta (*The Philosophy of Martin Heidegger* [New York: Harper and Row, 1971], p. 119n.) criticizes Versényi for taking the phrase out of context, but I think that Versényi is perfectly justified in the following comments: "In his attempt

to make visible what is Wholly Other, and to make us enter into an entirely different dimension, Heidegger engages in a kind of negative theology and mysticism: he gives forth sibylline utterances whose only concrete content is the rejection of all human experience and insight" (p. 163). "Heidegger is well aware of the fact that any justification of his choice of works and of his interpretations by way of an appeal either to philosophical tradition or to rational reflection on everyday experience would only make his thought liable to his own charges of humanism. To escape from this philosophical embarrassment, he takes the only logical step that is still open to him: he adopts the stance of a prophet and lays claim to mystic insight . . . ." (p. 162). One can say all this about Heidegger, however, without adopting what Mehta accurately describes as Versényi's "neo-classical position." From a Deweyan point of view, what is wrong with Heidegger is not, as Versényi suggests, that he gives up "rational reflection," but that he insists on claiming that he is somehow in a position to do better what rational reflection failed to do. In any sense in which mystic insight (or just plain insight, for that matter) does what philosophical argumentation traditionally tried to do, the common goal of both is something as vague as "lending meaning to life." What is objectionable about Heidegger is that such a vague and "humanist" goal is not enough for him. He wants Plato and Hegel and himself to be engaged in a common enterprise—speaking the words of Being—which is *not* just a fancy name for the common enterprise in which all of us, philosophers and plowmen, poets and ministers of state, are engaged.

70. *IM*, p. 36 (*EM*, p. 27).

71. *IM*, p. 37 (*EM*, p. 28).

72. Cf. *N*, I, pp. 585-586, esp. the following: " . . . [Nietzsche's] theory fits so closely into the matrix of Plato's Theory of Ideas that it remains only a specially contrived inversion of that Theory, and thus is in *essence* identical with it." (I owe my knowledge of this passage to Versényi's discussion of it at p. 70 of *Heidegger, Being and Truth*.) For the same point, see Bernd Magnus, *Heidegger's Metahistory of Philosophy* (The Hague: Nijhoff, 1970), pp. 131-132.

73. I am grateful to Marjorie Grene, Joan Stambaugh, Laszlo Versényi, and my late colleague Walter Kaufmann for helpful comment on a draft of this paper. I am also grateful to Frederick Olafson and Edward Lee, whose invitation to speak at a conference on Heidegger held at La Jolla in 1974 led me to write the paper.

4

Professionalized Philosophy and Transcendentalist Culture

Santayana's reflections on philosophy in the new world have two singular merits. First, he was able to laugh at us without despising us—a feat often too intricate for the native-born. Second, he was entirely free of the instinctive American conviction that the westering of the spirit ends here—that whatever the ages have labored to bring forth will emerge between Massachusetts and California, that our philosophers have only to express our national genius for the human spirit to fulfill itself. Santayana saw us as one more great empire in the long parade. His genial hope was that we might enjoy the imperium while we held it. In a famous essay on American philosophy, he suggested that we were still spoiling our own fun. We wanted to retain, he said, the "agonized conscience" of our Calvinist ancestors while keeping, simultaneously if illogically, the idealistic metaphysics of their transcendentalist successors. This metaphysics embodied what he called the "conceited notion that man, or human reason, or the human distinction between good and evil, is the centre and pivot of the universe."[1] The combination of Calvinist guilt and metaphysical egoism he called "The Genteel Tradition in American Philosophy." He opposed to it what he called "America's ruling passion, the love of business"—"joy in business itself and in its further operation, in making it greater and better organized and a mightier engine in the general life." "The American Will," he said, "inhabits the sky-scraper; the American Intellect inhabits the colonial mansion. The one is the sphere of the American man; the other, at least predominantly, of

60

the American woman. The one is all aggressive emphasis; the other is all genteel tradition."[2] The academic mind of 1911, he thought, counted as feminine in this respect: "The genteel tradition has subsisted in the academic mind for want of anything equally academic to take its place."[3]

We can afford to smile at all this, as we look about at the manly, aggressive and businesslike academics of our own time. The American academic mind has long since discovered the joy of making its own special enterprise "greater and better organized and a mightier engine in the general life." The well-funded professor, jetting home after a day spent advising men of power, is the envy of the provincial tycoon in the adjacent seat. If there is still something like a genteel tradition in American life, it cannot be identified with "the academic mind." Most academics now teach in skyscrapers. The public no longer associates our profession with epicene delicacy, but either with political violence and sexual license or with hard-nosed presidential advisors. If there is anything remotely analogous to what Santayana spoke of, it is the specifically highbrow culture—the culture which produces poems, plays and novels, literary criticism and what, for want of a better term, we can call "culture criticism." Some highbrows inhabit the academy, mostly in literature departments, but they are not academic entrepreneurs. They do not get grants; they have disciples rather than research teams; they inhabit whatever mansions may still be tucked away among the academic skyscrapers. Their more businesslike colleagues treat them alternately with the deference due from tradesmen to the clergy, and the contempt the successful feel for the shabby genteel.

Where, in the busy modern academy, do we find the philosophy professors? To treat this question properly we need to look at what has been going on in philosophy since Santayana wrote, and to divide it into two periods. The period between the World Wars was one of prophecy and moral leadership—the heroic period of Deweyan pragmatism, during which philosophy played the sort of role in the country's life which Santayana could admire. The period since the Second World War has been one of professionalization, in which philosophers have quite deliberately and self-consciously abdicated such a role. In the pre-World War I period which Santayana described, philosophy defined itself by its relation to religion. In the Deweyan period, it defined itself by its relation to the social sciences. At the beginning of the professionalizing period, philosophers attempted halfheartedly to define their activity in relation to mathematics and the natural sciences. In fact, however, this period has been marked by a withdrawal from the rest of the academy and from culture—an insistence on philosophy's autonomy.

The claim that philosophy is and ought to be a technical subject, that this recent professionalization is an important good, is usually not defended directly by pointing with pride to the importance of the issues philosophers discuss or to paradigms of successful philosophical inquiry. Rather, it is defended indirectly, by pointing with scorn to the low level of argumentative rigor among the competition —in the Deweyan philosophy of the thirties, in contemporary Continental philosophy, and in the culture criticism of the highbrows. Even philosophers who would like to break out of their professional isolation tend to insist that their special contribution will be in argumentative skill. It is not, they say, that philosophers know more about anything in particular, but that they have a kind of sensitivity to distinctions and presuppositions which is peculiarly their own.[4]

Since the highbrow culture critic has usurped many of the functions which traditional philosophers had fulfilled in the past, while remaining oblivious to what contemporary academic philosophers are actually doing, highbrows try to dismiss American philosophy with journalistic sneers about "irrelevance" or "scholasticism." Philosophers, in turn, try to dismiss the highbrow literary culture in the same way as Santayana dismissed the genteel tradition. They see this culture as palliating cranky hypersensitivity with aesthetic comfort, just as Santayana saw Royce and Palmer as palming the agonized conscience off with metaphysical comfort. Accusations of softness and sloppiness are exchanged for accusations of pedantry and narrowness.

When these accusations become self-conscious and explicit, they are usually offered as views about "the essence of philosophy," as if a niche in a permanent ahistorical schema of possible human activities were in danger of vacancy or of usurpation. I think that such disputes are pointless, since philosophy does not have an essence, any more than do literature or politics. Each is what brilliant men are presently making it. There is no common standard by which to compare Royce, Dewey, Heidegger, Tarski, Carnap, and Derrida in point of "being a *real* philosopher." But although philosophy has no essence, it does have a history. Although philosophical movements cannot be seen as departures from, or returns to, True Philosophy, and although their successes are as difficult to assess as those of literary or political movements, one can sometimes say something about their grosser sociological consequences. In what follows, I want to sketch some of the things that have happened in American philosophy since Santayana wrote, and to make some predictions about the consequences of professionalization.

Santayana noted that William James had already "turned the flank" of the genteel tradition. A decade after Santayana's essay, it became clear that Dewey had consolidated James's gains and succeeded in doing what Santayana had described as finding something "equally academic to take the place" of that tradition." Dewey made the American learned world safe for the social sciences. In the early 1900s the academy had to restructure itself to make room for half a dozen new departments, and for a new sort of academic who came to inhabit them. The American academy became the privileged sanctuary of attempts to reconstruct the American social order, and American philosophy became a call for such reconstruction. The Deweyan claim that moral philosophy was not the formulation of general principles to serve as a surrogate for divine commands, but rather the application of intelligence to social problems, gave American youth a new way of looking at the meaning of their education and their lives. With the New Deal, the social scientist emerged as the representative of the academy to the public, embodying the Deweyan promise. When, during the Depression, Stalinism recruited whole battalions of highbrows, a small circle around Sidney Hook—Dewey's chief disciple—kept political morality alive among the intellectuals. Philosophers like Max Otto, Alexander Meiklejohn, and Horace Kallen offered their students the possibility that "America's ruling passion, the love of business," might be transformed into a love of social reconstruction. Having sat at their feet, a whole generation grew up confident that America would show the world how to escape both Gradgrind capitalism and revolutionary bloodshed. In the years between the wars, American philosophy not only escaped from the genteel tradition, but provided moral leadership for the country. For the first time, American philosophy professors played the sort of role which Fichte and Hegel had once played in Germany.

By the end of the Second World War, however, the great days of Deweyan philosophy and social science were over. The strenuous reformist attitude which succeeded the genteel tradition was in turn succeeded by an urge to be scientific and rigorous. Both social scientists and philosophers wanted to stop striking public attitudes and start showing that they could be as thoroughly and exclusively professional, and preferably as mathematical, as the natural scientists. American sociology, whose early stages had been satirized as the expenditure of a five-thousand-dollar grant to discover the address of a whorehouse, came to be satirized as the expenditure of a five-million-dollar grant to plot the addresses of a thousand whorehouses against a multidimensional array of socio-economic variables. American philosophy students realized that the previous generation—Dewey's pupils—had exhausted the market for celebrations of American democracy, naturalism, and social reconstruction. Nobody could remember what an idealist, a subjectivist, a transcendentalist, or even an orthodox theist looked like, so nobody was interested in hearing them criticized. New heroes were needed, and they were found among that extraordinary body of men, the emigré scholars. A young American philosopher learning phenomenology from Gurwitsch or Schuetz, or logical empiricism from Carnap or Reichenbach, was trained to think of philosophy as a rigorous discipline, a matter of cooperation in joint inquiry and the production of agreed-upon results. By the mid-fifties, the victory which the pragmatists had won on native ground over the genteel tradition seemed as remote as Emerson's victory over the Calvinists. With exacting work to be done on the structure of visual awareness or on extensional criteria of nomologicality, there seemed no time and no need to ask what had happened in philosophy before Husserl or before Russell. As logical empiricism metamorphosed into analytic philosophy, and succeeded in driving phenomenology out into the academic shadows, American philosophers' disinterest in moral and social questions became almost total. Courses in moral philosophy were, for a time, little more than elaborate epistemological sneers at the common moral consciousness. Philosophers' contact with colleagues in the social sciences became as minimal and incidental as their contacts with colleagues in literature. Dewey had predicted that philosophy would turn away from the seventeenth-century tension between mathematical physics and the world of common sense, and would take up new problems arising from the social sciences and the arts. But this prediction was completely off target. On the contrary, all the good old Cartesian problems which Dewey thought he had disposed of were brought back, restated in the formal mode of speech and surrounded by new difficulties generated by the formalism.

What Dewey had predicted for American philosophy did, however, happen elsewhere: both in Continental philosophy and in American highbrow literary culture. Attention to interpretation rather than verification—to what the arts and the "sciences of man" have in common—was the mark of the literary intellectual. One result of this —the most important result for my present purposes—was that the history of philosophy began to be taken over by the highbrows. Whereas professionalized philosophers insisted on treating the great dead philosophers as sources of hypotheses or instructive examples of conceptual confusion, the highbrows still treated them in the old-fashioned way, as heroes or villains. Dewey had still attempted to tell a great sweeping story about philosophy from Plato to himself, but philosophers in the professionalizing period distrusted such stories as "unscientific" and "unscholarly." So they are, but they also form a genre of writing which is quite indispensable. Besides the need to ask whether certain propositions asserted by Aristotle or Locke or Kant or Kierkegaard are true or were validly inferred, there is also the need to adopt an attitude towards such men, just as one must adopt an attitude towards Alcibiades and Euripides, Cromwell and Milton, Proust and Lenin. Because the writings of the great dead philosophers form a bundle of intertwined dialectical sequences, one has to have attitudes towards many of them to justify one's attitude towards the others. Nor can one's attitude towards Kant, for example, be independent of one's attitudes towards Wordsworth and Napoleon. Developing attitudes towards the mighty dead and their living rivals—dividing the pantheon into the divine and the daemonic—is the whole point of highbrow culture. The kind of name-dropping, rapid shifting of context, and unwillingness to stay for an answer which this culture encourages runs counter to everything that a professionalized academic discipline stands for. Normally, the conflict between the academy and this culture can remain implicit. But in the case of philosophy it is bound to be expressed, if only because not even the most professionalized philosopher can stop seeing himself, if not as the contemporary counterpart of Plato and Kant, as at least their authorized commentator. So we have the conflict I described at the beginning of this essay—the highbrow and the academic philosopher viewing each other with equal suspicion, each harping on the vices of each other's virtues.

I want to claim that this is not a conflict which we need view with any great concern nor try to resolve. If we understand its historical background, we can live with its probable consequence—that philosophy as a technical academic subject will remain as remote from highbrow culture as is paleontology or classical philology. To defend this attitude, I want to go on to say why I think that the mode of treating the great philosophers characteristic of highbrow culture *is* indispensable, and also why one should not confuse this culture with the genteel tradition of which Santayana was complaining. I shall try to do this by sketching the history of the emergence of highbrow

culture, which seems to me as distinctively a nineteenth-century phenomenon as the New Science and the philosophical problematic which
it created were seventeenth-century phenomena.[5]

Beginning in the days of Goethe and Macauley and Carlyle and
Emerson, a kind of writing has developed which is neither the evaluation of the relative merits of literary productions, nor intellectual history, nor moral philosophy, nor epistemology, nor social prophecy,
but all these things mingled together into a new genre. This genre is
often still *called* "literary criticism," however, for an excellent reason.
The reason is that in the course of the nineteenth century imaginative literature took the place of both religion and philosophy in
forming and solacing the agonized conscience of the young. Novels
and poems are now the principal means by which a bright youth gains
a self-image. Criticism of novels is the principal form in which the
acquisition of a moral character is made articulate. We live in a culture in which putting one's moral sensitivity into words is not clearly
distinguishable from exhibiting one's literary sensibilities. Episodes
from the history of religion and from the history of philosophy are
seen as instantiating literary paradigms, rather than serving as sources
of literary inspiration. The creed or the philosophical doctrine becomes the emblem of the novelist's character or the poet's image, rather than converseley. Philosophy is treated as a parallel genre to the
drama or the novel or the poem, so that we speak of the epistemology common to Vaihinger and Valéry, the rhetoric common to
Marlowe and Hobbes, the ethics common to E. M. Forster and G. E.
Moore. What culture criticism does *not* do is to ask whether Valéry
wrote more beautiful lines than Marlowe, or whether Hobbes or
Moore told more truths about the good. In this form of life, the true
and the good and the beautiful drop out. The aim is to understand,
not to judge. The hope is that if one understands enough poems,
enough religions, enough societies, enough philosophies, one will have
made oneself into something worth one's own understanding.

To understand the relations between the genteel tradition of our
forebears and the highbrow culture criticism of the present, it helps
to look more closely at the good and the bad senses of the term
"transcendentalism" which Santayana distinguished. He contrasted
transcendentalist metaphysical systems, which he deplored as ego-
tistical, with what he called "transcendentalism proper." This, he
said,

> like romanticism, is not any particular set of dogmas about what things
> exist; it is not a system of the universe regarded as a fact. . . . It is a
> method, a point of view, from which any work, no matter what it might

contain, could be approached by a self-conscious observer. . . . It is the chief contribution made in modern times to speculation.[6]

This transcendentalist point of view is the mark of the highbrow. It is the attitude that there is no point in raising questions of truth, goodness, or beauty, because between ourselves and the thing judged there always intervenes mind, language, a perspective chosen among dozens, one description chosen out of thousands. On one side, it is the lack of seriousness which Plato attributed to poets, the "negative capability" for which Keats praised Shakespeare. On another, it is the Sartrean sense of absurdity which Arthur Danto suggests may befall us when we give up the picture theory of language and the Platonic conception of truth as accuracy of representation. In the later Wittgenstein, it was the wry admission that anything has a sense if you give it a sense. In Heidegger, who hated it, it was the charter of the modern—of what he called "the age of the worldview." In Derrida, it is the renunciation of "the myth of the purely maternal or paternal language belonging to the lost fatherland of thought." It is crystallized in Foucault's claim that he "writes in order to have no face."

Transcendentalism, in this sense, is the justification of the intellectual who has no wish to be a scientist or a professional, who does not think that intellectual honesty requires what Kuhn calls a "disciplinary matrix." It is what permits the attitude of the literary intellectual towards science which scandalizes C. P. Snow: the view of, say, quantum mechanics as a notoriously great, but quite untranslatable, poem, written in a lamentably obscure language. Transcendentalism is what gives sense to the very notion of the "highbrow"—a notion which is post-Romantic and post-Kantian. In the eighteenth century there were witty men and learned men and pious men, but there were no highbrows. Not until the Romantics did books become so various as to create readers who see what has been written as having no containing framework, no points of reference save the books one loves today but which may betray one tomorrow. Not until Kant did philosophy destroy science and theology to make room for moral faith, and not until Schiller did it seem possible that the room cleared for morality could be occupied by art. When Santayana traced "transcendentalism" (in the good sense) back to Kant, his point was that Kant's treatment of scientific truth makes science just one cultural manifestation among others. But since scientific truth has been, since the seventeenth century, the model for philosophical truth, Kant's treatment of scientific truth leads to Santayana's own aesthetic attitude towards philosophical vision. It was this sense of relativity and open possibility which Santayana thought we should admire in

Emerson—the side of Emerson that resembled Whitman rather than the side that resembled Royce. It was precisely the inability to maintain this splendidly aristocratic posture which made the genteel tradition merely genteel. That tradition claimed that one could take both scientific truth and religious truth with full seriousness and weave them together into something new—transcendental philosophy— which was higher than science, purer than religion, and truer than both. This claim was what Dewey and Russell were reacting against: Dewey by social concern, and Russell by inventing something scientific and rigorous and difficult for philosophy to become. By picking these men as heroes, two major movements in American philosophy became obsessed with the danger of a form of cultural life which no longer existed. American philosophers thought of themselves as guarding against idealistic speculations, long after such speculations had ceased to be written. They called "idealist" anything they didn't like—anything outside their own discipline which breathed the faintest trust in a larger hope.

The result was that culture criticism—the sort of writing done by T. S. Eliot and Edmund Wilson, by Lionel Trilling and Paul Goodman —was hardly visible to philosophers, though little else was visible to the best of the students they were teaching. When the Deweyan period ended, the moral sense of American intellectuals began to be formed without the intervention of the philosophy professors, who assumed that any decent kid would grow up to be the same sort of pragmatic liberal as themselves. As Harold Bloom writes,

> The teacher of literature now in America, far more than the teacher of
> history or philosophy or religion, is condemned to teach the presentness
> of the past, because history, philosophy and religion have withdrawn as
> agents from the Scene of Instruction. . . .[7]

Whatever species of professor takes on the task of teaching the presentness of the great dead philosophers, those philosophers will be present at the Scene of Instruction as long as we have libraries. There will be a Scene of Instruction as long as there is an agonized conscience in the young. This conscience is not something which was left behind with Calvinism in the eighteenth century nor with religion generally in the nineteenth. If this conscience is not induced by one's early betrayals of one's early loves, it will nevertheless be ensured, for example, by the well-funded American academic's realization that his colleagues in Chile and Russia are presently enduring humiliation and pain to amuse the guards at their prisons. Though Santayana hoped that American culture would stop trying to solace the agonized conscience with metaphysical comfort, he did not think that conscience would go away. But American philosophers came to fear that anything which even touched upon the agonized conscience might be construed as metaphysical comfort. They reacted either by ignoring the great dead philosophers or by reinterpreting them so that they would be seen as addressing properly professional issues. The result of such reinterpretation was to obscure the presentness of the past and to separate the philosophy professors from their students and from transcendentalist culture. Whether the sort of links between transcendentalist culture and academic departments of literature which presently exist will someday be paralleled by links with philosophy departments is not terribly important. It may be that American philosophy will continue to be more concerned with developing a disciplinary matrix than with its antecedents or its cultural role. No harm will be done by this, and possibly much good. The dialectical dramas which began with Plato will continue. They will be enacted; if not by people paid to teach Plato, then by others. These others may not be called "philosophers" but something else, possibly "critics." Possibly they will be given a name which would seem as odd to us as our use of "critic" would have seemed to Dr. Johnson, or our use of "philosopher" to Socrates.

This is the conclusion I wish to draw from my survey of what has happened in American philosophy since Santayana wrote. It amounts to saying that professionalized philosophy may or may not join transcendentalist culture, but that it should not try to beat it. I shall end by turning back to Santayana once again, and commending the second of the two virtues I initially attributed to him. This was his ability to avoid the conviction that America is what history has been leading up to, and thus that it is up to American philosophy to express the American genius, to describe a virtue as uniquely ours as our redwoods and our rattlesnakes. This mild chauvinism was in vogue during the Deweyan period, and occasionally we still feel nostalgia for it. But, *pace* Niebuhr, Deweyan philosophy did not start from the assumption that the American and the Industrial Revolutions had, between them, rendered the agonized conscience obsolete. Nor, despite a certain amount of hopeful rhetoric from Dewey and his disciples, did it really teach that the combination of American institutions and the scientific method would produce the Good Life for Man. Its attitude was best expressed by Sidney Hook in an essay called "Pragmatism and the Tragic Sense of Life," which closes by saying, "Pragmatism . . . is the theory and practice of enlarging human freedom in a precarious and tragic world by the arts of intelligent social control. It may be a lost cause. I do not know of a better one.[8] There is indeed no better cause, and the nostalgia which philosophers in the professionalizing period have felt for the prophetic Deweyan period comes from their sense that they are not doing as much for this cause as they would like. But the defense of this cause is only incidentally a matter of formulating moral principles, and moral education is only incidentally a matter of choosing and defending a cause. Further, although America will go down in history as having done more for this cause than any of the great empires so far, there is no particular reason why a nation's philosophers, or indeed its intellectuals, need be identified in the eyes of history with the same virtues as its political and social institutions. There is no reason to think that the promise of American democracy will find its final fulfillment in America, any more than Roman law reached its fulfillment in the Roman Empire or literary culture its fulfillment in Alexandria. Nor is there much reason to think that the highbrow culture of whatever empire does achieve that fulfillment will resemble our own, or that the professors of moral philosophy then will build on principles being formulated now. Even if, through some unbelievable stroke of fortune, America survives with its freedoms intact and becomes a rallying point for the nations, the high culture of an unfragmented world need not center around anything specifically American. It may not, indeed, *center* around anything more than anything else: neither poetry, nor social institutions, nor mysticism, nor depth psychology, nor novels, nor philosophy, nor physical science. It may be a culture which is transcendentalist through and through, whose center is everywhere and circumference nowhere. In such a culture, Jonathan Edwards and Thomas Jefferson, Henry and William James, John Dewey and Wallace Stevens, Charles Peirce and Thorstein Veblen will all be present. No one will be asking which ones are the Americans, nor even, perhaps, which ones are the philosophers.

Notes

1. George Santayana, *Winds of Doctrine* (London: J. M. Dent, 1913), p. 214.
2. *Ibid.*, p. 188.
3. *Ibid.*, p. 212.
4. I develop this theme at greater length in Essay 12, below.
5. I develop this contrast between the literary culture and the professional philosophers at greater length in Essay 8, below.

6. Santayana, *op. cit.*, 193-194.

7. Harold Bloom, *A Map of Misreading* (New York: Oxford University Press, 1975), p. 39.

8. Sidney Hook, *Pragmatism and the Tragic Sense of Life* (New York: Basic Books, 1974), p. 25.

5

Dewey's Metaphysics

Very near the end of his life, Dewey hoped to write a new edition of *Experience and Nature*, "changing the title as well as the subject matter from *Nature and Experience* [sic] to *Nature and Culture*." In a letter to Bentley, he says

> I was dumb not to have seen the need for such a shift when the old text was written. I was still hopeful that the philosophic word "Experience" could be redeemed by being returned to its idiomatic usages—which was a piece of historic folly, the hope I mean.

Around the same time, Dewey formally abjured his attempts to rehabilitate the word "metaphysics."[1] As he came to recognize, it is hard to say in what sense *Experience and Nature*, which is often called his "principal work on metaphysics,"[2] is to be assimilated to the genre which includes the central books of Aristotle's *Metaphysics*, Spinoza's *Ethics*, Royce's *The World and the Individual*, and similar paradigms. Dewey's book consists, very roughly, of accounts of the historical and cultural genesis of the problems traditionally dubbed "metaphysical," interspersed with recommendations of various pieces of jargon which, Dewey thinks, will help us to see the irreality (or, at least, the evitability) of these problems. It is easier to think of the book as an explanation of why nobody needs a metaphysics, rather than as itself a metaphysical system. If one thinks of it as a book which ought to have been called *Nature and Culture*, one will be tempted to assimilate it with what, for lack of a better name, we can call the history of ideas: works such as the first book of the *Metaphysics*, Kant's "Amphiboly of the Concepts of Reflection," Hegel's *Phenomenology*, Lovejoy's *Great Chain of Being*, and Foucault's *The Order of Things*. Given such an assimilation, one can see the book not as an "empirical metaphysics" but as a historico-sociological study of the cultural phenomenon called "metaphysics." It can be seen as one more version of the polemical critique of the tradition offered in *Reconstruction in Philosophy* and *The Quest for Certainty*.

For most of his life, however, Dewey would not have relished this assimilation. For better or worse, he *wanted* to write a metaphysical system. Throughout his life, he wavered between a therapeutic stance toward philosophy and another, quite different, stance—one in which philosophy was to become "scientific" and "empirical" and to do something serious, systematic, important, and constructive. Dewey sometimes described philosophy as the criticism of culture, but he was never quite content to think of himself as a kibitzer or a therapist or an intellectual historian. He wanted to have things both ways. When Santayana, reviewing *Experience and Nature*, remarked that "naturalistic metaphysics" was a contradiction in terms,[3] Dewey responded as follows:

> This is the extent and method of my "metaphysics":—the large and constant features of human sufferings, enjoyments, trials, failures and successes together with the institutions of art, science, technology, politics, and religion which mark them, communicate genuine features of the world within which man lives. The method differs no whit from that of any investigator who, by making certain observations and experiments, and by utilizing the existing body of ideas available for calculation and interpretation, concludes that he really succeeds in finding out something about some limited aspect of nature. If there is any novelty in *Experience and Nature*, it is not, I should say, this "metaphysics" which is that of the common man, but lies in the use made of the method to understand a group of special problems which have troubled philosophy.[4]

In this passage, Dewey wants to say simultaneously "I am just clearing away the dead wood of the philosophical tradition" and "I am using my own powerful invention—the application of scientific and empirical method in philosophy—to do so." But two generations of commentators have been puzzled to say what method might produce "a statement of the generic traits manifested by existences of all kinds without regard to their differentiation into mental and physical"[5] while differing "no whit" from that employed by the laboratory scientist. Nor has it been any clearer how displaying such generic traits could either avoid banality or dissolve traditional philosophical problems.

Yet another way of putting this tension in Dewey's thought is suggested by some remarks of Sidney Hook, describing Dewey's view of the place of philosophy in culture:

> Traditional metaphysics has always been a violent and logically impossible attempt to impose some parochial scheme of values upon the cosmos in order to justify or undermine a set of existing social institutions by a pretended deduction from the nature of Reality. . . . But once crack the shell of any metaphysical doctrine, what appears is not verifiable knowledge but a directing bias . . . the preeminent subject matter of philosophy has been the relation between things and *values*.[6]

Given this view, one has a dilemma: either Dewey's metaphysics differs from "traditional metaphysics" in not having a directing bias concerning social values because Dewey has found an "empirical" way of doing metaphysics which abstracts from any such biases and values, or else when Dewey falls into his vein of talking of the "generic traits manifested by existences of all kinds" he is in slightly bad faith. The first horn of this dilemma is not one which any Deweyan would want grasped. The best thing about Dewey, one may well feel, is that he did not, like Plato, pretend to be a "spectator of all time and eternity," but used philosophy (even that presumably highest and purest form of philosophy—metaphysics itself) as an instrument of social change. Even if, somehow, one could explain what "empirical method" in metaphysics came down to, it *ought* not (on Dewey's own principles) to be something with the magisterial neutrality which traditionally belongs to a discipline that offers us "generic traits of existence of all kinds." Even if Dewey *could* explain what is "observational and experimental" about *Experience and Nature*, his own remarks about observation and experiment as tools for solving some given problem involving social values should be brought to bear upon his own work. If, as I have said, the actual content of *Experience and Nature* is a series of analyses of how such pseudo-"problems of philosophy" as subject-object and mind-versus-matter arose and how they can be dissolved, the nature of that project is clear. But it is also clear that the talk of "observation and experiment" is as irrelevant to the accomplishment of the project as it was to the great predecessor of all such works of philosophy-as-criticism-of-culture, Hegel's *Phenomenology*.

This point is well brought out by Hook's contrast between the logical positivists' attitude toward philosophical problems and Dewey's own:

> Dewey had shown that most of the traditional problems of philosophy were pseudo-problems, i.e., they could not be solved even in their own terms. In a much more formal way the logical empiricists did the same thing and stopped. But instead of stopping with the demonstration of the logical futility of continuing the controversy over formulations which in principle could never be adequate to any concrete problems, Dewey went on to inquire what the genuine conflicts were which lay at the bottom of fruitless verbal disputes.[7]

This seems to me an accurate account of the relevant differences, and also to help explain various changes of fashion in the last forty years or so of the history of American philosophy. Deweyan naturalism, after a period of dominance, was shoved off the American philosophical scene for a couple of decades, during the heyday of logical empiricism. This can easily be explained if one is willing to grant that writers like Russell, Carnap, Ayer, and Black were doing a better job of showing the "pseudo-ness" of pseudo-problems than Dewey had been able to do. They could do so because they had the virtues of their vices. What now seems to us (in the light of, for example, Quine's and Sellars's criticisms of its assumptions) the dogmatism and artificiality of the logical empiricist movement was precisely what permitted this movement to criticize the tradition so sharply and so effectively. Following Kant in wishing to put philosophy upon the secure path of a science, and writing as if Hegel had never lived, the logical empiricists carried assumptions common to Descartes, Locke, and Kant to their logical conclusion and thus reduced the traditional problematic of philosophy to absurdity. By exhibiting the implications of the quest for certainty, and the inability to resist Hume's conclusions once one had adopted Descartes' spectatorial account of knowledge and what Austin called "the ontology of the sensible manifold," they made clear what Dewey had been unable to make clear: just why the pictures common to the great philosophers of the modern period had to be abandoned.

But in doing this, the logical empiricists encompassed their own destruction, as Austin pointed out against Ayer, and Wittgenstein against Russell, Moore, and his earlier self. "Oxford philosophy," an even shorter-lived movement than logical empiricism, helped us see how logical empiricism had been the *reductio ad absurdum* of a tradition, not the criticism of that tradition from the standpoint of magisterial "logical" neutrality which it had thought itself to be. The narrowness and artificiality of the dualisms which logical empiricists presupposed enabled them to do what Dewey, precisely because of his broader scope and his ability to see the tradition in perspective, had not. Dewey's inquiry into "the genuine conflicts which lay at the bottom of fruitless verbal disputes" had the vices of its virtues: it distracted attention from the way in which, *in their own terms*, the Cartesian-Humean-Kantian assumptions were self-refuting. The positivists and later the "Oxford philosophers" brought these internal contradictions to much sharper focus than had Dewey and his followers, just because their vision was so much narrower.

Hook's account also helps explain the current revival of interest in Dewey. The working out of the pseudo-ness of pseudo-problems is by now familiar. Philosophers would like something new to do. As usual when their fountains of inspiration dry up, English-speaking philosophers are looking to the Continent for some new ideas, and what they find there is just what Dewey hoped for. In 1930, Dewey wrote:

> Intellectual prophecy is dangerous; but if I read the signs of the times aright, the next synthetic movement in philosophy will emerge when the significance of the social sciences and arts has become the object of reflective attention in the same way that mathematical and physical sciences have been made the objects of thought in the past, and when their full import is grasped.[8]

In such writers as Habermas and Foucault, we find just the sort of attention Dewey wanted paid to the cultural matrix in which "the idea of a social science" arose and to the problems which the dubious self-understanding of the social sciences engenders in debates on social and political questions. In writers like Derrida (and some American philosophers who admire Derrida's work, like Cavell and Danto), one finds questions about the relation between philosophy and novels, philosophy and theater, philosophy and film, emerging to replace the traditional Kantian, Husserlian, and Carnapian questions about the relation between philosophy on the one hand, and mathematical physics and introspective psychology on the other. This is not, obviously, the first time in the history of philosophy that such questions have been raised; one need only think of Nietzsche, Dilthey, and Cassirer. So I do not want to prophesy that, having finally overcome the Kantian obsession with modeling philosophy on "the mathematical and physical sciences" and with the data and methods of these sciences as principal loci of philosophical inquiry, we are now about to enter a golden age of philosophy under the aegis of Hegelian historicism. I confess I *hope* that that is the case, but the hope may be idle. For present purposes, I simply note that Dewey is just the philosopher one might want to reread if one were turning from Kant to Hegel, from a "metaphysics of experience" to a study of cultural development.

This contrast brings me back from an excursus on recent philosophical fashions to the tension in Dewey's thought which I want to discuss. To give one more illustration of this tension, consider Dewey's devastating remark about the tradition: "Philosophy has assumed for its function a knowledge of reality. This fact makes it a rival instead of a complement to the sciences."[9] To pursue this line of thought consistently, one must renounce the notion of an "empirical metaphysics" as wholeheartedly as one has already renounced a "transcendental account of the possibility of experience." I see no way to reconcile such passages as this, which I think represent Dewey at his best, with his answer to Santayana—his talk of "generic traits." Sympathetic expositors of Dewey-as-metaphysician—such as Hofstadter, who describes "the aim of metaphysics, as a general theory of existence" as "the discovery of the basic types of involvements and their relationships"[10] —cannot, I think, explain why we *need* a discipline at that level of generality, nor how the results of such "discoveries" can be anything but trivial. Would anyone—including Dewey himself— really believe that there is a discipline that could somehow do for "the basic types of involvement," something left undone by novelists, sociologists, biologists, poets, and historians? All one might want a philosopher to do is to synthesize the novels, poems, histories, and sociologies of the day into some larger unity. But such syntheses are, in fact, offered us on all sides, in *every* discipline. To be an intellectual, rather than simply to "do research," is precisely to reach for some such synthesis. Nothing save the myth that there is something special called "philosophy" that provides the paradigm of a synthetic discipline, and a figure called "the philosopher" who is the paradigm of the intellectual, suggests that the professional philosopher's work is incomplete unless he has drawn up a list of the "generic traits of all existence" or discovers "the basic types of involvements."[11]

So far I have been saying that it is unlikely that we shall find, in *Experience and Nature*, anything which can be called a "metaphysics of experience" as opposed to a therapeutic treatment of the tradition —on the ground that Dewey's own view of the nature and function of philosophy precludes it. To confirm this, one needs to look at what Dewey actually says about experience in this book, and I shall do so shortly. But first I want to insert an account of one of Dewey's earlier views—the notion of "philosophy as psychology" which he held in the 1880s and which became the center of a controversy with Shadworth Hodgson. Turning back the pages to the beginnings of Dewey's philosophical career will show us, I think, why he thought it was so important to "redescribe experience" and will also suggest why he was tempted to describe that redescription as "the whole of philosophy." Dewey was a hedgehog rather than a fox; he spent his life trying to articulate and restate a single vision, and in the writings of his third decade he already exhibits the tension I have claimed to find in the later writings.

Hodgson reacts indignantly to Dewey's youthful claim that "Psychology is the completed method of philosophy, because in it science and philosophy, fact and reason, are one." He writes:

> The passage [in Dewey's articles] which comes nearest to a description of the method of psychology is the following:
>
>> But the very essence of psychology as method is that it treats of experience in its absolute totality, not setting up some one aspect of it to account for the whole, as, for example, our physical evolutionists do, nor yet attempting to determine its nature from something outside and beyond itself, as, for example, our so-called empirical psychologists have done.
>
> The method is here described by negatives only. It consists in the precepts to avoid the faults exemplified by the physical evolutionists on the one hand and the empirical psychologists on the other. But as to any positive direction how to go to work in investigation, there is a blank. This is quite what we should expect from the identification of psychology with transcendental philosophy.[12]

Hodgson's criticism is, I think, entirely justified. It parallels Santayana's criticism of the possibility of a "naturalistic metaphysic," and neatly singles out a recurrent flaw in Dewey's work: his habit of announcing a bold new positive program when all he offers, and all he needs to offer, is criticism of the tradition. "Psychology as method" was only the first of a series of resounding but empty slogans that Dewey employed, but it is important to see why this particular slogan attracted him. He ends one of the articles attacked by Hodgson by saying:

> The conclusion of the whole matter is that a "being like man," since self-conscious, is an individualized universe, and hence that his nature is the proper material of philosophy, and in its wholeness the only material. Psychology is the science of this nature, and no dualism in it, or in ways of regarding it, is tenable.[13]

In this passage, and in the pages leading up to it, we get the following doctrines: (1) most of the troubles philosophy has encountered stem from untenable dualisms; (2) traditional empiricism (as represented by Hume, Bain, and Hodgson) puts forward a "partial account of experience" which separates percepts from concepts;[14] (3) the way to overcome such dualisms as those produced by empiricism's separation of percepts from concepts, and thus of consciousness from self-consciousness, is "psychology," the discipline which tells us that no such separations are possible. In his reply to Hodgson, Dewey never really answers Hodgson's question about what the method of psychology might be, but blandly says

> I speak, not as a Germanizing transcendentalist, but according to my humble lights as a psychologist, when I say that I know nothing of a perceptual order apart from a conceptual, and nothing of an agent or bearer apart from the content which it bears. As a psychologist, I see the possibility of abstractly analyzing each from the other, and if I were as fond of erecting the results of an analysis into real entities as Mr. Hodgson believes me to be, I should suppose that they were actually distinct as concrete experiences. But, sticking fast to what Psychology teaches me, I must hold that they are aspects, analytically arrived at, of the one existing reality — conscious experience.[15]

It was not, of course, "psychology" which taught Dewey this, but rather T. H. Green, who had spent a great deal of energy reiterating Kant's criticism of Hume, viz. that no set of percepts juggled about could produce self-consciousness, and who drew the moral that the British empiricist notion of a sensory impression was a confusion between a physiological causal process and a self-conscious perceptual belief.[16] Dewey, however, is not content to let Green's analysis of experience be a better one than Bain's and Hodgson's Humean account: he needs to insist that what Green tells us is also told us by experience itself:

> We may see how the matter stands by inquiring what would be the effect upon philosophy if self-consciousness were not an *experienced fact*, i.e., if it were not one actual stage in that realization of the universe by an individual which is defined as constituting the sphere of psychology. The result would be again, precisely, that no such thing as philosophy, under any theory of its nature whatever, is possible. Philosophy, it cannot be too often repeated, consists simply in viewing things *sub specie aeternitatis* or *in ordine ad universum*. . . . To deny, therefore, that self-consciousness is a matter of psychological experience is to deny the possibility of any philosophy.[17]

Though Dewey was soon to recant this definition of philosophy, he was never to escape the notion that what he himself said about experience described what experience itself looked like, whereas what others said of experience was a confusion between the data and the products of their analyses. Others might be transcendentalizing metaphysicians, but he was a "humble psychologist." Other philosophers produced dualisms, he was to insist throughout his life, because they "erected the results of an analysis into real entities." But a nondualistic account of experience, of the sort Dewey himself proposed, was to be a true return to *die Sache selbst*. Though he gave up the term "psychology" for his own "philosophical method," replacing it with still vaguer notions like "scientific method in philosophy" and "experimentalism in metaphysics," he was always to insist that his opponents were those who erected dualisms because they "abandoned the acknowledgement of the primacy and ultimacy of gross experience—primary as it is given in an uncontrolled form, ultimate as it is given in a more regulated and significant form—a form made possible by the methods and results of reflective experience."[18] What exasperated Hodgson in the 1880s was to exasperate another generation of critics in the 1930s. These critics welcomed with enthusiasm Dewey's suggestions about the cause and cure of traditional empiricisms and rationalisms, but were unable to see much point in Dewey's own "constructive" attempts to produce a philosophical jargon that was dualism-free, nor in his claim to be more "empirical" in method than his opponents.

To conclude this look at Dewey's earliest formulation of a program and method, I think we can see from the passages I have cited how easy it would have been for him, once he had, as he put it, "drifted away from Hegelianism,"[19] to have tried to do justice both to his earlier belief that the Kant-Hegel-Green critique of empiricism was the key to an understanding of man, and to his growing distrust of philosophy as a view of the universe *sub specie aeternitatis*. His resolution of the conflict amounted to saying: there must be a standpoint from which experience can be seen in terms of some "generic traits" which, once recognized, will make it impossible for us to describe it in these misleading ways which generate the subject-object and mind-matter dualisms that have been the dreary topics of traditional philosophical controversy. This viewpoint would not be *sub specie aeternitatis*, since it would emphasize precisely the temporality and contingency which Augustine and Spinoza used the notion of "eternity" to exclude. But it would resemble traditional metaphysics in providing a permanent neutral matrix for future inquiry. Such a naturalistic metaphysics would say, "Here is what experience is really like, before dualistic analysis has done its fell work." Such a philosophy would thus enjoy the benefit of that "immense release and liberation"[20] which young Dewey had found in Hegel, while spurning all temptations toward "German transcendentalizing."

Some such notion of doing equal justice to Hegel and to "naturalism" lies behind the project Dewey set himself in *Experience and Nature*, and I hope this backward look at the young Dewey may have helped lend additional plausibility to the criticisms I now want to make of that book. The first and most general criticism just repeats Santayana's claim that "naturalistic metaphysics" is a contradiction in terms. One can put this point best, perhaps, by saying that no man can serve both Locke and Hegel. Nobody can claim to offer an "empirical" account of something called "the inclusive integrity of 'experience,'" nor take this "integrated unity as the starting point for philosophic thought,"[21] if he also agrees with Hegel that the starting point of philosophic thought is bound to be the dialectical situation in which one finds oneself caught in one's own historical period—the problems of the men of one's time. Only someone who thought, with Locke, that we can free ourselves from the problems of the day and pursue a "plain, historical method" in examining the emergence of complex experiences out of simple ones would have written the following:

> That the physiological organism with its structure, whether in man or in the lower animals, is concerned with making adaptations and uses of material in the interest of maintenance of the life-process, cannot be denied. The brain and nervous system are primarily organs of action-undergoing; biologically it can be asserted without contravention that primary experience is of a corresponding type. Hence, unless there is breach of historic and natural continuity, cognitive experience must originate within that of a noncognitive sort.[22]

Again, only someone who thought that a proper account of the "generic traits" of experience could cross the line between physiology and sociology—between causal processes and the self-conscious beliefs and inferences that they make possible—would have written the chapter in *Experience and Nature* called "Nature, Life and Body-Mind," or have attempted to develop a jargon that would apply equally to plants, nervous systems, and physicists.[23] But this return to Lockean modes of thought, under the aegis of Darwin, betrayed precisely the insight which Dewey owed to Green: that nothing is to be gained for an understanding of human knowledge by running together the vocabularies in which we describe the causal antecedents of knowledge with those in which we offer justifications of our claims to knowledge. Dewey's naturalistic metaphysics hoped to eliminate epistemological problems by offering an up-to-date version of Locke's "plain, historical method." But what Green and Hegel had seen, and Dewey himself saw perfectly well except when he was sidetracked into doing "metaphysics," was that we can eliminate epistemological problems by eliminating the assumption that justification must repose on something other than social practices and human needs. To say, as Dewey wants to, that to gain knowledge is to solve problems, one does not need to find "continuities" between nervous systems and people, or between "experience" and "nature." One does not need to justify our claim to know that, say, a given action was the best we could take by noting that the brain is an "organ of action-undergoing," any more than by pointing out that the particles which make up the brain are undergoing some actions themselves. Dewey, in short, confuses two ways of revolting against philosophical dualisms. The first way is to point out that the dualism is imposed by a tradition for specific cultural reasons, but has now outlived its usefulness. This is the Hegelian way—the way Dewey adopts in "An Empirical Survey of Empiricisms." The second is to describe the phenomenon in a nondualistic way which emphasizes "continuity between lower and higher processes." This is the Lockean way—the way which led Locke to assimilate all mental acts to raw feels, thus paving the way for Humean skepticism. It was this assimilation which provoked Kant's remark that whereas Leibniz "intellectualized" appearances, "Locke sensualized all concepts of the understanding"[24] and which led German thought to turn away from the "naturalism" which Locke seemed to represent. Its reappearance in *Experience and Nature* led the logical empiricists to accuse Dewey of confusing "psychological" with "conceptual" issues.

Dewey wanted to be as naturalistic as Locke and as historicist as Hegel. This can indeed be done. One can say with Locke that the causal processes that go on in the human organism suffice, without the intrusion of anything non-natural, to explain the acquisition of knowledge (moral, mathematical, empirical, and political). One can also say, with Hegel, that rational criticism of knowledge-claims is always in terms of the problems that human beings face at a particular epoch. These two lines of thought neither intersect nor conflict. Keeping them separate has the virtue of doing just what Dewey wanted to do—preventing the formulation of the traditional, skeptically motivated "problems of epistemology." But it also leaves "systematic philosophy" or "metaphysics" with little to do. Dewey never quite brought himself to adopt the Bouwsma-like stance that philosophy's mission, like that of therapy, was to make itself obsolete. So he thought, in *Experience and Nature*, to show what the discovery of the *true* "generic traits" of experience could do.

To make this line of criticism a bit more specific, consider Dewey's treatment of the mind-body problem. He thought to "solve" this problem by avoiding both the crudity and paradox of materialism and the "unscientific" theorizing offered by traditional dualisms. The solution is to say that

> Feelings make sense; as immediate meanings of events or objects, they are sensations, or more properly, sensa. Without language, the qualities of organic action that are feelings are pains, pleasures, odors, noises, tones, only potentially and proleptically. With language, they are discriminated and identified. They are then "objectified"; they are immediate traits of things. This "objectification" is not a miraculous ejection from the organism or soul into external things, nor an illusory attribution of psychical entities to physical things. The qualities never were "in" the organism; they always were qualities of interactions in which both extra-organic things and organisms partake.[25]

Such phrases as "qualities of interactions" soothe those who do not see a mind-body problem and provoke those who do. Tell us more, the latter say, about these interactions: are they interactions between people and tables, say? Is my *interaction* with this table brown, rather than, as I had previously thought, the *table* being brown? Is Dewey saying something more than that nobody would know that the table was brown unless he understood what the word "brown" meant? Is *that*, in turn, to make the Kantian point that there are no divisions between objects, or between objects and their qualities, until concepts have been used to give sense to feelings? But can that point be made without committing oneself to transcendental idealism? Have we solved the problem of the relation between the empirical self and the material world only to wind up once again with a transcendental ego constituting both?

This sequence of rhetorical questions expresses the exasperation which readers of Dewey often feel at his attempt to be as commonsensically realistic as Aristotle while somehow sounding as idealistic as Kant and Green. There is obviously *some* sense in which Dewey agrees with Kant that only the transcendental idealist can be an empirical realist. I think the sense is this: Dewey believed that only someone who broke with Humean empiricism in the way in which Kant and Green did, who recognized that intuitions without concepts were blind, and that no data were ever "raw," could say that both brown tables and swirls of colorless atoms were equally "given in experience." That is, he thought that what Sellars has called "the clash between the scientific and the manifest images of man" could be resolved only by taking commonsense concepts like "brown" and "ugly" and "painful" and "table" as qualities of one sort of interaction and scientific concepts like "atom" and "mass" as qualities of another. What Kant had called "the constitution of the empirical world by synthesis of intuitions under concepts," Dewey wanted to call "interactions in which both extra-organic things and organisms partake." But he wanted this harmless-sounding naturalistic phrase to have the same generality, and to accomplish the same epistemological feats, which Kant's talk of the "constitution of objects" had performed. He wanted phrases like "transaction with the environment" and "adaptation to conditions" to be simultaneously naturalistic and transcendental—to be common-sensical remarks about human perception and knowledge viewed as the psychologist views it and also to be expressions of "generic traits of existence." So he blew up notions like "transaction" and "situation" until they sounded as mysterious as "prime matter" or "thing-in-itself." He made it sound as if what the table *really* was, was neither an ugly brown thing whose hard edges bumped people, nor yet a swirl of particles, but something common to both—sheer potentiality, ready to be transformed in a situation. He wanted, in a way, just what he had wanted in the 1880s —that psychology and metaphysics should be one. But the way in which they were to be made one consisted merely in lifting the vocabulary of the evolutionary biologist out of the laboratory and using it to describe everything that could ever count as "Knowledge." It can, of course, be so used. But no problems are solved by doing so, any more than they were solved by Locke's "sensualization" of concepts.

To return to the mind-body problem, the passage I quoted about secondary qualities as "qualities of interactions in which both extra-organic things and organisms partake" leads one naturally to ask: what qualities do those two sorts of things have when they are not interacting? And here Dewey always turns naturalistic and common-sensical on us. Suddenly dropping talk of the "generic traits of existences," we are told that what is interacting is just the good old table, and the good old human body of common sense, or else two swirls of particles, or any other nongeneric description you like. If Dewey had, like Ryle and Sellars and Wittgenstein and Heidegger, confined himself to remarking that without the spectator model of knowledge we should never have had a mind-body problem in the first place, he would have been on firm ground, and would (I think) have said all that needs to be said. But, once again, he wanted not merely skepti-cal diagnosis but also constructive metaphysical system-building. The system that was built in *Experience and Nature* sounded idealistic, and its solution to the mind-body problem seemed one more invoca-tion of the transcendental ego, because the level of generality to which Dewey ascends is the same level at which Kant worked, and the model of knowledge is the same—the constitution of the knowable by the cooperation of two unknowables. Sounding like Kant is a fate that will overtake *any* systematic account of human knowledge which purports to supplant both physiological Lockean accounts and soci-ological Hegelian accounts by something still more generic. The "ontology of the sensible manifold" is the common destiny of all philosophers who try for an account of subject-and-object, mind-and-body, which has this generic quality.

I have now made all the criticisms of Dewey's "naturalistic meta-physics" which I have to make, and I should like to end by offering a brief encomium on what Dewey accomplished, sometimes despite himself. Dewey set out to show the harm which traditional philo-sophical dualisms were doing to our culture, and he thought that to do this job he needed a metaphysics—a description of the generic traits of existences that would solve (or dissolve) the traditional prob-lems of philosophy, as well as open up new avenues for cultural de-velopment. I think that he was successful in this latter, larger, aim; he is one of the few philosophers of our century whose imagination was expansive enough to envisage a culture shaped along lines different from those we have developed in the West during the last three hun-dred years. Dewey's mistake—and it was a trivial and unimportant mistake, even though I have devoted most of this essay to it—was the notion that criticism of culture had to take the form of a rede-scription of "nature" or "experience" or both. Had Dewey written the book called *Nature and Culture*, which was to replace *Experience and Nature*, he might have felt able to forget the Aristotelian and Kantian models and simply have been Hegelian all the way, as he was in much of his other (and best) work.

By being "Hegelian" I mean here treating the cultural develop-ments which Kant thought it was the task of philosophy to preserve and protect as simply temporary stopping-places for the World-Spirit. Kant thought that there were three permanent data of philosophy: (1) Newtonian physics and the resulting conception of a unified sci-ence centering on mathematical descriptions of micro-structures; (2) the common moral consciousness of a North German Pietist; (3) the sense of delicacy, of playful freedom from the imperatives of scientific inquiry and moral duty, offered by the eighteenth-century aesthetic consciousness. The aim of philosophy was to preserve these cultural accomplishments by drawing the lines between them (preferably writing a separate book about each) and showing how they could be rendered compatible with one another and made "necessary." Philosophy, for Kant, as it had been for Aristotle, was a matter of drawing boundaries to keep scientific inquiry from interfering with morals, the aesthetic from interfering with the scientific, and so on. For Hegel, on the other hand, Newtonian physics, the contrite consciousness, and the delight in landscape gardens were brief episodes in the development of spirit: stepping-stones on the way to a culture that would encompass all of these without dividing them from one another. For Dewey, the quests for truth, for moral virtue, and for aesthetic bliss are seen as distinct and potentially competing activities only if one thinks of truth as "accuracy of representation," of moral virtue as purity of heart, and of beauty as "purposiveness without purpose." He did not question the accuracy of Kant's description of the eighteenth century's ways of thinking of these things, but with Hegel, he questioned the necessity of staying in the eighteenth century.

If one abandons the Kantian distinctions, one will not think of philosophy as a matter of solving philosophical problems (for example, of having a theory of the relation between sense-experience and theoretical knowledge which will reconcile rationalists and empiricists, or a theory of the relation between mind and body which will reconcile materialists and panpsychists). One will think of it as a matter of putting aside the distinctions that permitted the formulation of the problems in the first place. Dewey, I suggested earlier, was not as good at dissolving philosophical problems as the followers of either the early or the later Wittgenstein—but he had a larger aim in view. He wanted to sketch a culture that would not continually give rise to new versions of the old problems, because it would no longer make the distinctions between Truth, Goodness, and Beauty which engender such problems.

In doing this larger job, his chief enemy was the notion of Truth as accuracy of representation, the notion later to be attacked by Heidegger, Sartre, and Foucault. Dewey thought that if he could break down this notion, if scientific inquiry could be seen as adapting and coping rather than copying, the continuity between science, morals, and art would become apparent. We would no longer ask ourselves questions about the "purity" of works of art or of our experience of them. We would be receptive to notions like Derrida's—that language is not a device for representing reality, but a reality in which we live and move. We would be receptive to the diagnosis of traditional philosophy which Sartre and Heidegger offer us—as the attempt to escape from time into the eternal, from freedom into necessity, from action into contemplation. We would see the social sciences not as awkward and unsuccessful attempts to imitate the physicists' elegance, certainty, and freedom from concern with "value," but as suggestions for ways of making human lives into works of art. We would see modern physics both as Snow sees it—as the greatest human accomplishment of the century—and as Kuhn sees it, as one more episode in a series of crises and intervening calms, a series that will never terminate in "the discovery of the truth," the finally accurate representation of reality.

Finally, we might move out from under the shadow of Kant's notion that something called a "metaphysics of experience" is needed to provide the "philosophical basis" for the criticism of culture, to the realization that philosophers' criticisms of culture are not more "scientific," more "fundamental," or more "deep" than those of labor leaders, literary critics, retired statesmen, or sculptors. Philosophers would no longer seem spectators of all time and eternity, or (like social scientists) unsuccessful imitators of the physical sciences, because the scientists themselves would not be seen as spectators or representers. Philosophers could be seen as people who work with the history of philosophy and the contemporary effects of those ideas called "philosophic" upon the rest of the culture—the remnants of past attempts to describe the "generic traits of existences." This is a modest, limited enterprise—as modest and limited as carving stones into new shapes, or finding more basic elementary particles. But it sometimes produces great achievements, and Dewey's work is one of those achievements. It is great not because it provides an accurate representation of the generic traits of nature or experience or culture or anything else. Its greatness lies in the sheer provocativeness of its suggestions about how to slough off our intellectual past, and about how to treat that past as material for playful experimentation rather than as imposing tasks and responsibilities upon us. Dewey's work helps us put aside that spirit of *seriousness* which artists traditionally lack and philosophers are traditionally supposed to maintain. For the spirit of seriousness can only exist in an intellectual world in which human life is an attempt to attain an end beyond life, an escape from freedom into the atemporal. The conception of such a world is still built into our education and our common speech, not to mention the attitudes of philosophers toward their work. But Dewey did his best to help us get rid of it, and he should not be blamed if he occasionally came down with the disease he was trying to cure.

Notes

1. Cf. John Dewey and Arthur F. Bentley, *A Philosophical Correspondence 1932-1951*, ed. S. Ratner and J. Altman (New Brunswick: Rutgers University Press, 1964), p. 643, for the suggested title change. Cf. "Experience and Existence: A Comment," *Philosophy and Phenomenological Research*, 9 (1949): 712 ff., for a renunciation of "metaphysics."

2. E.g., by Arthur E. Murphy, in "Dewey's Epistemology and Metaphysics" in *The Philosophy of John Dewey*, ed. P. A. Schilpp (Evanston and Chicago: Tudor Publishing Co., 1939), p. 219.

3. "Dewey's Naturalistic Metaphysics," reprinted in Schilpp, *op. cit.*, p. 245.

4. Dewey, "'Half-Hearted Naturalism'," *Journal of Philosophy*, 24 (1927): 59.

5. Dewey, *Experience and Nature* (New York: W. W. Norton, 1929), p. 412.

6. Sidney Hook, *John Dewey* (New York: John Day, 1939), pp. 34-35.

7. *Ibid.*, p. 44.

8. "From Absolutism to Experimentalism" (1930), reprinted in *John Dewey on Experience, Nature and Freedom*, ed. Richard J. Bernstein (New York: The Library of Liberal Arts, 1960), p. 18.

9. *The Quest for Certainty* (New York: Minton, Balch, 1929), p. 309. I pursue the analogies between this strand in Dewey's thought and Heidegger's criticism of "metaphysics" in Essay 3, above.

10. Albert Hofstadter, "Concerning a Certain Deweyan Conception of Metaphysics," in *John Dewey: Philosopher of Science and Freedom*, ed. Sidney Hook (New York: Dial Press, 1949), p. 269. For criticism of this sort of view, see Hook's discussion of Randall in *The Quest for Being* (New York: St. Martin's Press, 1961), pp. 163 ff.

11. Here again there is a useful analogy to be drawn with Heidegger. The notion that one should discover "the basic types of involvements" is just what led Heidegger to draw up a list of *Existentiale* in *Sein und Zeit*. The realization that this was part of the "humanist" tradition of metaphysics which he wished to set aside led him, in his later work, to renounce any such project.

12. Shadworth Hodgson, "Illusory Psychology," an attack on Dewey originally published in *Mind* for 1886, and reprinted in *The Early Works of John Dewey*, 1 (Carbondale: Southern Illinois University Press, 1969). This passage appears in that volume at p. lvi, and the two passages cited from Dewey at pp. 157-158 and pp. 161-162 respectively.

13. From "Psychology as Philosophic Method," *Early Works*, 1, pp. 166-167.

14. For the notion of "empiricism" as the view in which a "partial account of experience, or rather account of partial experience, is put forward as the totality," see *Early Works*, 1, p. 161.

15. *Early Works*, 1, pp. 171-172.

16. Cf. T. H. Green, *Works*, 1 (London, 1885), pp. 13-19. Green's point in this passage is made explicitly by Dewey in one of the essays which Hodgson is criticizing ("The Psychological Standpoint," *Early Works*, 1, pp. 125-126). Note also Dewey's often cited tribute to Green (*Early Works*, 1, p. 153). For Green's and Dewey's central point against Hume clothed in modern dress, see Sellars, "Empiricism and the Philosophy of Mind," sect. VI (reprinted in his *Science, Perception and Reality* [London: Routledge and Kegan Paul,

1963]) and J. Bennett, *Locke, Berkeley, Hume* (Oxford: Oxford University Press, 1971), sect. 4.

17. *Early Works*, 1, p. 152.

18. *Experience and Nature*, p. 15.

19. The phrase is from the autobiographical essay "From Absolutism to Experimentalism," reprinted in Bernstein, *op. cit.*, p. 12. On the same page he remarks that "I should never think of ignoring, much less denying, what an astute critic occasionally refers to as a novel discovery—that acquaintance with Hegel has left a permanent deposit in my thinking."

20. "From Absolutism to Experimentalism," p. 10.

21. *Experience and Nature*, p. 9.

22. *Ibid.*, p. 23.

23. The sort of jargon which Dewey and Bentley were still aiming for in *Knowing and the Known*.

24. Kant, *Kritik der reinen Vernunft*, A271 = B327.

25. *Experience and Nature*, pp. 258-259.

6

Philosophy as a Kind of Writing: An Essay on Derrida

Here is one way to look at physics: there are some invisible things which are parts of everything else and whose behavior determines the way everything else works. Physics is the search for an accurate description of those invisible things, and it proceeds by finding better and better explanations of the visible. Eventually, by way of microbiological accounts of the mental, and through causal accounts of the mechanisms of language, we shall be able to see the physicists' accumulation of truths about the world as itself a transaction between these invisible things.

Here is another way of looking at physics: the physicists are men looking for new interpretations of the Book of Nature. After each pedestrian period of normal science, they dream up a new model, a new picture, a new vocabulary, and then they announce that the true meaning of the Book has been discovered. But, of course, it never is, any more than is the true meaning of *Coriolanus* or the *Dunciad* or the *Phenomenology of Spirit* or the *Philosophical Investigations*. What makes them physicists is that their writings are commentaries on the writings of earlier interpreters of Nature, not that they all are somehow "talking about the same thing," the *invisibilia Dei sive naturae* toward which their inquiries steadily converge.

Here is a way of thinking about right and wrong: the common moral consciousness contains certain intuitions concerning equality, fairness, human dignity, and the like, which need to be made explicit through the formulation of principles—principles of the sort which

90

can be used to write legislation. By thinking about puzzle-cases, and by abstracting from differences between our (European) culture and others, we can formulate better and better principles, principles corresponding ever more closely to the moral law itself.

Here is another way of thinking about right and wrong: the longer men or cultures live, the more φρόνησις they may, with luck, acquire —the more sensitivity to others, the more delicate a typology for describing their fellows and themselves. Mingling with others helps; Socratic discussion helps; but since the Romantics, we have been helped most of all by the poets, the novelists, and the ideologues. Since the *Phenomenology of Spirit* taught us to see not only the history of philosophy, but that of Europe, as portions of a *Bildungsroman*, we have not striven for moral knowledge as a kind of ἐπιστήμη. Rather, we have seen Europe's self-descriptions, and our own self-descriptions, not as ordered to subject matter, but as designs in a tapestry which they will still be weaving after we, and Europe, die.

Here is a way of looking at philosophy: from the beginning, philosophy has worried about the relation between thought and its object, representation and represented. The old problem about reference to the inexistent, for example, has been handled in various unsatisfactory ways because of a failure to distinguish properly philosophical questions about meaning and reference from extraneous questions motivated by scientific, ethical, and religious concerns. Once these questions *are* properly isolated, however, we can see philosophy as a field which has its center in a series of questions about the relations between words and the world. The recent purifying move from talk of ideas to talk of meanings has dissipated the epistemological skepticism which motivated much of past philosophy. This has left philosophy a more limited, but more self-conscious, rigorous, and coherent area of inquiry.

Here is another way of looking at philosophy: philosophy started off as a confused combination of the love of wisdom and the love of argument. It began with Plato's notion that the rigor of mathematical argumentation exposed, and could be used to correct, the pretensions of the politicians and the poets. As philosophical thought changed and grew, inseminated by this ambivalent ἐρῶς, it produced shoots which took root on their own. Both wisdom and argumentation became far more various than Plato dreamed. Given such nineteenth-century complications as the *Bildungsroman*, non-Euclidean geometries, ideological historiography, the literary dandy, and the political anarchist, there is no way in which one can isolate philosophy as occupying a distinctive place in culture or concerned with a distinctive subject or proceeding by some distinctive method. One cannot even seek an essence for philosophy as an academic *Fach* (because one would first have to choose the country in whose universities' catalogs one was to look). The philosophers' own scholastic little definitions of "philosophy" are merely polemical devices—intended to exclude from the field of honor those whose pedigrees are unfamiliar. We can pick out "the philosophers" in the contemporary intellectual world only by noting who is commenting on a certain sequence of historical figures. All that "philosophy" as a name for a sector of culture means is "talk about Plato, Augustine, Descartes, Kant, Hegel, Frege, Russell . . . and that lot." Philosophy is best seen as a kind of writing. It is delimited, as is any literary genre, not by form or matter, but by tradition—a family romance involving, e.g., Father Parmenides, honest old Uncle Kant, and bad brother Derrida.

There, then, are two ways of thinking about various things. I have drawn them up as reminders of the differences between a philosophical tradition which began, more or less, with Kant, and one which began, more or less, with Hegel's *Phenomenology.* The first tradition thinks of truth as a vertical relationship between representations and what is represented. The second tradition thinks of truth horizontally —as the culminating reinterpretation of our predecessors' reinterpretation of their predecessors' reinterpretation. . . . This tradition does not ask how representations are related to nonrepresentations, but how representations can be seen as hanging together. The difference is not one between "correspondence" and "coherence" theories of truth—though these so-called theories are partial expressions of this contrast. Rather, it is the difference between regarding truth, goodness, and beauty as eternal objects which we try to locate and reveal, and regarding them as artifacts whose fundamental design we often have to alter. The first tradition takes scientific truth as the center of philosophical concern (and scorns the notion of incommensurable scientific world-pictures). It asks how well other fields of inquiry conform to the model of science. The second tradition takes science as one (not especially privileged nor interesting) sector of culture, a sector which, like all the other sectors, only makes sense when viewed historically. The first likes to present itself as a straightforward, down-to-earth, scientific attempt to get things right. The second needs to present itself obliquely, with the help of as many foreign words and as much allusiveness and name-dropping as possible. Neo-Kantian philosophers like Putnam, Strawson, and Rawls have arguments and theses which are connected to Kant's by a fairly straightforward series of "purifying" transformations, transformations which are thought to give clearer and clearer views of the persistent problems. For the non-Kantian philosophers, there are no persistent problems—save perhaps the existence of the Kantians. Non-Kantian philosophers like Heidegger and Derrida are emblematic figures who not only do not solve problems, they do not *have* arguments or theses. They are connected with their predecessors not by common subjects or methods but in the "family resemblance" way in which latecomers in a sequence of commentators on commentators are connected with older members of the same sequence.

To understand Derrida, one must see his work as the latest development in this non-Kantian, dialectical tradition—the latest attempt of the dialecticians to shatter the Kantians' ingenuous image of themselves as accurately representing how things really are. Derrida talks a lot about language, and it is tempting to view him as a "philosopher of language" whose work one might usefully compare with other inquiries concerning the relations between words and the world. But it would be less misleading to say that his writing about language is an attempt to show why there should be no philosophy of language.[1] On his view, language is the last refuge of the Kantian tradition, of the notion that there is something eternally present to man's gaze (the structure of the universe, the moral law, the nature of language) which philosophy can let us see more clearly. The reason why the notion of "philosophy of language" is an illusion is the same reason why philosophy—*Kantian* philosophy, philosophy as more than a kind of writing—is an illusion. The twentieth-century attempt to purify Kant's general theory about the relation between representations and their objects by turning it into philosophy of language is, for Derrida, to be countered by making philosophy even more impure—more unprofessional, funnier, more allusive, sexier, and above all, more "written." Thus, insofar as he has an attitude towards, for example, the mini-tradition which stretches from Frege to Davidson, it is the same as his attitude towards Husserl's discussion of language. The attitude, roughly, is that most twentieth-century concern with language is Kantian philosophy in extremis, a last desperate attempt to do on a pathetically small scale what Kant (and before him Plato) attempted to do on a large scale—show how the atemporally true can be contained in a spatio-temporal vehicle, regularize the relation between man and what man seeks by exhibiting its "structure," freezing the historical process of successive reinterpretations by exhibiting the structure of all possible interpretation.

Derrida, then, has little to tell us about language, but a great deal to tell us about philosophy. To get a handle on his work, one might take him as answering the question, "Given that philosophy *is* a kind of writing, why does this suggestion meet with such resistance?" This becomes, in his work, the slightly more particular question, "What must philosophers who object to this characterization think *writing* is, that they should find the notion that that is what they are doing so offensive?" Whereas Heidegger, Derrida's great father-figure, was the first to "place" (or if you prefer, "transcend" or "castrate") Hegel by giving a historical characterization of Hegel's historicism, Derrida wishes to "place" (or whatever) Heidegger by explaining Heidegger's distrust of writing. Heidegger, it is true, wrote a lot, but always (after the "turn") in the interests of urging us to be still and listen to the single line of verse, the individual Greek word. Derrida is suspicious of Heidegger's preference for the simplicity and splendor of the word spoken on the hill, and also of his contempt for the footnote scribbled in the ergastulum down in the valley. The preference, he thinks, betrays a fatal taint of Kantianism, of the Platonic "metaphysics of presence." For it is characteristic of the Kantian tradition that, no matter how much writing it does, it does not think that philosophy *should* be "written," any more than science should be. Writing is an unfortunate necessity; what is really wanted is to show, to demonstrate, to point out, to exhibit, to make one's interlocutor stand at gaze before the world. The copy theory of ideas, the spectator theory of knowledge, the notion that "understanding representation" is the heart of philosophy, are expressions of this need to substitute an epiphany for a text, to "see through" representation. In a mature science, the words in which the investigator "writes up" his results should be as few and as transparent as possible. Heidegger, though struggling manfully against this cluster of notions, and especially against the notion of the "research project" as model for philosophical thinking, in the end succumbed to the same nostalgia for the innocence and brevity of the spoken word. His substitution of auditory for visual metaphors—of listening to the voice of Being for being a spectator of time and eternity—was, Derrida thinks, only a dodge. The Kantian urge to bring philosophy to an end by solving all its problems, having everything fall into place, and the Heideggerian urge towards *Gelassenheit* and *Unverborgenheit*, are the same urge. Philosophical writing, for Heidegger as for the Kantians, is really aimed at putting an end to writing. For Derrida, writing always leads to more writing, and more, and still more—just as history does not lead to Absolute Knowledge or the Final Struggle, but to more history, and more, and still more. The *Phenomenology*'s vision of truth as what you get by reinterpreting all the previous reinterpretations of reinterpretations still embodies the Platonic ideal of the Last Re-interpretation, the *right* interpretation at last. Derrida wants to keep the horizontal character of Hegel's notion of philosophy without its teleology, its sense of direction, its seriousness.

II

So far in this paper I have merely been trying to locate Derrida in philosophical space. Now I want to focus on a few of his remarks about writing, with an eye to seeing more clearly how he answers the question, "What must philosophers think writing is that they resent so much the suggestion that this is what they do?" His answer is, roughly, that they think that writing is a means of representing facts, and that the more "written" writing is—the less transparent to what it represents and the more concerned with its relation to others' writings —the worse it must be. The way he spells out his answer, I think, can help us see why he thinks writing about writing will help to "decon-struct" the Kantian way of looking at things. Consider, to begin with, the following passage:

> There is therefore good and bad writing: the good and natural is the divine inscription in the heart and the soul; the perverse and artful is technique, exiled in the exteriority of the body. A modification well within the Platonic diagram: writing of the soul and of the body, writing of the in-terior and of the exterior, writing of conscience and of the passions, as there is a voice of the soul and a voice of the body. . . .
>
> The good writing has therefore always been comprehended. Compre-hended as that which had to be comprehended: within a nature or a natu-ral law, created or not, but first thought within an eternal presence. Com-prehended, therefore, within a totality, and enveloped in a volume or a book. The idea of the book is the idea of a totality, finite or infinite, of the signifier; this totality of the signifier cannot be a totality, unless a to-tality constituted by the signified preexists it, supervises its inscriptions and its signs, and is independent of it in its ideality. The idea of the book, which always refers to a natural totality, is profoundly alien to the sense of writing. . . . If I distinguish the text from the book, I shall say that the destruction of the book as it is now under way in all domains, denudes the surface of the text.[2]

Consider Derrida as trying, in such passages as this, to create a new thing for writing to be about—not the world, but texts. Books tell the truth about things. Texts comment on other texts, and we should stop trying to test texts for accuracy of representation:

"reading . . . cannot legitimately transgress the text toward some-thing other than it, toward the referent (a reality that is metaphysical, historical, psychobiographical, etc.) or toward a signifier outside the text whose content could take place, could have taken place outside of language, that is to say, in the sense that we give here to that word, outside of writing in general. . . . There is nothing outside of the text."[3] Derrida regards the need to overcome "the book"—the no-tion of a piece of writing as aimed at accurate treatment of a subject, conveying a message which (in more fortunate circumstances) might have been conveyed by ostensive definition or by injecting knowledge straight into the brain—as justifying his use of any text to interpret any other text. The most shocking thing about his work—even more shocking than, though not so funny as, his sexual interpretations of the history of philosophy—is his use of multilingual puns, joke ety-mologies, allusions from anywhere to anywhere, and phonic and typographical gimmicks. It is as if he really thought that the fact that, for example, the French pronunciation of "Hegel" sounds like the French word for "eagle" was supposed to be relevant for compre-hending Hegel. But Derrida does not want to comprehend Hegel's books; he wants to play with Hegel. He doesn't want to write a book about the nature of language; he wants to play with the texts which other people have thought they were writing about language.

At this point one can imagine serious-minded philosophers on both sides of the Channel murmuring about "idealism." There is a deep terror among Kantian philosophers of a certain job-related health hazard: the philosopher, after overstrenuous inquiry into our relation to the world, may lose his nerve, his reason, and the world simulta-neously. He does this by withdrawing into a dream world of ideas, of representations—even, God help us, of texts. To guard against this temptation, Kantian philosophers tell us, we must remember that only the transcendental idealist can be an empirical realist. Only the man who comprehends the relation between representation and repre-sented, in that arduous but rigorously scientific way characteristic of the epistemologist in the last century and the philosopher of language in this, can be transcendental in the required sense. For only he can represent *representing itself* accurately. Only such an accurate tran-scendental account of the relationship of representation will keep the Knowing Subject in touch with the Object, word with world, scientist with particle, moral philosopher with the Law, philosophy itself with reality itself. So whenever dialecticians start developing their coher-entist and historicist views, Kantians explain that it is another sad case of Berkeley's Disease, and that there is no cure save a still better, more luminously convincing, more transparent philosophical account of representation.

When dialectical philosophers are accused of idealism, they usually reply as Berkeley replied to his critics—by explaining that they are only protesting against the errors of a certain philosophical school and that they are really not saying anything at which the plain man would demur. As Austin said in this connection, "There's the bit where you say it and the bit where you take it back." The nice thing about Derrida is that he doesn't take it back. He has no interest in bringing "his philosophy" into accord with common sense. He is not writing a philosophy. He is not giving an account of anything; he is not offering a comprehensive view of anything. He is not protesting against the *errors* of a philosophical school. He is, however, protesting against the notion that the philosophy of language, pursued "realistically" as the study of how language hooks on to the world, is something more than one more quaint little genre, that it is first philosophy. But the protest is not because he has a different candidate for the position of "first philosophy," it is against the notion of "first philosophy." He could, if he liked, say that he, too, can pass judgments within this genre—that he recognizes better and worse "realistic" philosophy of language, that he agrees with all up-to-date philosophers of language that Strawson and Searle were terribly wrong about the referents of proper names, and so on. But what he really wants to do is to say, "You used to think that it was terribly important to get meaning and reference, and all that, right. But it isn't. You only thought that because . . ." He might be compared with the secularist who says not "There is no God" but rather "All this talk about our relation to God is getting in our way." James, when he said that "the true is what is good in the way of belief" was simply trying to debunk epistemology; he was not offering a "theory of truth." So Derrida, when he says "il n'y a pas de hors-texte," is not putting forward an ontological view; he is trying to debunk Kantian philosophy generally.

Well then, one might reply, he *does* take it back. For he admits that all this stuff about there not being any such thing as accuracy of representation is *metaphorical*, just a way of speaking. But why doesn't he say what he means? Why doesn't he come right out and tell his views about language and about reality? To this one can only reiterate that Derrida is in the same situation in regard to language that many of us secularists are in in regard to God. It isn't that we believe in God, or don't believe in God, or have suspended judgment about God, or consider that the God of theism is an inadequate symbol of our ultimate concern; it is just that we wish we didn't have to have a view about God. It isn't that we know that "God" is a cognitively meaningless expression, or that it has its role in a language-game other than the fact-stating, or whatever. We just regret the fact that the word is used so much. So it is for Derrida with the vocabulary of Kantian philosophy. His attitude towards centuries of worry about the relation between subject and object, representations and the real, is like the Enlightenment attitude toward centuries of worry about the relation between God and man, faith and reason. Indeed, for Derrida as for Heidegger, these worries are all the same worry: the worry that we may lose touch with certain exigencies, conformity with which is the whole duty of man. For Derrida as for Freud, these are all forms of the worry about what our fathers require of us. For Derrida as for Sartre, these are all forms of the attempt to know oneself by transforming oneself into a knowable object—an *être-en-soi* which obeys the laws of its kind.

So, to sum up the gloss I want to put upon the texts I have quoted from Derrida, Derrida is trying to do for our highbrow culture what secularist intellectuals in the nineteenth century tried to do for theirs. *He is suggesting how things might look if we did not have Kantian philosophy built into the fabric of our intellectual life, as his predecessors suggested how things might look if we did not have religion built into the fabric of our moral life.* The secularists I speak of were continually assailed by the question, "What argument do you have for not believing in God?" Derrida is continually assailed by the question, "What argument do you have for saying that we should not refer the text to something which is not a text?" Neither has any interesting arguments, because both are not working by the same rules as their opponents. They are trying to make up some new rules. Lack of seriousness, in the sense in which I just attributed it to Derrida, is simply this refusal to take the standard rules seriously, conjoined with the refusal to give a clear answer to the question, "Is it the old game played differently, or rather a new game?"

There is another sense, however, in which Derrida is very serious indeed—as serious as the prophets of secularization. He is serious about the need to change ourselves, serious about what he calls "deconstruction." Thus he warns us against taking "grammatology" as the name of a new research program, as an attempt at doing something constructive and progressive, when he speaks of "the systematic crossing-out of the ἀρχή and the transformation of general semiology into a grammatology, the latter performing a critical work upon everything within semiology—right down to its matrical concept of signs—that retains any metaphysical presuppositions incompatible with the theme of differance."[4] One can easily conclude from such passages as this that Derrida conceives of his work as purely negative —deconstructing the metaphysics of presence in order to leave the texts bare, unburdened by the need to represent. Such a view is also suggested by his excusing his high-handed treatment of Saussure in this way: "My justification would be as follows: This [a text of Saussure's] and some other indices (in a general way the treatment of the concept of writing) already give us the assured means of broaching the de-construction of *the greatest totality*—the concept of the episteme and logocentric metaphysics—from which are produced, without ever posing the radical question of writing, all the Western methods of analysis, explication, reading, or interpretation."[5] This passage conforms to the picture of Derrida I have offered so far—one in which he wants to do better than Heidegger the job of "overcoming the tradition of Western metaphysics" which Heidegger attempted. This picture may, however, be too charitable. For there is a side of Derrida which looks unfortunately constructive, a side which makes it look as if he in the end succumbs to nostalgia, to the lure of philosophical system-building, and specifically that of constructing yet another transcendental idealism. I turn now, therefore, to a discussion of the luminous, constructive, bad side of Derrida's work, as opposed to the shadowy, deconstructive, good side which I have been discussing so far.

III

To explain where and why Derrida seems to get constructive, I need to go back to the point I was making earlier about his attitude towards "the philosophy of language." One can see Derrida's attempt to "deconstruct the greatest totality" as an attempt to get rid of the notion that language is an attempt to represent something nonlinguistic. He is taking the Wittgensteinian doctrine which Sellars calls "psychological nominalism"—the doctrine that "all awareness is a linguistic affair"—to its extreme.[6] But he sees the recent attention to language (as a general subject matter of inquiry, comparable in scope to God, nature, history, or man) as a kind of pseudonominalism.[7] It is as if the Kantians had been forced, by attacks on the notions of "thought" and "the mind," to see that there is no way to cut beneath language to the thought which language expresses, no way, as Wittgenstein said, to "get between language and its object." But instead of concluding that we should stop viewing language as representing something, the Kantian response has been to say something like, "Now that we see that language is not the expression of thought, but since we know that language *does* represent the world, we can now be properly serious about language, can pay language the attention it deserves, by exploring *direct* word-world connections." What looks to modern philosophers of language like a new-found respect for language is, for Derrida, simply a disguised attempt to put language in its place, to insist that language has responsibilities to something outside itself, that it must be "adequate" to do its representative job. Derrida thinks that the proper moral to draw is that language is *not* a tool, but that in which we live and move. So to ask "how does language manage to do its job?" betrays psychological nominalism. If all awareness is a linguistic affair, then we are never going to be aware of a word on the one hand and a thing-denuded-of-words on the other and see that the first is adequate to the second. But the very notions of "sign" and "representation" and "language" convey the notion that we *can* do something like that. The notion of philosophy of language as the successor-subject to epistemology suggests that we have now found out how to study representation *properly*, and thus to do properly the job which Kant saw needed to be done.

Given this situation, Derrida looks about for a way to say something about language which will *not* convey the idea of "sign" or "representation" or "supplement." His solution consists in such notions as *trace*, which have, recently, become something very much like a new "subject matter" for his followers. But in developing this alternative, Derrida comes perilously close to giving us a philosophy of language, and thereby perilously close to slipping back into what he and Heidegger call "the tradition of onto-theology." That tradition is kept going by the following dialectical movement: first one notices that something all-encompassing and unconditioned is being treated as if it were just one more limited and conditioned thing. Then one explains that this thing is so distinctive that it requires an entirely different vocabulary for its description, and proceeds to create one. Finally, one's disciples become so bemused by one's new vocabulary that they think one has invented a new field of inquiry, and the whole sequence starts up once again. This happened to "God" when the Platonism of the Church Fathers lifted the divine out of space and time and insisted on His consequent ineffability. God thus became a pigeon for Doctors of the Church who had read Aristotle; they explained how the ineffable *could* be effed after all, but only *analogically*. It happened to "Mind" when Kant explained (in the "Paralogisms") that the subject was not a substance, thus permitting

Fichte and the nineteenth century to explain that really there was a lot to say about the Subject, but only *transcendentally*. In both cases, somebody (Augustine, Kant) warns us against trying to describe the unconditioned, and somebody else (Aquinas, Fichte) dreams up a special technique designed especially for the purpose. If I am right in my suspicions about Derrida, we are in some danger of seeing this same pattern repeated by Heidegger and Derrida. We may find ourselves thinking that what Heidegger thought could not be effed really can be, if only *grammatologically*.

Heidegger spent his life explaining that all his predecessors had ignored the "ontological difference" between beings and Being, and finally wound up suggesting that one should only write the word *Being* X-ed out.[8] Heidegger kept trying to fend off disciples who said, "Now that we have the ontological difference clearly in mind, tell us something about Being." Finally he said that the attempt to say that the tradition of metaphysics, of onto-theology, had confused beings with Being was itself a misleadingly metaphysical attempt. He ends his "Time and Being" by saying:

> To think Being without beings means: to think Being without regard to metaphysics. Yet a regard for metaphysics still prevails even in the intention to overcome metaphysics. Therefore, our task is to cease all overcoming, and leave metaphysics to itself.
>
> If overcoming remains necessary, it concerns that thinking that explicitly enters Appropriation in order to say It in terms of It about It.
>
> Our task is unceasingly to overcome the obstacles that tend to render such saying inadequate.
>
> The saying of Appropriation in the form of a lecture remains itself an obstacle of this kind. The lecture has spoken merely in propositional statements.[9]

But, of course, Appropriation (*Ereignis*) looks like one more name for the goal of our inquiries. This movement of Heidegger's thought back from one ineffable to another (e.g., from "Being" to "Appropriation") just as soon as people begin to eff the first ineffable, can be viewed as an attempt to find *something* which cannot be the subject of a commentary, something which cannot be the subject of an inquiry into, for example, "Heidegger's doctrine of *Ereignis*." Derrida thinks, or at least thought when he began *De la Grammatologie*, that the only way to solve Heidegger's problem was to get away from terminology borrowed from the visual and aural imagery of earlier authors and invent a new way which had to do *only* with writing. One can see this impulse in the following passages:

The reassuring evidence within which Western tradition had to organize itself and must continue to live would therefore be as follows: the order of the signified is never contemporary, is at best the subtly discrepant inverse or parallel—discrepant by the time of a breath—from the order of the signifier. And the sign must be the unity of a heterogeneity, since the signified (sense or thing, noeme or reality) is not in itself a signifier, a *trace*: in any case is not constituted in its sense by its relationship with a possible trace. The formal essence of the signified is *presence*, and the privilege of its proximity to the logos as *phonè* is the privilege of presence. This is the inevitable response as soon as one asks: "what is the sign?," this is to say, when one submits the sign to the question of essence, to the "ti esti." The "formal essence" of the sign can only be determined in terms of presence. One cannot get around that response, except by challenging the very form of the question and beginning to think that the sign that ill-named thing, the only one, that escapes the instituting question of philosophy: "what is . . . ?"[10]

What should give one pause in this passage is the phrase "the only one." It is as if Derrida thought he had done the one thing Heiddegger failed to do—find the one word which cannot be the subject of a commentary, a Ph.D. thesis on "Derrida's doctrine of the sign," the one expression of the unconditioned which nobody will ever be able to treat as if it were the name of one more conditioned. In the following passage also one can see such a notion: "The movement of the effacement of the trace has been, from Plato to Rousseau to Hegel, imposed upon writing in the narrow sense; the necessity of such a displacement may now be apparent. Writing is one of the representatives of the trace in general, it is not the trace itself. *The trace itself does not exist.* (To exist is to be, to be an entity, a being-present, *to on*.")[11] One can comment cynically on this passage that, if you want to know what notion takes the place of God for a writer in the onto-theological tradition, always look for the one which he says does not exist. That will be the name of the Ineffable, of what can be shown but not said, believed but not known, presupposed but not mentioned, that in which we live and move and have our being. It is the need to express the unconditioned while realizing that it is inexpressible which brings us to the point described by Wittgenstein: "Sometimes, in doing philosophy, one just wants to utter an inarticulate sound."[12] But that will not prevent somebody from writing a thesis on whatever sound one makes.

Fortunately, however, Derrida was the first to warn us against the temptation I have just described—the temptation to divinize the *trace*, and to treat writing as "one of the representatives of the trace in general, but not the trace itself" (a passage which seems to make *trace* one of the *invisibilia Dei*, which *per ea quae factae sunt cognoscuntur*). In "Differance," published just after *On Grammatology*, he identifies the difference he hoped to find between "the sign" as the only thing that escapes the instituting question of philosophy and all the other failed candidates for this role with Heidegger's "ontological difference." He turns himself, in this essay, from something dangerously like a philosopher of language, into a philosopher of philosophy, where philosophy is just the self-consciousness of the play of a certain kind of writing. *Différance*, unlike *trace*, has no more to do with signs than it does with things or gods or minds or any of the other things for which Kantian philosophy has sought the unconditioned conditions. *Différance* is a name of the situation which the dialectical philosopher starts from—the wish to revolt against the eternalization and cosmologization of the present vocabulary by creating a new vocabulary which will not permit the old questions to be asked. In "Differance," Derrida has a passage which forms a splendid rebuke both to Heidegger and to his previous self:

> For us, differance remains a metaphysical name; and all the names that it receives from our language are still, so far as they are names, metaphysical. . . .
>
> "Older" than Being itself, our language has no name for such a differance. But we "already know" that if it is unnamable, this is not simply provisional; it is not because our language has still not found or received this *name*, or because we would have to look for it in another language, outside the finite system of our language. It is because there is no *name* for this—not even essence or Being—not even the name "differance," which is not a name, which is not a pure nominal unity, and continually breaks up in a chain of different substitutions. . . .
>
> There will be no unique name, not even the name of Being. It must be conceived without *nostalgia*; that is, it must be conceived outside the myth of the purely maternal or paternal language belonging to the lost fatherland of thought. On the contrary we must *affirm* it—in the sense that Nietzsche brings affirmation into play—with a certain laughter and with a certain dance.[13]

IV

Let me now turn to what may seem the chief question raised by what I've said so far: granted that Derrida is the latest and largest flower on the dialectical kudzu vine of which the *Phenomenology of Spirit* was the first tendril, does that not merely show the need to uproot this creeping menace? Can we not now see all the better the need to strip the suckers of this parasitic climber from the still unfinished walls and roofs of the great Kantian edifice which it covers and conceals? Granted that if all this nonsense about language not being a system of representations were true, Derrida would have drawn some interesting consequences from it, cannot we now return to sanity and say that it is false, and that philosophy would do well to return to the slow and patient work of understanding how representation is accomplished?

The dialectical response to this should, I think, be twofold. First, one can reply that the question of whether language is a system of representations is not the sort of question *anybody* (Kantian or non-Kantian) knows how to answer, and so whatever is at issue, that cannot be it. The question is not whether "language is a system of representations" is a correct representation of how things are. Second, one can reply that *of course* language can usefully, for many purposes, be viewed as a system of representations, just as physical theory can usefully be seen as an approximation to what we would see if we could get down there among the quanta, moral philosophy as an approximation to the Moral Law, and philosophy as a quest for a purer and better way to answer traditional questions. All that one has to do to make *any* of these approaches useful and productive is to take the vocabulary of the present historical period (or class or society or academy) for granted and to work within it. Once one is safely ensconced within this language-game, questions about what correctly represents what, how we know that it does, and how it manages to do so will make admirable sense and will get useful answers. There is nothing done within the Kantian tradition which the dialectical tradition cannot treat as the description of the practices of a certain historical moment—the sort of description one gets when one blinkers one's historical consciousness temporarily for the sake of getting a clear view of what is currently going on. The traditions come into real conflict *only* when the Kantian tradition cosmologizes and eternalizes its current view of physics, or right and wrong, or philosophy, or language. Thus, for example, if we freeze physics at a period of what Kuhn calls "normal science," we can describe the practice of justifying theories in terms of a determinate observation-language, a list of meaning-rules, and some canons of theory-choice. If we try to bring this heuristic apparatus to bear on all the things that might count as explaining nature in various periods and cultures, however, we either become viciously anachronistic or fall into pointless puzzlement about, e.g., "criteria for change of reference of theoretical terms." Analogously, if we take as data a range of assertions running the gamut from "the cat is on the mat" to "the particle went through the left-hand slit," we may be able to construct an account of the contribution of the parts of the expressions to the wholes, and of the conditions under which a language-user would be justified in employing them. We go wrong only when we invoke this account to be condescending about, or be baffled by, such assertions as "caloric fluid is just a lot of moving molecules," "language speaks man," or "God's essence is His existence." If we then try to be systematically invidious or reductive by talking about "literal vs. metaphorical" or "non-statement-making uses of declarative sentences," or the like, philosophy of language will begin to seem relevant to epistemology, controversial, and essential to our self-understanding. It will also seem to come into conflict with the sort of thing that Heidegger and Derrida are telling us. Worse yet, the sort of thing Heidegger and Derrida are saying may seem to be in competition with what, e.g., Frege and Carnap and Putnam say.

No such competition exists. There is no topic—and in particular not that of the relation between sign and signified, language and the world—on which Derrida holds a different view than that of any of the philosophers of language I have mentioned. Nor does he have any insights which complement theirs. He is not, to repeat, a philosopher of language. The closest Derrida comes to the philosophy of language is his interest in the historical question of why a view about the relation between sign and signified, the nature of representation, could ever have been thought to have been essential to our self-understanding, the starting point of the love of wisdom, first philosophy. He is interested in the connection between the "Kantian" view of philosophy and the "Kantian" view of language—in why the latest Kantian effort to cosmologize or eternalize the present should have centered on language. Here he *does* have something to say—but it is something about philosophy, not about language.

Kantian philosophy, on Derrida's view, is a kind of writing which would like not to be a kind of writing. It is a genre which would like to be a gesture, a clap of thunder, an epiphany. *That* is where God and man, thought and its object, words and the world meet, we want speechlessly to say; let no further words come between the happy pair. Kantian philosophers would like not to write, but just to *show*. They would like the words they use to be so simple as to be presuppositionless. Some of them like to think that physics, too, is not a kind of writing. So they cherish the thought that, at least in some countries, philosophy has no literary pretensions because it has attained the secure path of a science. Just as, on the Kantian view of physics, physics has no need of a historical self-understanding to enable it to point straight to the heart of matter, so, on the Kantian view of philosophy, philosophers need not be concerned with their own Kantian motives in order to point straight to the heart of spirit —the relation of representation itself. Derrida's reply is that anybody can get along without literary pretensions—without writing—if he is content simply to demonstrate how something falls into place in a previously established context. In normal physics, normal philosophy, normal moralizing or preaching, one hopes for the normal thrill of just the right piece fitting into just the right slot, with a shuddering resonance which makes verbal commentary superfluous and inappropriate. Writing, as Derrida says in commenting on Rousseau, is to this kind of simple "getting it right" as masturbation is to standard, solid, reassuring sex. This is why writers are thought effete in comparison with scientists—the "men of action" of our latter days. The important thing to notice is that the difference between the two forms of activity is not subject matter—not, for instance, a matter of the difference between the flinty particles of the hard sciences and the flexible behavior of the soft ones—*but rather is determined by normality or abnormality.* Normality, in this sense, is accepting without question the stage-setting in the language which gives demonstration (scientific or ostensive) its legitimacy. Revolutionary scientists need to write, as normal scientists do not. Revolutionary politicians need to write, as parliamentary politicians do not. Dialectical philosophers like Derrida need to write, as Kantian philosophers do not.

The Freudian distinction between the normal and the abnormal, drawn with the concreteness which is given by Derrida's exhibition of the sexual overtones of most metaphilosophical debate, seems to me just what is needed to be properly playful about the difference between the Kantians and the dialecticians. If one thinks of this difference as that between the partisans of Eternity and of Time, or those of Theory and of Practice, Nature and History, Permanence and Change, Intellect and Intuition, the Sciences and the Arts, it all looks too momentous, too much as if there were a serious and debatable issue around. The issue between Kantian and non-Kantian philosophy is, I think, about as serious as the issue between normal and deviant sexual practices.

It is, to be sure, an issue upon which men may well feel their identity and their integrity depend. ("Men," rather than "people," since taking how and what one does in bed as definitive of one's being seems a specifically masculine trait.) So it is not unserious in the sense of unimportant. But it is *not* a serious issue in the sense of a debatable one, on which there is much to be said on both sides. It is not an issue which we ought all to pitch in and try to resolve (in some more discursive way than massacring the opposition). Indeed, we had better not. For if the issue *were* ever resolved, there might not be any more philosophy. (Or any more interesting writing at all. Philosophy is, after all, *dominatrix disciplinarum* if no longer *regina scientiarum*; nobody does any really "written" writing without timidly hoping that what he writes may have "philosophical implications.") Similarly, if the difference between normal and deviant sex ever got settled —not by massacre, but by rational demonstration of the moral superiority of one side or the other, or of their being morally equivalent— then it is not clear that sex would matter nearly as much as it does now. When Freud told us that we had sexual repression to thank for the hang-ups of the neurotics who created European culture, he meant exactly what he said. If Derrida is on the right track in his post-*Grammatology* treatment of philosophical texts, we can be a bit more specific about just how this culture was fed by sublimated sexuality. The Kantian versus non-Kantian contrast now appears as that between the man who wants to take (and see) things as they are, and thus make sure that the right pieces go in the right holes, and the man who wants to change the vocabulary presently used for isolating pieces and holes. This helps us see why the dialectic of the conditioned and the unconditioned, the effable and the ineffable, has the peculiar thrill that it does. Unspeakable possibilities, unmentionable acts are those which are spoken and mentioned in the new, revolutionary, Hegelian, abnormal vocabulary. Sartre's account of the attempt of the philosopher to become God by recreating himself as a *pour-soi-en-soi* joins up with Freud's to suggest that the Kantian tradition plays the role in recent European culture of the normal man, the man whose respect for the law is such that he would wish the natural and the moral law to be as one.

This Freudian twist also helps us see why, even given the compatibility of, e.g., everything which Derrida says and everything Quine says, we cannot relax and split the difference. We cannot just let Kantians have their (self-eliminating) kind of writing and the Hegelians their (self-extending, kudzu-like) alternative kind. Being conciliatory in this way would obscure the fact that these traditions live each other's death, die each other's life—the same relation which holds between normal and abnormal sex. The dialectician will always win if he waits long enough, for the Kantian norm will in time become tedious, full of anomie and anomaly. The Kantian, on the other hand, escapes triviality, and achieves self-identity and self-conscious pride, only by the contrast between his mighty deeds and the mere words of the dialectician. *He* is no effete parasite, but one who does his share in the mighty time-binding work of building the edifice of human knowledge, human society, the City of Real Men. The non-Kantian knows that the edifice will itself one day be deconstructed, and the great deeds reinterpreted, and reinterpreted again, and again. But of course the non-Kantian *is* a parasite—flowers could not sprout from the dialectical vine unless there were an edifice into whose chinks it could insert its tendrils. No constructors, no deconstructors. No norms, no perversions. Derrida (like Heidegger) would have no writing to do unless there were a "metaphysics of presence" to overcome. Without the fun of stamping out parasites, on the other hand, no Kantian would bother to continue building. Normal philosophers need to think, for example, that in forging the powerful tools of modern analytic philosophy, they are developing weapons to ensure victory in the coming final struggle with the decadent dialecticians. Everybody needs everybody else.

Kantian and non-Kantian metaphilosophers, when this point in the development of their self-consciousness is reached, like to explain that their opponents really want to do what they themselves are doing. The Kantian thinks of the non-Kantian as somebody who would like to have a proper, disciplined, philosophical view about, e.g., words and the world, but can't quite manage to get it together into a coherent, rigorous form. The Hegelian likes to think that there is not really a contrast between the vine and the edifice it covers—rather, the so-called edifice is just accumulated dead wood, parts of the Great Vine itself, which once were fresh and flower-laden but now have come to lie in positions which suggest the outlines of a building. So the normal man sees the abnormal as not quite up to it—more to be pitied than censured. The abnormal sees the normal as someone who never had the courage to come out, and so died inside while his body lived on—more to be helped than despised.

This kind of crosstalk can continue indefinitely. Derrida's point, I take it, is that that crosstalk is all that we are going to get, and that no gimmick like "the new science of grammatology" is going to end or *aufheben* it. Once one thinks of philosophy as a kind of writing, one should not be surprised at this result. For to think this is to stop trying to have a philosophy of language which is "first philosophy," a view of all possible views, an ἐπιστήμη ἐπιστήμης, a bootstrap self-elevation to a point from which all past and future writing can be seen as contained within a permanent framework. Only one who *had* levitated to such a point would have the right to look down on writing, to view it as a second-best (like Plato) or as an abnormal activity to which sin has condemned him (like Rousseau), or as something which a discipline can dispense with on reaching the secure path of a science. Derrida's polemic against the notion that speech is prior to writing should be seen as a polemic against what Sartre calls "bad faith"—the attempt to divinize oneself by seeing in advance the terms in which all possible problems are to be set, and the criteria for their resolution. If the "logocentric," Platonic notion of speech as prior to writing were right, there might be a last Word. Derrida's point is that no one can make sense of the notion of a last commentary, a last discussion note, a good piece of writing which is more than the occasion for a better piece.

Notes

1. On Derrida's relation to contemporary philosophy of language, and especially to Wittgenstein, see Newton Garver, Preface to Jacques Derrida, *Speech and Phenomenon, and Other Essays in Husserl's Theory of Signs*, trans. David B. Allison (Evanston: Northwestern University Press, 1972), and "Derrida on Rousseau on Writing," *Journal of Philosophy*, 74 (1977): 663-673; Marjorie Grene, "Life, Death and Language: Some Thoughts on Wittgenstein and Derrida," in *Philosophy in and out of Europe* (Berkeley and Los Angeles: University of California Press, 1976), pp. 142-154; John Searle's exchange with Derrida in the first two volumes of *Glyph*; Richard Rorty, "Derrida on Language, Being, and Abnormal Philosophy," *Journal of Philosophy*, 74 (1977): 673-681.

2. Derrida, *Of Grammatology*, trans. Gayatri Chakravorty Spivak (Baltimore: Johns Hopkins University Press, 1976), pp. 17-18.

3. *Ibid.*, p. 158.

4. From "Differance," translated in Derrida, *Speech and Phenomenon*, p. 146.

5. *Of Grammatology*, p. 46.

6. See Wilfrid Sellars, *Science, Perception and Reality* (London and New York: Routledge and Kegan Paul, 1963), pp. 160ff.

7. *Of Grammatology*, p. 6.

8. Cf. Martin Heidegger, *The Question of Being*, trans. William Kluback and Jean T. Wilde (New York: Twayne, 1958), a translation of *Zur Seinsfrage* (Frankfurt: Klostermann, 1959).

9. Heidegger, *On Time and Being*, trans. Joan Stambaugh (New York: Harper and Row, 1972), p. 24.

10. *Of Grammatology*, pp. 18-19.

11. *Ibid.*, p. 167.

12. Ludwig Wittgenstein, *Philosophical Investigations* (New York and London: Macmillan, 1953), pt. 1, sect. 261.

13. *Speech and Phenomenon*, pp. 158-159.

7

Is There a Problem
about Fictional Discourse?

1. Introductory

Contemporary analytic philosophy has given rise to a good deal of discussion of "truth about fictional objects," but the motives of this discussion are fairly remote from literary theory. Within Anglo-Saxon philosophy of language, the topic of fiction usually arises in connection with such banal questions as: what must be said about truth such that the sentences "Gladstone was born in England" and "Sherlock Holmes was born in England" can both be true?

The importance for philosophy of truth about fictions lies in the role which solutions to this problem play in deciding what to say about truth in general. If truth is "correspondence to reality," we seem to have a problem—for to what reality does the second sentence correspond? If truth is simply "warranted assertibility," however, we have what may seem a less difficult problem; we need merely distinguish the situation, or conventions, or presuppositions, relevant to asserting each of the sentences.

The question whether to view truth as "correspondence to reality" or as "warranted assertibility" is the question of whether to treat language as a picture or as a game. This latter issue—very roughly, that between the younger and the older Wittgenstein—is brought to a head by debates about "truth in fiction" because the whole problematic of realism vs. idealism, or of "representationalism" vs. "pragmatism," can be crystallized in the question: what, if anything, turns on the difference between being "really there" and being "made up"? For what purposes is a convenient fiction as good as reality? Discussions of quite picky and technical issues within semantics can, in this way, suddenly provoke reflection on Heideggerian truth-as-*Unverborgenheit* vs. truth as *adequatio intellectus et rei*.

The paths which lead from the technical issues to the larger, vaguer, and more interesting ones are complicated. Further, one can avoid taking any of them simply by fixing in advance what is going to count as a solution to a puzzle within a given semantical research program. I have no attachment to any such program, so I shall not be arguing for the virtues of a certain solution to the problem about Gladstone and Sherlock Holmes, much less claiming that this solution dictates, or follows from, a general view about language or truth. Rather, I shall survey four solutions to this problem which have been offered in the recent literature, with an eye to the presuppositions of the philosophers who offer them. I shall argue that a central set of "Parmenidean" presuppositions is common to all four. I do not accept these presuppositions, but they seem to me too abstract to argue against. So I shall merely try to show how things look if they are *not* made. I shall conclude by suggesting why this Parmenidean outlook is important for fictions which self-consciously reflect on the fact that they are made rather than found—that is, works of fiction which make much of *being* fictional.

The four solutions to the problem about Gladstone and Holmes which I shall take up are: (1) the standard Russellian view that "talk about Holmes is really about Conan Doyle's stories," (2) John Searle's notion of "pretended assertion," (3) a "physicalist" view of reference to the inexistent offered by Keith Donnellan in protest against the view common to Russell and Searle that reference is determined by the speaker's intentions, (4) a recent version of "Meinongianism"— the view that reference may be made to *any* intentional object—offered by Terence Parsons. The last three of these views are reactions against one or another element in Russell's view, which was "standard" for many years and provides the common background for discussion of this topic.

2. Russell: Semantics as Epistemology

Bertrand Russell held various doctrines about both semantics and epistemology at various times during his life, but he did not waver from the view that

(1) Whatever is referred to must exist

and that it follows that

(2) Statements apparently referring to something which does not exist must really be abbreviations for, be "analyzed as," statements referring to existents.

Further, and more controversially, Russell sometimes held that

(3) One can only talk about what is directly given in "knowledge by acquaintance" (in the sense in which the intellect is "acquainted" with universals and the senses with particular sense-data)

which entails that

(4) All statements can be analyzed into statements which contain "genuine names" (e.g., such "logically proper names" as demonstratives like "this").

In defense of (1) Russell put forward his "theory of descriptions," which construed such apparently referring expressions as "the round square" and "the golden mountain" as predicative expressions. Statements using such expressions were analyzed as containing explicit assertions of the existence of entities of which the relevant predicates ("roundness and squareness," "being gold and a mountain") were true. This meant that all statements about the inexistent came out false, on Russell's view, a claim which went largely unchallenged within analytic philosophy until Strawson argued that

The golden mountain is in Africa

presupposed rather than *asserted*

There exists something which is both a mountain and gold.

On Strawson's view, if the second statement is false, the first is neither true nor false. I shall take up Strawson's point shortly in connection with Searle's attempt to reinforce it, but for the moment let me simply note that, putting aside (3) and (4) for the moment, Russell's (2) "solves the problem of fictional discourse" by analyzing

Holmes lived on Baker Street

as

There is a set of stories by Conan Doyle which either contains the statement "Sherlock Holmes lived on Baker Street" or other statements which entail this statement.

Since the latter is true, so is the former. When we turn to examples of the inexistent outside of deliberate fiction—e.g., entities falsely believed to exist such as "Zeus" or "caloric"—we see that we can construe such statements as

Zeus hurled lightning bolts

and

Caloric naturally rises

as *false* because asserting existence of the inexistent, *or* as *true* because analyzable as "really" statements about certain myths or about certain false chemical theories. The former treatment is appropriate for occurrences of these statements in some conversations, and the latter for occurrences in others.

If we now ask *why* Russell held (1), an important part of the answer is that he held (3). That is to say, he put Frege's semantical notion of "reference" at the service of an epistemological view whose core was traditional British empiricism. Whereas Frege, and later Wittgenstein in the *Tractatus*, had kept the question "what object is referred to?" distinct from questions of how the object is known, or even whether it *can* be known, Russell firmly identified knowing what proposition a statement expressed—what it meant—with knowing which objects one would have to be acquainted with in order to find out whether the statement was true. Much of the history of reactions against Russell's view consists in attempts to "purify" semantics of epistemology, and to describe "reference" in such a way as to free it from problems about verification. But—and this is the point I wish to emphasize—those who criticize Russell usually still insist on the truth of (1). For, as Donnellan puts it, Russell's notion of "genuine names" incorporates a certain "natural view" about "the relation between language and the world" which is independent of epistemology and which presumably motivated Frege and the young Wittgenstein: the view that "there must be the possibility, at least, of singular terms that do not introduce quantifiers." Donnellan emphasizes this supposed core of truth in Russell's theory by saying that in a sentence like "Socrates is snub-nosed," the singular expression "Socrates" is "simply a device used by the speaker to pick out what he wants to talk about." Or again, "in using such simple sentences . . . we are not saying something general about the world."[1] This view that there is a relation called "reference" which picks out entities in the world is the essence of the "picture" view of language which Wittgenstein developed in the *Tractatus*. It can be (and is) held even if one maintains that the user of a referring expression may have no idea what object he is referring to, nor even any idea of how to go about finding this out.

Notice that unless one held that a relation which satisfied (1) formed the "tie" between words and the world, one would not see any interesting problem about truths about Sherlock Holmes. One would not, like Searle, write articles about "the logical status" of fictional discourse, nor bother to be "Meinongian" like Parsons or "physicalist" like Donnellan, Putnam, and Field. But if one holds a *pure* "language-game" view of language, so that questions about "ties with the world" do not arise, then to know methods of verification would be to know *all* there was to know about the semantical features of statements. Such knowledge would not be a matter of semantical *theory*, but simple "know-how." Something like this was the attitude of the older Wittgenstein. Wittgenstein came to think that his younger self, Frege, and Russell had all been "held captive by a picture," and he meditated on why he and Russell had been so devoted to "the idea that names really signify simples."[2] I shall come back to the later Wittgenstein's criticism of the *Tractatus* in section 6, below, but here it is enough simply to note that the very idea of "explaining how words relate to the world" is bound up with belief in something like (1) So, *a fortiori*, is the view that there is something philosophically puzzling about *fictional* discourse.

3. Searle and Language-Games

Searle's book *Speech Acts* opens with the question "How do words relate to the world?"[3] The book offers the sort of answer which became popular as a result of a reaction against Russell's logical empiricism: the relation between words and the world is to be understood by seeing how words are *used*, rather than by starting with the point at which they attach to reality (as in Russell's "genuine names"). Austin's polemic against sense-data and Wittgenstein's against the "picture theory" of language form the background of Austin's and Searle's notion that philosophy of language should center around the notion of "speech act." Their strategy is to see language as behavior governed by conventions, like games, and to see "reference" in terms of conventions which must be obeyed if one is to make a successful move in the game. Not just sense-data empiricism, but epistemology itself, is moved firmly to one side. Thus we may hope to avoid confusion between, on the one hand, descriptions of the conventions of the game which is our language and, on the other, speculation about the motives for, or the rewards of, playing it.

Searle follows Strawson in objecting to the unnaturalness of Russell's "theory of descriptions," arguing against the claim that

The golden mountain is in Africa

asserts (has as part of its analysis) that

There exists something which is both a mountain and gold.

One argument offered is the *prima facie* absurdity of saying that "every illocutionary act in which a definite description is used refer-ringly is to be construed as the assertion of an existential proposition plus some other speech act about the object asserted to exist."[4] Russell's notion of "analysis" revealing unsuspected complexity in simple predicative sentences has no place in speech-act theory, so Searle asks why Russell was driven to such a paradoxical claim. The answer is that

> The whole plausibility of the theory of descriptions, once the paradoxes have been removed, derives from the fact that a precondition of any suc-cessfully performed reference is the existence of the object referred to (axiom of existence). And consequently the proposition containing that reference cannot be true if the proposition that the object exists is not true.

But, Searle continues,

> It never simply follows from the fact that a type of act can only be per-formed under certain conditions, that the performance of that act is itself an assertion that those conditions obtain.[5]

So Searle then goes on to give his own theory of proper names. He holds that they neither pick out objects without benefit of de-scriptions, nor are shorthand for descriptions, but rather *evoke* identifying descriptions in both speaker and hearer, though not necessarily the *same* descriptions, nor necessarily *accurate* descrip-tions.[6] This theory incorporates "the principle of identifying de-scriptions" attacked as "idealistic" by Putnam, Kripke, and Donnellan. I shall return to it below. For the moment, however, I want to dwell on the fact that what Searle calls the "axiom of existence" is simply Russell's

(1) Whatever is referred to must exist.

To this first axiom, Searle adds two more: the "axiom of identity" —

(5) If a predicate is true of an object it is true of anything identical with that object regardless of what expressions are used to refer to that object

and the "axiom of identification" —

(6) If a speaker refers to an object, then he identifies or is able
on demand to identify that object for the hearer apart from
all other objects.[7]

Before going on to see how Searle handles reference to fictional entities, we should note that on a *pure* "language-game" approach (6)
could take the place of (1). That is, as long as we view language as
conventional behavior, rather than as hooking on to the world at
designated spots, ability to identify should be enough to keep conversation going, existence or no existence. To put this still another
way, conversations about Holmes or caloric conducted by those who
believe that these entities actually exist, are, *qua* games, just like conversations about Gladstone or electrons. (5) and (6) seem sufficient
conventions to regulate such conversations. So we shall shortly have
to ask why Searle wants to preserve (1) rather than resting content
with (5) and (6).

But, before doing so, consider what Searle says about Holmes. In
an article called "The Logical Status of Fictional Discourse," Searle
has spelled out the view he suggested in *Speech Acts* — that we engage
in two distinct games, "fictional discourse" and "real world talk,"
and that

> in real world talk both "Sherlock Holmes" and "Mrs. Sherlock Holmes"
> fail of reference because there never existed any such people. In fictional
> talk "Sherlock Holmes" refers, for such a character really does exist in
> fiction, but "Mrs. Sherlock Holmes" fails of reference because there is no
> such fictional character.[8]

He begins his later article by saying that he believes that

> there is a systematic set of relationships between the meanings of the
> words and sentences we utter and the illocutionary acts we perform in the
> utterance of those words and sentences.
>
> Now for anybody who holds such a view the existence of fictional
> discourse poses a difficult problem . . . how can it be the case that
> words and other elements in a fictional story have their ordinary meanings
> and yet the rules that attach to those words and other elements and de-
> termine their meaning are not complied with . . . ?[9]

The answer, he goes on to say, must be that "in fictional speech
semantic rules are altered or suspended in some way." To see how,
we must first see that "the author of a work of fiction pretends to
perform a series of illocutionary acts, normally of the representative
type," and then that

the pretended illocutions which constitute a work of fiction are made possible by the existence of a set of conventions which suspend the normal operation of the rules relating illocutionary acts and the world. In this sense, to use Wittgenstein's jargon, telling stories really is a separate language game; to be played it requires a separate set of conventions, though these conventions are not meaning rules; and the language game is not on all fours with illocutionary language games, but is parasitic upon them.[10]

So "what makes fiction possible is a set of extralinguistic, non-semantic conventions that break the connection between words and the world established by the rules"[11] which govern assertions—e.g., the rule that "the maker of an assertion commits himself to the truth of the expressed proposition."[12]

This solution to Searle's original problem is sensible enough. But it will nevertheless seem trivial if one thinks of "determining meaning" as "determining word-world relationships." Searle tells us that words can mean the same when the rules governing their use changes, because we pretend to obey the old rules. But if pretense is as good as reality, we may have doubts about the original claim that rules for performing speech-acts determine meaning. To see this issue more clearly, consider Searle's claim that "one of the conditions on the successful performance of the speech act of reference is that there must exist an object that the speaker is referring to."[13] Searle has to say that this condition can be fulfilled in fictional discourse: "Because the author has created these fictional characters, we on the other hand can make true statements about them as fictional characters."[14] Thus "the world" whose connection with words is established by the rules for performing speech-acts is one which contains fictional objects. "I did not *pretend* to refer to a real Sherlock Holmes; I *really referred* to the fictional Sherlock Holmes."[15]

But what is the difference supposed to be between saying, with Russell, that to assert

Holmes lived in Baker Street

is to assert, roughly,

The Holmes stories contain such statements as "Holmes lived in Baker Street"

and saying, with Searle and against Russell, that we are "really referring" to Holmes? Well, there is at least this difference. When Russell formulated (1) he meant to use such "analyses" as the above to

protect it against counter-examples. But for reasons we have already looked at, a speech-act theory cannot resort to this strategy of
"analyzing away" unwelcome referring expressions. So Searle *has* to
construct the notion of "existence-in-fiction" and "reference with
fictional discourse" to substitute for such analyses if (1) is to be
saved. But it has been saved at the cost of ambiguity and triviality.
Russell meant by "existence" plain ordinary spatio-temporal existence (with qualifications to allow for mathematical objects, knowledge of which he thought rested on direct acquaintance with "logical"
universals). If we are to allow the results of "creation of fictional
characters" to satisfy (1) we shall have to say that "existence" now
means something like "either spatio-temporal existence *or* ability to
be referred to in a language-game parasitic on real world (spatio-
temporal) talk and known to its speakers to be distinct from such
talk." (The last qualification is necessary to prevent caloric being created as an object of reference by chemists who thought it real; it is
only so created, presumably, by historians of science who assert
"caloric naturally rises" in the context of discussion of a theory
which they do not accept.)

The trouble with revising (1) by broadening the sense of "exists"
is that it brings to a head the question I raised above about language-
game approaches: is there any real difference between (1) and (6)—
the axioms of, respectively, existence and identifiability? For "ability to refer to X" in fictional discourse (or in any other parasitic
language-game) seems just "ability to keep up a coherent conversation about X." This, in turn, seems just possession of an identifying
description full enough to let us see what would count for or against
various assertions using the term in question. If we agree that Holmes
is a fictional character, we shall settle debates about his habits by
turning to Conan Doyle, we shall not inquire whether he and Gladstone
ever met, and so on. That is, we shall conduct successful conversation
about him in a way which would not be possible with someone who
took him to be an historical personage. In general, if we ask "what is
enough of an identifying description to satisfy Searle's (6)?" the answer would seem to be that it would have to at least give us a sense
of what is relevant to answering questions about the referent. But
that seems to say that one can successfully refer to anything if one
knows how to play the standard language-game about that thing.
(Though this may be a different game at different times, as the example of caloric shows.)

The conclusion I want to draw is that just those considerations
which moved Searle away from Russell's picture of language hooking

on to the world with "genuine names" and towards a "language-game" approach make it impossible for him to give a nontrivial sense to his "axiom of existence," Russell's (1). His attempt to do so works perfectly well as long as he simply remarks that there are conventions which permit you to talk as if you believed that something existed even when you don't. But this sensible remark is too slight to count as part of a general theory about "how words relate to the world" or of the "logical status" of kinds of discourse. All that Searle's approach permits him to say is that they relate to the world by being counters used in games of assertion and denial, where any game can be played as long as there are conventions to tell one what moves to make. But if this were enough to say (as I, in fact, think it), no one would have dreamed of a discipline called "philosophy of language" which answered questions about how language works. Searle falls between two stools by retaining a Russellian notion of reference, contextually defined in part by (1), while abjuring Russellian notions of "implicit assertions" about the spatio-temporal world.

4. Donnellan and Physicalist Semantics

I turn now to a reaction against the notion, common to Russell *and* Searle, that we use proper names (of either real or fictional objects) by virtue of our possession of identifying descriptions of them. This reaction is associated with the names of Kripke, Putnam, Field, and Donnellan. I shall discuss Donnellan because he is the only member of the group associated with the so-called "causal theory of reference" to have published an explicit discussion of reference to fictional entities. Donnellan would presumably agree with Russell that there are conventions such that we can properly assent to "Holmes lived on Baker Street" by treating it as an abbreviation for "According to the Holmes stories, . . ." But Donnellan wants to answer the further question: how, in the *absence* of such conventions (as in the case of a fiction which has successfully imposed itself as reality), "can one even speak and be *understood* when using a singular expression with no referent[?] "[16] Donnellan is unwilling to allow that when the child who *believes* in Santa Claus says "Santa Claus will come tonight" a proposition has been expressed, much less a true one.[17] The child's disbelieving parents may use the same form of words to abbreviate "According to the legend, Santa Claus will come tonight" and thereby say something true. But the truth of "Santa Claus does not exist" is not a function of what the legend says. Nor, on Donnellan's account, is it an abbreviation for the Russellian "There is no entity such that . . ."; for Donnellan views the Russellian notion of reference as accomplished through "identifying descriptions" as fundamentally erroneous. He presumably would view the defects of Searle's view as an indication of the hidden errors in Russell's. More generally, he would regard the relation between Russell and Searle as analogous to that between Sin and Death.

To understand Donnellan's solution to his problem, we must understand the underlying criticism of Russell. Those who favor "causal theories of reference" think that Russell strayed into something like idealism by thinking that reference is established by "something in the speaker's mind." Specifically, this error led him to disjoin "reference" from a word-world connection, and thus to mislocate the "tie" between language and the world in the epistemological notion of "acquaintance"—a notion which gave rise to Russell's notoriously obscure and unworkable theory that only demonstratives like "this" were "genuine names." Donnellan wants to preserve what he calls the "natural" view which Russell tried to hang on to by invoking this latter notion, but to do so consistently with the central theses of his own "historical explanation" view. This view says that

> when there is an absence of historical connection between an individual and the use of a name by a speaker, then, be the speaker's descriptions ever so correct about a certain individual, that individual is not the referent; . . . on the other hand, a certain historical connection between the use of a name and an individual can make the individual the referent even though the speaker's descriptions would not by themselves single out the individual.[18]

This view contrasts sharply with Searle's, since it disjoins the "condition of identification" entirely from the "condition of existence." Whereas it was natural for Searle to think that our ability to conduct successful convention-regulated conversations about fictional characters was a reason for saying that the existence condition is satisfied in fictional discourse, Donnellan sees no necessary connection between what is being referred to and what the speaker would pick out as what he was talking about. So his solution to his chosen problem of how one can "speak and be understood" when using a singular expression with no reference will have nothing to do with the speaker's or the hearer's intentions or dispositions or knowledge. Part of his solution goes as follows:

> If N is a proper name that has been used in predicative statements with the intention to refer to some individual, then "N does not exist" is true if and only if the history of those uses ends in a block[19]

where "ending in a block" is defined as "ending with events that preclude any referent being identified."[20] Thus if Holmes had been generally thought a real contemporary of Gladstone's but historical investigation had subsequently proved that people only speak of Holmes because of Doyle's stories, we should have encountered a block. At that point we should conclude that all statements such as "Holmes lived in Baker Street" are false, unless intended as abbreviations for "According to the Holmes stories, Holmes lived in Baker Street."

To evaluate this solution, recall that the "natural" view which Searle and Donnellan both wish to preserve is that

> in using such simple sentences (as "Socrates is snub-nosed") we are not saying something general about the world—that is, not saying something that would be correctly analyzed with the aid of quantifiers; . . . in such cases the speaker could, in all probability, have said the same thing, expressed the same proposition, with the aid of other and different singular expressions, so long as they are being used to refer to the same individual.[21]

This view, when conjoined with the anti-Russellian claim that "proper names have no descriptive content,"[22] makes Dennellan say that "Santa Claus will not come tonight" cannot express a proposition. If one has no "descriptive content" in the subject-term, then no proposition is expressed unless the proper historical connection is present. This means that for "Santa Claus does not exist," and existential statements involving proper names generally, "we cannot preserve a clear notion of what proposition is expressed." *So we must disjoin knowing how to use a statement from knowing what proposition it expresses.* The price we pay for retaining the "natural view" while rejecting the view, common to Russell and Searle, that "meaning is in the mind" is twofold:

(a) we must adopt the counter-intuitive notion that our knowledge of what is referred to depends upon historical inquiry

(b) we must drop the assimilation of "knowing what proposition is expressed by S" to "knowing the truth-conditions for S."

We can hook up this result with the result of our discussion of Searle by saying that if we reject Searle's claim that in talk of fictional entities we "really refer," then we are driven to a notion of reference which ties it (as in Russell) to epistemological notions of direct acquaintance or (as in Donnellan) to the view that we can understand the "tie between language and the world" only for predicative statements and not for existential statements. To put it another way, if we insist against Searle that only spatio-temporal existence will suffice to satisfy the "existence condition" on reference, then we shall either have to say with Russell that

(i) The notion of reference needs to be fleshed out with "analyses" of what sentences are really about

or to say with Donnellan that

(ii) The notion of reference which specifies the "tie between language and the world" has no application for such true and intelligible statements as "Holmes did not exist."

If we adopt (ii), we must recognize that Russell's (1)—the claim that we can only refer to what exists—has now been preserved only at the cost of serious concessions. For Russell thought that reference in the sense governed by (1) was a prerequisite for significant talk about the world. On Donnellan's view, we can make true and intelligible assertions about the spatio-temporal world which contain no referring expressions. Here we see a result of a sharp divergence in motive between Russell and advocates of "causal theories" of reference. Russell wanted semantics in order to do "verificationist" epistemology better, and so he aimed for a general account of all true and intelligible statements about the world which would exhibit our methods of understanding and verifying them. The price Russell paid for (1) was paradoxically complex "analyses" of some statements. Most admirers of Donnellan and Kripke, however, want semantics in order to do what Putnam calls "realist" epistemology better, where being "realist" means a full-fledged return to "picture" theories of language.[23] So the price Donnellan pays for (1) is to be unable to say what propositions are expressed by many statements which are both intelligible and true. Russell's paradoxes come when he reads more into our speech-act than we had thought was there. Donnellan's come when he declines to provide a "tie between language and the world" for many true statements which look as if they were asserting such ties.

The notion of a "realist" epistemology, in the sense intended by Putnam, Kripke, and Donnellan, is complex and obscure. But for present purposes it may suffice to say that it is an attempt to expound the consequences of the following theses:

(7) Knowledge gives us a picture of physical reality

(8) Anything can be a picture of reality according to certain conventions

(9) So to avoid a relativism of "alternative conceptual schemes" we must say that there are word-world relationships which hold independently of any choice of conventions, conceptual schemes, identifying descriptions, or other "subjective" factors, and are themselves physical relationships.

In short, a realistic epistemology and/or philosophy of language wants to develop an account of "how words relate to the world" which would *not* work equally well for a fictional world and for a real one. In realist eyes, the fatal flaw of the Russell-Searle way of looking at language is that it *would* work equally well if life were a dream, or if Descartes' demon were real, or if we were all brains preserved in vats. For reasons I have set out elsewhere,[24] I do not think this sort of realism is a coherent project, but I shall put off further discussion of it until section 7. In the following section I want to take up one more account of truth about fictions in order to round out my presentation of the standard strategies for dealing with this problem.

5. Meinongianism and "Incomplete Objects"

Russell originally proposed his theory of descriptions as a way of avoiding granting existence to all intentional objects, a view he attributed to Meinong. He gave neither an accurate account of Meinong's views nor a clear argument against them, nor shall I. I shall simply follow custom in using the label "Meinongian" for any view of reference which holds that reference to Gladstone and to Holmes occurs in exactly the same way, and that the difference between real and fictional persons is irrelevant to semantics. The most recent exponent of such a view is Terence Parsons.[25] I shall sketch the general lines of Parsons' treatment of truth about fiction very briefly, and then quickly focus on a Meinongian notion which most philosophers find counter intuitive, that of "incomplete objects."

The basic Meinongian strategy is to substitute

(1′) Whatever is referred to must be an object

for Russell's

(1) Whatever is referred to must exist.

The idea is to take the "identifying description" we use to "pick out" a referent as enumerating the members of a subset of a (possibly) larger set of properties which is the object itself — the remainder of the set being composed of all its as yet unmentioned properties. Meinongianism can be thought of as saying: If you have enough identifying properties, you can forget about particulars to bear those properties. Berkeley said, in the same spirit, that if you had enough ideas you could forget about the material substrata in which qualities inhere; and Kant, that if you had enough coherent representations you could forget about the thing-in-itself.

The effect of this strategy is to make it possible to refer to, and thus to tell truths about, practically anything. The only sorts of expressions which Parsons would exclude from referring are ones like "the thing which is round and not round." Yet he happily includes "the round square." On his view, it is true that the round square is round in just the same sense that it is true of Henry James that, in addition to the various properties by which we usually identify him, he includes the property of having encountered Charles Sanders Peirce on a visit to Paris. In just that sense, it is true that Sherlock Holmes has the property of being of matrilineal French descent. Trouble arises for this strategy only when one begins to consider properties like "existent" and ask whether there is a set of properties which includes all the properties of Sherlock Holmes plus one extra — the property of existence. Again, one can generate problems by including the property "being as yet unthought of." Parson's strategy here is to excise all such paradoxes by treating this sort of "special" troublemaking property as "extranuclear" and saying that "objects are composed of nuclear properties only,"[26] e.g., the sort of properties which occur in ordinary nonintensional predicative judgments.

Skipping blithely over both the details and the difficulties of this nuclear-extranuclear distinction, I shall pass at once to the application of Parsons' theory to fictional characters. Parsons thinks[27] that this application is confirmation of the truth of his view. He regards the intuition that talk about fictional objects should be "analysed away . . . in such a way that the paraphrase refers only to real objects — perhaps to novels, or sentences in novels . . ." as an "idiosyncrasy of recent Anglo-American philosophy."[28] He urges that his view lets us say a lot of things which the Russellian tradition forbids — e.g., that Holmes is a detective, Pegasus a winged horse, and so on. On his view,

[in] the case of "Sherlock Holmes" we get an incomplete, possible, nonexistent object, some of whose nuclear properties are: being a detective, catching criminals, smoking a pipe, etc. Typically, fictional objects will be incomplete, for the body of literature in question will not determine all of their properties. For example, it is not true that according to the Conan Doyle novels, Holmes had a mole on his left leg, nor is it true that according to those novels he didn't have a mole on his left leg . . . he is *indeterminate with respect to* that property.[29]

Parsons wishes us to accept this outcome with equanimity, but there is obviously something troubling in the notion of an "incomplete" object. The difficulty becomes extreme in the cases of "too simple" stories—like that cited by Parsons from David Lewis: "Staub was a dragon who had ten magic rings. The end." One is tempted to say that there is a minimum number of properties which even an *incomplete* object must have, and that Staub does not qualify. Further, there is a converse difficulty, also pointed out by Lewis: we can construct two objects, one of which is the set of all properties Holmes is said to have in the stories and the other is all these plus having a mole on the left leg. Indeed, by placing moles elsewhere we can construct indefinitely many objects of this Holmesian sort. Which is the object of which the Holmes stories are true? It is natural to say: only the first. But though natural, it seems arbitrary. Once we connive at the notion that there is truth-by-correspondence-to-an-object about Holmes, why should we think that Conan Doyle knew all such truths? Suppose we try to avoid incomplete objects. We might just construct a *complete* object on the basis of the properties attributed to Holmes in the stories. For every sensible question which can reasonably be raised about Henry James (did he meet Gladstone? did he shave twice a day?), there is an answer, although usually unknown to us. That is why Henry James is a complete object. If, *per impossibile*, we list all the questions we can ask about James, raise them about Holmes, and assign arbitrary answers, we shall have a complete object. Unfortunately, of course, Lewis' point applies here also. If we give a different arbitrary answer to one question, we shall have a different complete object. The practical impossibility of listing all the questions should be no more of a barrier to saying that there are such objects than is the practical impossibility of thinking of all the properties attributed to Holmes by the stories.

What bothers us, I think, in considering these consequences of Parsons' theory is just that the pleasure of being able to say "Holmes is a detective" and "Pegasus is a winged horse" without having to think of them as Russellian abbreviations of statements about stories is diminished by the strain of regarding truth about Holmes as a relation between a sentence and an object. If we let the object be simply "that of which all *and only* the sentences in the stories are true," as Parsons does, then the strain will not arise. But as soon as we contemplate the difficulty of picking out *which* object the sentences are true of, the notion of truth-by-correspondence suddenly seems altogether out of place. So does the notion of "corresponding to an incomplete object," particularly because, even if we throw in billions of arbitrary extra properties in hopes of a complete Holmes, we shall never construct an object which can be fitted into a complete story of nineteenth-century London (all the space-time intervals being, alas, already full of other objects). To do so we would have to construct a complete new *world*, one in which no space-time interval is identical with any in the actual world. But when we think of building up a "new" space and time by adding together properties, we run up against all the intuitions which Kant mustered in the "Transcendental Aesthetic": there cannot be more than one space or time. The basic Meinongian strategy of substituting clusters of properties for individuals breaks down as soon as we come to spatio-temporal relationships.

There are various Meinongian things which might be said to allay these qualms, most of them insisting that we should not confuse "being an object of reference" with "being a spatio-temporal object." For Meinongian purposes, we want a notion of "object" at least as vague as Wittgenstein's use of *Gegenstand* in the *Tractatus*. If one views semantical notions like "truth" and "reference" as applying equally to mathematical equations and reports of spatio-temporal events, for example, one will want a notion of truth-as-correspondence-to-reality which floats free of constructing linguistic pictures of physical reality. So one will want to disassociate (1) from the "natural view" described by Donnellan—a view which insists on the possibility "of singular terms which do not introduce quantifiers," of simply "picking something out" without "saying something general." Or, at least, one will want to disassociate this notion of "picking out" from the commonsensical activity of "isolating the relevant spatio-temporal region" one is talking about. "Picking out" will have to extend to, e.g., picking out a possible world, or an item in "logical space."

Rather than examining how far one could go in defending Meinongianism, however, I shall rest content with this bare indication of the line of objections and replies which Meinongian proposals generate. I want to press on, in the next section, to a more general discussion of whether and how the notion of truth-by-correspondence (and thus of "reference" as a notion needed to explicate the correspondence in question) can be disassociated from physicalism—from the intuition that all truth is, somehow, truth about the layout of the spatio-temporal world. I shall be arguing that the notions of "correspondence" and "reference," in the senses in which all four of the authors I have discussed use them, cannot be so disassociated: that Donnellan is, to this extent, right. So I shall argue that we have only *two* alternatives: a "pure" language-game approach which dispenses with these notions altogether, or a rigidly physicalist approach which interprets them in terms of physical causality. To put it in terms of my main topic: The alternatives are to separate semantics from epistemology so drastically that semantics will have no interesting distinctions to make between truth about fact and about fiction, or to bring semantics together with a realistic epistemology of "picturing" which, in the manner of Donnellan, will disallow truth about fiction altogether.

6. The Parmenidean Picture Picture

Let me try to bring out the moral of the complicated story I have been telling by putting forward a very simple-minded view of language and truth—one which avoids all the problems discussed so far. This view follows Dewey, Sellars, and the later Wittgenstein in taking all assertions as moves in a game. What Dewey called "the warranted assertions"—the ones we normally call "true"—are warranted in as many various ways as there are topics of discourse. Consider the following examples: "2 plus 2 is 4"; "Holmes lived in Baker Street"; "Henry James was born in America"; "There ought to be more love in the world"; "Vermeer's straightforward use of light is more successful than La Tour's trickery." These are all warranted assertions, and all true in exactly the same sense. The differences between them are revealed by sociological study of the way in which people would justify each assertion—but not by semantics. Or, to put it another way, whatever semantics (or "philosophy of language") may be good for, it will not tell you anything about "how words relate to the world"—for there is nothing *general* to be said. On this view, the notion of "reference," as a relation satisfying (1), is pointless, a philosopher's invention. All we need is the commonsensical notion of "talking about," where the criterion for what a statement is "about" is just whatever its utterer "has in mind"—that is, whatever he *thinks* he's talking about. The philosopher's notion of truth as "correspondence to reality" is a pointless attempt to press sentences like the one about Vermeer above into the same mold as sentences like "The cat is on the mat."

This view is amiably simple-minded, completely unhelpful if one hopes that light will be shed on the nature of fictions by analytic philosophy of language, and, I think, correct. What *is* helpful for purposes of thinking about fiction, I believe, is asking why the phenomenon of analytic philosophy of language exists—or, more precisely, why (1) was ever taken seriously. Why should the perfectly reasonable epistemological point that

The best way to find out about Sherlock Holmes is to read Conan Doyle's stories

ever have been expressed as the semantical claim that

Statements about Sherlock Holmes are really about Conan Doyle's stories?

Well, perhaps for the same bad reasons as

The best way to find out about the stars is to use your senses

was expressed as

Statements about stars are really statements about sense-data.

But why, once semantics was separated off from epistemology in the enlightened post-war, post-positivistic era of analytic philosophy, did not Searle and Strawson rest content with language-as-game rather than attempting "theory of reference"? Why would anyone still bother to be Meinongian—creating objects to refer to in order to save an analogue of (1)—rather than simply saying that we can have warranted assertions (e.g., "Love is better than hate") which only a diehard Platonist would insist are "about objects"?

The answer, I think, is that semantics has *not* become completely disjoined from epistemology, despite advertisements to that effect. Most philosophers of language want the same thing out of semantics that epistemologists from Descartes to Chisholm wanted: an account of our representations of the world which guarantees that we have not lost touch with it, an answer to the skeptic which flows from a general account of the nature of representation. The difference between mental representations and linguistic representations has not changed the motive of an inquiry into representation; whereas once we had theories about privileged "ideas" or *Vorstellungen* (simple ideas of sensation, clear and distinct ideas, categories) with which to argue against the skeptic, we now have theories about those privileged elements of discourse (e.g., names, identifying descriptions) which "tie language to the world." In both traditional epistemology and recent semantics there is a self-deceptive attempt to conceal this motive by describing the activity as simply an explanation of how the mind or the language works, but the account offered always betrays the need to answer the skeptic who asks: how would it be different if everything were a dream? How would it be different if it were all *made up*? How would it be different if there were nothing there to be represented? How does having knowledge differ from making poems and telling stories?

Only the urge to answer such questions keeps a notion like (1) alive —or, more precisely, makes philosophers think that there is an interesting notion called "reference" in addition to the commonsensical notion of "talking about." For only the notion that where there is truth there is "correspondence to an object" would have made Searle think that an understanding of the language-game played with, e.g., "Sherlock Holmes" required the notion of "existence-in-fiction." Only the same notion would make it seem worthwhile to challenge the Russellian "analyses" by supplying Meinongian "objects" rather than simply denying (1) and sweeping away Russell's (2), (3), and (4) along with it. Only this notion gives plausibility to Donnellan's claim that "Santa Claus comes tonight" does not express a proposition, or that we do not know what proposition "Santa Claus does not exist" expresses. For only the rather desperate fear that language will lose touch with the world could make one think that "knowing what proposition is expressed by 'S'" has nothing to do with knowing how to use "S" and everything to do with picking out something in the world for "S" to be true of. The insistence on preserving (1) can only be explained as an expression of the captivating picture which is sketched in Wittgenstein's *Tractatus*:

> The object is simple.
>
> Every statement about complexes can be analysed into a statement about their constituent parts, and into those propositions which completely describe the complexes.
>
> Objects form the substance of the world. Therefore they cannot be compound.
>
> If the world had no substance, then whether a proposition had sense would depend on whether another proposition was true.
>
> It would then be impossible to form a picture of the world (true or false).
>
> It is clear that however different from the real world an imagined one may be, it must have something—a form—in common with the real world.
>
> This fixed form consists of the objects.[30]

The language-game approach of the *Investigations* abandons this "picture picture" of language precisely in allowing that whether a sentence has sense (i.e., can be intelligible and true or false) *may* be dependent upon whether another sentence is true. Since this possibility is paradigmatically actual in the case of fictional discourse (taken at face value and neither "analyzed" à la Russell nor assigned special referents as in Searle and Parsons), philosophical problems about fiction simply do not arise once the picture picture is dropped. Nor, for parallel reasons, do sceptical problems about life being a dream, nor the problem of how scientific theories may be "philosophically" distinguished from poems.

The common root of all these problems is the fear that the manifold possibilities offered by discursive thought will play us false, will make us "lose contact" with the real. This fear is, as Heidegger has argued, definatory of the Western philosophical tradition. To see why Wittgenstein feared that nonpicture, "game" theories would lose touch with "the fixed form of the world"[31] and would make impossible "determinacy of meaning,"[32] we need to look back all the way to Parmenides. Parmenides' fear of the poetic, playful, arbitrary aspects of language was so great as to make him distrust predicative discourse itself. This distrust came from the conviction that only being seized, compelled, gripped, by the real could produce Knowledge rather than Opinion. When Parmenides says that we "cannot speak of what is not," I take him to be saying that discourse which is not so gripped is not even a candidate for expressing Knowledge. Since discourse which uses two different expressions to apply to the real is, Parmenides thought, committed either to negative predication or to redundancy, no predicative sentence can do more than express Opinion. The multiplicity of things which predicative discourse can say shows Parmenides that such discourse depends upon *conventions* of representation, and thus is νόμῳ rather than φύσει. If Heidegger is right in suggesting that this dread of losing the "essential togetherness of Being and Apprehension" is Plato's inheritance from Parmenides, then we can see the history of epistemology and semantics as the attempt to "ground" predicative discourse on a nonconventional relation to reality. Such a grounding will divide predicative discourse into two parts, one corresponding to the Way of Truth, because "anchored" epistemologically or semantically by unmediated relationships, and the other corresponding to the Way of Opinion, because lacking such anchorage. Ἐπιστήμη, science, will be the paradigm of the first sort, and ποίησις, poetry, what has been made up, the paradigm of the second.

This need for a division between two sorts of discourse is, I think, the link between the twentieth-century semantical tradition of adherence to Russell's (1) and the old epistemological tradition which thinks of some sort of "vision" as the relationship which hooks mental representations to reality. Following Heidegger once again, it seems natural to see Russell's notion of "knowledge by acquaintance" as the heir of Plato's attempt to model Knowledge on vision—thus securing the sort of *compulsion* to believe the truth which occurs when what is before our eyes makes it impossible to doubt the truth of a proposition. Plato and Russell both think that unless this analogue to the *forced* character of visual perception occurs, there will be no distinction between knowledge and opinion, logic and mysticism, science and poetry. Heidegger sketches the relation between Parmenides' original distrust of language and predication and Plato's as follows:

> The word ἰδέα means that which is seen in the visible, the aspect it offers. What is offered is the appearance, εἶδος, of what confronts us.[33]

> The crux of the matter is not that φύσις should have been characterized as ἰδέα but that the ἰδέα should have become the sole and decisive interpretation of being.[34]

> Φύσις is the emerging power, the standing-there-in-itself, stability. Ἰδέα, appearance as what is seen, is a determination of the stable insofar and only insofar as it encounters vision.[35]

From this adoption of vision as the model for our relation to Being, Heidegger continues, was to come the Aristotelian notion of truth as accuracy of representation (ὀρθότης rather than ἀλήθεία): "The truth becomes the correctness of the logos."[36]

But Plato himself was still Parmenidean enough to reject the view which both Aristotle and contemporary analytic philosophy of language take for granted: that there can be fully meaningful uses of language which are *bad* representations of reality (either because they are false or because they are phrased in inappropriate vocabulary)—but nevertheless "hook on" to reality by a relation of reference and serve as hypotheses, stepping-stones to *better* representations. Thus Nicholas White says that Plato

> does not accord full meaningfulness to languages that are not perfect and final representations of reality. . . . Not only is the true theory of the knowable world, i.e., of the world of the Forms, without genuine precursors, but it is also without genuine alternatives.[37]

White explains that Plato is led eventually to reject the notion of hypotheses because he thinks that "we have, in our ability to apprehend Forms, an avenue to knowledge of them which is independent of language" and so we may

> simply hope to happen on what we can know, without worrying about whether it answers to a previous inquiry, or how it would be described in terms to which we are accustomed.
> It is Plato's picture of the nature of intelligible reality that makes this

last expedient one that he can contemplate. For he can think of the Forms
as somehow lying plainly open to one's mental gaze, if one could only
clear away the obstructions.[38]

This epistemology-of-vision brings the following semantical consequence, which Alexander Nehamas calls Plato's "One-Name Assumption":

> If w is the name of a, then w is the only name a has, and a is the only ob-
> ject named by w.[39]

Nehamas makes the same point when he says that Plato

> thinks of an ὄνομα as revealing the nature of what it names, and that it is
> only if this very strong semantical relation obtains that a word can pick
> out an item in reality.[40]

This "very strong semantical relation" is the heir of the even
stronger Parmenidean relation of being-undiscursively-gripped-by,
and the ancestor of the weaker Russellian relation of "reference"
which dominates recent semantics. All three notions contrast with
the *weakest* semantical relation in the area—mere "talking about," in
the sense in which we can talk about, but not refer to, nonexistent,
and specifically fictional, entities. *That* relation is one which may be
constituted by discourse—since no more is required for talking about
Sherlock Holmes or caloric than that the *words* "Sherlock Holmes"
and "caloric" be systematically bandied about. The Parmenidean,
Platonic, and Russellian relations, by contrast, are word-world relationships which are *presuppositions* and *foundations* of discourse.
They are relations which purport to make truth possible—or, more
exactly, to make possible first-class truth, as opposed to the parasitic
and second-rate sort of truth possessed by "Holmes lived in Baker
Street." To understand the need which the young Wittgenstein felt
for such a relation we must understand the need for a distinction
between "responsible" and "irresponsible" discourse—that need to
distinguish sharply between science and poetry which makes us distinctively Western.

7. Physicalism and Factuality

Were it not for our Parmenidean need to be constrained to truth,
compelled by things to call them by their proper names, we should
never have thought that a discipline called "theory of knowledge"
might tell us about "objectivity," nor that another called "philosophy of language" could tell us how words hook on to the world. The

very idea that we could have a theory about mental or linguistic representations which would *not* be a "game" theory—which would find
representations which stood in "natural" rather than merely conventional relations to the objects represented—is so odd that only
something like Heidegger's view of the West as obsessed by the "metaphysics of presence" can account for it. But given this commitment
plus the idea, current since Frege, that semantics rather than epistemology is "first philosophy," plus the further idea that Russell's approach confuses epistemological with purely semantical considerations, it is natural that the demand for a "causal theory" should be
the final formulation of our Parmenidean yearnings. The argument
offered in propositions (7)-(9) above is that a picture picture of language will only be possible if physical relationships are substituted
for conventional ones in explaining how words hook up with the
world. This argument is, I think, valid, but constitutes a *reductio
ad absurdum* of (7). What I have said so far is simply that attempts
(like Searle's and Parsons') to avoid the physicalism to which this argument leads are pointless. To say with Searle that Russell's (1)—"the
axiom of existence"—can be satisfied by fictitious characters, or to
say with Parsons that it can be satisfied by nonspatio-temporal objects, is to deprive this axiom of any point. For that axiom was formulated as an attempt to make sure that language was hooked up to
the spatio-temporal world by such nonconventional relationships as
Russellian "knowledge by acquaintance." Once such epistemological
notions are gone, the only nonconventional relationship which is
even a candidate for the desired hook-up is ordinary physical causality.

What, then, can we say about the success of physicalism in giving
satisfaction to our Parmenidean urges? If we view physicalistic semantics as some of its proponents view it—as a prolegomenon to a
"realistic" epistemology—its prospects are dim. For our ability to
give a causal account (e.g., an evolutionary account) of how we came
to use the words we do and to assert the propositions we assert
shows nothing whatever about whether we are representing reality
accurately. *Any* community with a reasonably complete language
and a reasonably imaginative scientific world-story will be able to
give such an account of how it came to speak and believe as it does.
What Putnam calls "internal realism"—the ability of science to double
back on itself and explain its own genesis—has nothing to do with
the Parmenidean need to feel that reality has constrained us, or is in
the process of constraining us, to pick the One Right Representation
of itself. (The latter is what Putnam calls "metaphysical realism,"
which he has come to regard as incoherent.)[41] The Cartesian and

Kantian urge to slide a philosophical foundation underneath our science or our culture will not be gratified by a physicalistic semantics.

Another sort of urge, however, *will* be. This is the urge to find a principled differentiation between science and nonscience, between first-rate picturing discourse and second-rate nonpicturing discourse, between talking about the world and talking about what we have "made up." If physicalistic semantics cannot guarantee that we are getting the world right, it can at least give us a way of quashing the fear that science itself is simply a form of myth-making—the fear that there is no distinction between ἐπιστήμη and ποίησις to be made at all. This is the fear which both idealism and a thorough-going "language-game" approach inspire, the fear that there are simply no ties at all between language and the world, that we are wandering about among our own creations rather than being constrained to truth. A physicalist semantics offers, by contrast, an account of the distinction between ἐπιστήμη and ποίησις in terms of the notion of an Ideal Causal Explanation of Linguistic Behavior. Such an explanation is a part of the Ideal Explanation of All Events—that part which explains why human beings say the things they do. Some of the things they say are to be explained on the basis of reality being as they say it is. Other things are to be explained in other ways. The former things make up first-class picturing discourse; the latter, second-class gamesome discourse. Intuitively, the idea is that where there are causal lines between referring expressions and entities mentioned in the Ideal Explanation, there we have picturing. Where there are not, where tracing causal pathways is prevented by what Donnellan calls "blocks," we do not. True statements containing expressions which are thus "blocked off" from reality are "truths in fiction"—truths in the language-game sense, statements whose truth is *mere* warranted assertibility.

The most explicit statement of the relevant physicalist intuitions has been given by Dagfinn Føllesdal, in an attempt to explain what Quine is getting at in his mysterious doctrine of the "double indeterminacy of translation"—the claim that "the totality of truths of nature, known and unknown, observable and unobservable, past and future leaves translation undetermined." On the question "Does 'rouge' mean *red*?," Quine tells us, "there is no fact of the matter even to *within* the acknowledged underdetermination of a theory of nature."[42]

Føllesdal glosses this as follows:

All the truths there are, are included in our theory of nature. . . . And the only entities we are justified in assuming are those that are appealed to in the simplest theory that accounts for all this evidence. These entities and their properties are all there is to the world, and all there is to be right or wrong about. All truths about these are included in our theory of nature. In translation we are not describing a further realm of reality, we are just correlating two comprehensive theories concerning all there is. . . . This is, I think the reason for the difference between theory of nature and translation, and thereby for the indeterminacy of translation.[43]

The principle that only the entities appealed to "in the simplest theory that accounts for all this evidence" are such that one can be right or wrong about them is the claim that the Ideal Causal Explanation determines the limits of picturing discourse. There are plenty of other things one can speak truly about—e.g., the meanings of words and the moral worth of actions—but these true statements do not picture reality any more than does "Holmes lived in Baker Street." They are true by virtue of something other than The Way The World Is.

This minimal gratification of Parmenidean needs permits us to give something like sense to the claim that statements which are not about "atoms and the void" are only "true by convention." The relation of "reference"—the world-word hook-up—which is secured by this physicalism is merely one which meets the condition that

(10) Whatever is referred to must be the sort of object which we have to talk about in order to give the Ideal Causal Explanation of our saying what we say.

These objects, if reductionist hopes come true, will be some up-to-date counterpart of "atoms and the void." Donnellan, Kripke, and other physicalists do not pretend to give any argument for (10) which *grounds* this ancient Democritean intuition; they merely offer a way of explicating this intuition within a certain philosophical vocabulary.

8. The Poet's Debt to Parmenides

I want to bring this paper to a close by noting the importance of such intuitions for the development of modern literature, offering a few reminders about the way in which the existence within our culture of these Parmenidean intuitions serves as a foil for poets, novelists, and critics. Since Mallarmé and Joyce, a whole series of writers have blurred the representational function of language by making words both object and representation at once. A whole tradition of storytellers, notably Borges and Nabokov, have achieved their effects by violating the space defined by the proscenium arch. In the wake of

Nietzsche's questioning of "the will to truth" and Heidegger's questioning of the "metaphysics of presence," a series of critics (notably Derrida) have been trying to do away with the notion of "referent" and saying things like "There is nothing outside the text." One could see this swelling chorus as auguring "the end of metaphysics"—as signaling the beginning of our liberation from the Parmenidean tradition. One could see Borges and Nabokov, Mallarmé and Valéry and Wallace Stevens, Derrida and Foucault, as guiding us out of the world of subject-and-object, word-and-meaning, language-and-world, and into a newer and better intellectual universe, undreamt of since the Greeks first made those fateful distinctions between νόμος and φύσις, ἐπιστήμη and ποίησις, which have haunted the West. But this would, I think, be a great mistake. It would be better to see these people as using the Parmenidean tradition as a dialectical foil, in whose absence they would have nothing to say. In a culture in which the notion of "hard fact"—the Parmenidean notion of compulsion to truth by reality—had less of a place, the whole genre of "modernist" writing would make no sense. The notion of "intertextuality" would have no deliciously naughty thrill.

In particular, the ironic attitude towards "truth" which "modernism" exhibits would be impossible without a lively philosophical tradition which keeps the picture picture of mind or language alive. Without the foredoomed struggle of philosophers to invent a form of representation which will constrain us to truth while leaving us free to err, to find pictures where there are only games, there would be nothing to be ironic about. In a culture lacking the contrast between science and poetry, there would be no poetry about poetry, no writing which was a glorification of writing itself. That contrast is just what our Parmenidean philosophers keep alive for us. By constantly attempting to distinguish between first- and second-rate discourse, they make possible, so to speak, better second-rate discourse than we could have had otherwise.[44]

If the absurdity of the picture picture were ever universally acknowledged, if we became wholeheartedly pragmatic in science and morals, if we ever *simply* identified truth with warranted assertibility, our fantasts would have no theme, our modernists no irony. Neither William nor Henry James would have had anything to say in a world without Russells, nor would Borges in a world without Donnellans. What is most distinctively modern in modern literature depends for its effect upon straight men, and especially upon philosophers who defend "common-sense realism" against idealists, pragmatists, structuralists, and all others who impugn the distinction between the scientist and the poet. The modern revolt against what Foucault calls "the sovereignty of the signifier" helps us think of the creation of new descriptions, new vocabularies, new *genres* as the essentially human activity—it suggests the poet, rather than the knower, as the man who realizes human nature. But this is dangerous; the poet needs to be saved from his friends. If the picture picture is as absurd as I think it, it would be well that this absurdity should not become widely known. For the ironist poet owes far more to Parmenides and the tradition of Western metaphysics than does the scientist. The scientific culture could survive a loss of faith in this tradition, but the literary culture might not.[45]

Notes

1. Keith Donnellan, "Speaking of Nothing," *Philosophical Review*, 83 (1974): 11.

2. Ludwig Wittgenstein, *Philosophical Investigations* (London: Macmillan, 1953), pt. 1, sect. 46.

3. John R. Searle, *Speech Acts* (Cambridge: Cambridge University Press, 1969), p. 162.

4. *Loc. cit.*

5. *Ibid.*, p. 160.

6. *Ibid.*, pp. 170-171.

7. *Ibid.*, pp. 77-79.

8. *Ibid.*, p. 78.

9. Searle, "The Logical Status of Fictional Discourse," *New Literary History*, V (1974): 319. See Stanley Fish, *Is There a Text in the Class?* (Cambridge, Mass.: Harvard University Press, 1980), chap. 9, for criticisms of this article which parallel those I shall be making.

10. Searle, *op. cit.*, pp. 325-326.

11. *Ibid.*, p. 326.

12. *Ibid.*, p. 322.

13. *Ibid.*, p. 330.

14. *Ibid.*, p. 329.

15. *Ibid.*, p. 330.

16. Donnellan, "Speaking of Nothing," pp. 6-7.

17. *Ibid.*, pp. 20-21.

18. *Ibid.*, p. 18.

19. *Ibid.*, p. 19.

20. *Ibid.*, p. 23.

21. *Ibid.*, p. 11.

22. *Ibid.*, p. 21n.

23. See Hilary Putnam, *Meaning and the Moral Sciences* (London and New York: Routledge and Kegan Paul, 1978).

24. See Rorty, "Realism and Reference," *The Monist*, 59 (1976): 321-340; and *Philosophy and the Mirror of Nature* (Princeton: Princeton University Press, 1979), chap. 6. See also Donald Davidson, "Realism Without Reference," in *Reference, Truth and Reality*, ed. Mark Platts (London: Routledge and Kegan Paul, 1980), pp. 131-140.

25. Terence Parsons, "A Prolegomenon to Meinongian Semantics," *Journal of Philosophy*,

71 (1974): 551-560, and "A Meinongian Analysis of Fictional Objects," *Grazer Philosophische Studien*, 1 (1974): 73-86.

   26. Parsons, "Prolegomenon," p. 573.

   27. Parsons, "Meinongian Analysis," p. 74.

   28. *Ibid.*, p. 77.

   29. *Ibid.*, p. 80.

   30. Wittgenstein, *Tractatus Logico-Philosophicus* (London: Routledge, 1922), 2.02-2.023.

   31. *Ibid.*, 2.026.

   32. *Ibid.*, 3.23.

   33. Martin Heidegger, *Introduction to Metaphysics* (New Haven: Yale University Press, 1959), p. 180.

   34. *Ibid.*, p. 182.

   35. *Loc. cit.*

   36. *Ibid.*, p. 186.

   37. Nicholas White, *Plato on Knowledge and Reality* (Indianapolis: Hackett, 1976), p. 228.

   38. *Ibid.*, p. 230.

   39. Alexander Nehamas, "Self-Predication and Plato's Theory of Forms," *American Philosophical Quarterly*, 16 (1979): 101.

   40. *Ibid.*, p. 100.

   41. See Putnam, *Meaning and the Moral Sciences*, pt. 4.

   42. Willard V. O. Quine, "Reply to Chomsky" in *Words and Objections: Essays on the Work of W. V. Quine*, ed. Donald Davidson and Jaako Hintikka (Dordrecht: Reidel, 1969), p. 303.

   43. Dagfinn Føllesdal, "Meaning and Experience," *Mind and Language*, ed. Samuel Guttenplan (Oxford: Oxford University Press, 1975), p. 32.

   44. I develop this theme further in Essay 6, above.

   45. I am grateful to Barbara Herrnstein Smith for comments on a draft of this paper which led to useful revisions.

8

Nineteenth-Century Idealism
and Twentieth-Century Textualism

I

In the last century there were philosophers who argued that nothing exists but ideas. In our century there are people who write as if there were nothing but texts. These people, whom I shall call "textualists," include for example, the so-called "Yale school" of literary criticism centering around Harold Bloom, Geoffrey Hartmann, J. Hillis Miller, and Paul De Man, "post-structuralist" French thinkers like Jacques Derrida and Michel Foucault, historians like Hayden White, and social scientists like Paul Rabinow. Some of these people take their point of departure from Heidegger, but usually the influence of philosophers is relatively remote. The center of gravity of the intellectual movement in which these people figure is not philosophy, but literary criticism. In this paper I want to discuss some similarities and differences between this movement and nineteenth-century idealism.

The first similarity is that both movements adopt an antagonistic position to natural science. Both suggest that the natural scientist should not be the dominant cultural figure, that scientific knowledge is not what really matters. Both insist that there is a point of view other than, and somehow higher than, that of science. They warn us against the idea that human thought culminates in the application of "scientific method." Both offer to what C. P. Snow called "the literary culture" a self-image, and a set of rhetorical devices.

The second similarity is that both insist that we can never compare human thought or language with bare, unmediated reality. The idealists started off from Berkeley's claim that nothing can be like an idea

139

except another idea. The textualists start off from the claim that all problems, topics, and distinctions are language-relative—the results of our having chosen to use a certain vocabulary, to play a certain language-game. Both use this point to put natural science in its place. The concepts of natural science, idealists pointed out, were shown by Kant to be merely instruments which the mind uses to synthesize sense-impressions; science, therefore, can know only a phenomenal world. In textualist terms, this becomes the claim that the vocabulary of science is merely one among others—merely the vocabulary which happens to be handy in predicting and controlling nature. It is not, as physicalism would have us think, Nature's Own Vocabulary. Both use the same point to exalt the function of art. For the idealists, art could put us in touch with that part of ourselves—the noumenal, free, spiritual part—which science cannot see. For the textualists, the literary artist's awareness that he is making rather than finding, and more specifically the ironic modernists's awareness that he is responding to texts rather than to things, puts him one up on the scientist. Both movements treat the scientist as naive in thinking that he is doing something *more* than putting together ideas, or constructing new texts.

I hope that these two similarities are enough to justify my attempt to view textualism as the contemporary counterpart of idealism—the textualists as spiritual descendants of the idealists, the species having adapted to a changed environment. The differences in environment, I shall claim, consist in the fact that in the early nineteenth century there was a well-defined and well-regarded discipline, philosophy, which had claims to be architectonic for culture, and within which metaphysical theses could be argued. In our culture there is no such discipline. Idealism was based upon a metaphysical thesis, but textualism is not. When philosophers like Derrida say things like "there is nothing outside the text" they are not making theoretical remarks, remarks backed up by epistemological or semantical arguments. Rather, they are saying, cryptically and aphoristically, that a certain framework of interconnected ideas—truth as correspondence, language as picture, literature as imitation—ought to be abandoned. They are not, however, claiming to have discovered the *real* nature of truth or language or literature. Rather, they say that the very notion of discovering the *nature* of such things is part of the intellectual framework which we must abandon—part of what Heidegger calls "the metaphysics of presence," or "the onto-theological tradition."

If one repudiates that tradition, one repudiates the notion which once held realists and idealists together in a single enterprise called "philosophy"—the notion that there is a nonempirical quasi-science which can weigh the considerations for and against a certain view of what reality or knowledge is like. When textualists claim that issues such as those between nineteenth-century idealists and positivists were created by an outdated vocabulary, and are to be dismissed rather than (as some contemporary analytic philosophers would wish) reformulated and made precise, they do not attempt to defend this claim by anything one could call a "philosophical argument." Textualists sometimes, it is true, claim that Heidegger ended metaphysics, just as positivists used to smugly claim that Carnap had. Smugness, however, is all the cases have in common. Heidegger did not announce a new philosophical discovery, in the way in which Carnap claimed to have discovered something about language. The whole idea of adopting a new vocabulary because *something has been discovered to be the case* is just one more element in that "metaphysics of presence" which Heidegger wants to deconstruct.

I have been saying, first, that idealism and textualism have in common an opposition to the claim of science to be a paradigm of human activity, and, second, that they differ in that one is a philosophical doctrine and the other an expression of suspicion about philosophy. I can put these two points together by saying that whereas nineteenth-century idealism wanted to substitute one sort of science (philosophy) for another (natural science) as the center of culture, twentieth-century textualism wants to place literature in the center, and to treat both science and philosophy as, at best, literary genres. The rest of my paper will be an attempt to refine this crude formula and to make it plausible. I shall begin by defining its component terms in the senses in which I wish to use them.

By 'science' I shall mean the sort of activity in which argument is relatively easy—in which one can agree on some general principles which govern discourse in an area, and then aim at consensus by tracing inferential chains between these principles and more particular and more interesting propositions. Philosophy since Kant has purported to be a science which could sit in judgment on all the other sciences. As the science of knowledge, the science of science, *Wissenschaftslehre, Erkenntnistheorie*, it claimed to discover those general principles which made scientific discourse scientific, and thus to "ground" both the other sciences and itself.

It is a feature of a science that the vocabulary in which problems are posed is accepted by all those who count as contributing to the subject. The vocabulary may be changed, but that is only because a new theory has been discovered which explains the phenomena better by invoking a new set of theoretical terms. The vocabulary in which the *explananda* are described has to remain constant. It is a feature of what I shall call "literature" that one can achieve success by introducing a quite new genre of poem or novel or critical essay *without* argument. It succeeds simply by its success, not because there are good reasons why poems or novels or essays should be written in the new way rather than the old. There is no constant vocabulary in which to describe the values to be defended or objects to be imitated, or the emotions to be expressed, or whatever, in essays or poems or novels. The reason "literary criticism" is "unscientific" is just that whenever somebody tries to work up such a vocabulary he makes a fool of himself. We don't *want* works of literature to be criticizable within a terminology we already know; we want both those works and criticism of them to give us *new* terminologies. By 'literature', then, I shall mean the areas of culture which, quite self-consciously, forego agreement on an encompassing critical vocabulary, and thus forego argumentation.

Though obviously crude, this way of separating science and literature has at least the merit of focusing attention on a distinction which is relevant to both idealism and textualism—the distinction between finding out whether a proposition is true and finding out whether a vocabulary is good. Let me call "romanticism" the thesis that what is most important for human life is not what propositions we believe but what vocabulary we use. Then I can say that romanticism is what unites metaphysical idealism and literary textualism. Both, as I said earlier, remind us that scientists do not bring a naked eye to nature, that the propositions of science are not simple transcriptions of what is present to the senses. Both draw the corollary that the current scientific vocabulary is one vocabulary among others, and that there is no need to give it primacy, nor to reduce other vocabularies to it. Both see the scientists' claim to discover the ways things really are as needing qualification, as a pretension which needs to be curbed. The scientist, they say, is discovering "merely scientific" or "merely empirical" or "merely phenomenal" or "merely positive" or "merely technical" truths. Such dismissive epithets express the suspicion that the scientist merely goes through mechanical procedures, checking off the truth-value of propositions—behaving like a glorified stock-room clerk inventorying the universe in accord with a predetermined scheme. The sense that science is banausic, except perhaps in those rare creative moments when a Galileo or a Darwin suddenly imposes a new scheme, is the essence of romanticism. Romanticism inverts the values which, in the third *Critique*, Kant assigned to the determinate and the reflective judgment. It sees the determinate judgment—the activity which ticks off instances of concepts by invoking common, public criteria—as producing merely *agreement*. Kant thought "knowledge," the name for the result of such activity, was a term of praise. Romanticism accepts Kant's point that objectivity is conformity to rule, but changes the emphasis, so that objectivity becomes *mere* conformity to rule, merely going along with the crowd, merely consensus. By contrast, romanticism sees the reflective judgment—the activity of operating without rules, of searching for concepts under which to group particulars (or, by extension, of constructing new concepts which are "transgressive" in that they do not fit under any of the old rules)—as what really matters. Kant, in saying that aesthetic judgment is noncognitive because it cannot be brought under rules, is assigning it a second-best status—the status which the scientific culture has always assigned to the literary culture. Romanticism, on the other hand, when it says that science is *merely* cognitive, is trying to turn the tables.

I can sum up by saying that post-Kantian metaphysical idealism was a specifically philosophical form of romanticism whereas textualism is a specifically post-philosophical form. In the next section I shall argue that philosophy and idealism rose and fell together. In section III I shall discuss the relation between textualism as post-philosophical romanticism and pragmatism, arguing that pragmatism is, to speak oxymoronically, post-philosophical philosophy. Finally, in section IV, I shall take up some criticisms which apply equally to textualism and to pragmatism.

II

Maurice Mandelbaum, in his *History, Man and Reason*, tells us that in the post-Enlightenment period "there arose significantly new forms of thought and standards for evaluation" and that throughout this period of about one hundred years—roughly, though not exactly, coincident with the nineteenth century—"there existed only two main streams of philosophic thought, each of which possessed a relatively high degree of continuity . . . metaphysical idealism and positivism." He defines metaphysical idealism as the view that

> within natural human experience one can find the clue to an understanding of the ultimate nature of reality, and this clue is revealed through those traits which distinguish man as a spiritual being.[1]

As Mandelbaum stresses, to take this seriously one has to think that there might *be* such a thing as "the ultimate nature of reality." One also has to think that science might not be the last word on the

subject, even though one does remain "within natural human experience" and does not look for supernatural sources of information. Why
would anyone hold either of these beliefs? Why did anyone think that
in addition to science there might also be something called "metaphysics"?

If you just spring the question "what is the ultimate nature of reality?" on somebody, he won't know where to begin. One needs a
sense of what some possible answers might be. The Enlightenment
had had a simple contrast with which to explain and give sense to the
question, the contrast between the world-picture offered by Aquinas
and Dante and that offered by Newton and Lavoisier. The one was
said to have been produced by superstition and the other by reason.
Nobody before Kant suggested that there could be a discipline called
"philosophy" which might offer you a third alternative. The so-called
"modern philosophers" prior to Kant were not doing something
clearly distinguishable from science. Some were psychologists in the
manner of Locke and Hume—providing what Kant called a "physiology of the human understanding" in the hope of doing for inner
space what Newton had done for outer space, giving a quasi-mechan-
ical account of the way in which our minds worked. But this was a matter of extending the scientific world-picture, rather than of criticizing
or grounding or replacing it. Others were scientific apologists for the
religious tradition in the manner of Leibniz, trying to smuggle enough
Aristotelian vocabulary back into Cartesian science to have things
both ways. But this was, once again, not a matter of criticizing or
grounding or replacing science but of tinkering with it in the hope of
squeezing in God, Freedom, and Immortality. Locke's and Leibniz's
conceptions of science were like those of, respectively, B. F. Skinner,
and LeComte de Noüy. Neither thought that some autonomous discipline, distinct in subject and method from natural science, might demonstrate the truth of a third view about the ultimate nature of reality.

In order to have such a notion one needs an idea of what such an
alternative view might be. Idealism—the view that the ultimate nature of reality is "revealed through those traits which distinguish
man as a spiritual being" is not just *a* possibility; it is pretty much
the *only* possibility which has ever been offered. But, in Berkeley
and Kant, idealism becomes something very different from the tradition which starts with Anaxagoras and runs through Plato and various forms of Platonism. None of these various suggestions that the
material world is unreal were presented as the outcome of scientific
argumentation—as a solution to an outstanding scientific difficulty.
For Berkeley, however, this is just what idealism was—a neat way of

coping with the difficulty which had been created by the new and "scientific" doctrine that the mind perceives only its own ideas. As George Pitcher says, the "beautiful and extravagant" Berkeleian philosophy has among its roots a "sober, well-informed account of . . . sense-perception."[2] The problem which Berkeley confronted was raised by the fact that, as Hume put it "'tis universally allowed by philosophers that nothing is ever really present with the mind but its perceptions or impressions and ideas, and that external objects become known to us only by those perceptions they occasion."[3] The "philosophers" in question were people like Locke, who were doing what we would call psychology, and especially perceptual psychology. Berkeley took himself out of the running as a psychologist by proposing too "quick and dirty" a solution to the puzzle about which ideas resembled their objects—namely, that *nothing* can be like an idea except an idea." This struck his contemporaries as the panpsychist suggestion that all matter is alive strikes present-day evolutionary biologists. The problem is not that it's a silly idea, but that it is so abstract and empty that it simply doesn't *help*.

Berkeley, however, is important for an understanding of why idealism was taken seriously, even though his own version is only a curiosity. Berkeley's idealism is not Platonic other-worldliness but a sober answer to a scientific question, Locke's question about the resemblance of ideas to their objects. Hume proceeded to generalize Locke's question into the question of whether we were entitled to speak of "objects" at all, and this enabled Kant to change a scientific question about psychophysiological mechanisms into a question about the legitimacy of science itself. He did so by making three points:

(a) One can solve the problem of the nature of scientific truth only by saying that science corresponds to a world which is transcendentally idea, made rather than found

(b) One can explain the contrast between making and finding, transcendental ideality and transcendental reality, only by contrasting the use of *ideas* to *know* with the use of the *will* to *act*—science with morality

(c) Transcendental philosophy, as the discipline which can rise above both science and morality to allot their respective spheres, replaces science as the discipline which tells us about the ultimate nature of reality.

Kant thus finessed the Enlightenment notion of an opposition between science and religion, reason and superstition, by taking over an unsolved scientific problem—the nature of knowledge—and transmuting it into an issue about the *possibility* of knowledge. This transmutation was made possible by taking seriously Berkeley's suggestion that "nothing can be like an idea except an idea," while revising it to read "no idea can be true of anything except a world made of ideas." But this latter notion of a world made of ideas needs to be backed up with an explanation of whose ideas these are. Since Berkeley's God was not available to Kant, he had to create the transcendental ego to do the job. As Kant's successors were quick to point out, the only way we could make sense of the transcendental ego was to identify it with the thinkable but unknowable self who is a moral agent—the autonomous noumenal self.

At this point idealism ceases to be a mere intellectual curiosity. For now it offers us not *just* Berkeley's gimmicky *ad hoc* solution to the problem of the relation between sensations and external objects, but a solution to the problem of how to fit art, religion, and morality into the Galilean world-picture. Once one could see a solution to this slightly shamefaced spiritual difficulty as a corollary to the solution of a perfectly respectable scientific problem, one could see the discipline which offered both solutions as *replacing science*, and making respectable Rousseau's distrust of the Enlightenment. Philosophy thus gets to be both a *science* (for has it not solved a problem science was unable to solve?) and a way to regain what science had seemed to take away—morality and religion. Morality and religion could now be encompassed within the bounds of reason alone. For reason had been discovered by philosophy to be wider than science, and philosophy had thus shown itself to be a *super*-science.

So far I have been arguing that transcendental idealism was necessary to make sense of the notion that a discipline called "philosophy" could transcend both religion and science by giving you a third, decisive view about the ultimate nature of reality. The Kantian system, on my account, began by borrowing the prestige of science through its solution to a scientific problem, and then proceeded to demote science to the second rank of cultural activities. It promoted philosophy to the first rank by showing you how to have the best of both religion and science, while looking down on both. Idealism seemed a scientific thesis—a thesis for which one might actually *argue*—because of what Berkeley and Kant had in common, namely, a concern with Locke's psychological problem about the relation of sensations to their objects. Philosophy came to look like a super-science because of what Kant and Hegel had in common—namely, a solution to the problem of the relation of science to art, morality, and religion. One side of transcendental idealism is turned toward Newton, Locke, the way of ideas, and the problem of perception. The other faces toward Schiller, Hegel, and romanticism. This ambivalence helps explain why, in the first decades of the nineteenth century, transcendental idealism could look like demonstrable truth. It also helps explain why transcendental philosophy could seem as dramatically new and permanent an addition to culture as Newtonian science had seemed a century earlier. Both illusions were possible only because the prestige of one side of Kant was borrowed by the other side. The argumentative character which the first *Critique* shares with Newton's *Principia* and Locke's *Essay* created an aura of *Wissenschaftlichkeit* which stretched over the second and third *Critiques*, and even over Fichte.

The next step in the development of idealism, however, was the beginning of the end for both idealism and philosophy. Hegel decided that philosophy should be speculative rather than merely reflective, changed the name of the Transcendental Ego to "the Idea," and began treating the vocabulary of Galilean science as simply one among dozens of others in which the Idea chose to describe itself. If Kant had survived to read the *Phenomenology* he would have realized that philosophy had only managed to stay on the secure path of a science for about twenty-five years. Hegel kept the name of "science" without the distinctive mark of science—willingness to accept a neutral vocabulary in which to state problems, and thereby make argumentation possible. Under cover of Kant's invention, a new superscience called "philosophy," Hegel invented a literary genre which lacked any trace of argumentation, but which obsessively captioned itself *System der Wissenschaft* or *Wissenschaft der Logik*, or *Encyklopädie der philosophischen Wissenschaften*.

By the time of Marx and Kierkegaard, everybody was saying that the emperor had no clothes—that whatever idealism might be it was not a demonstrable, quasi-scientific thesis. By the end of the century (the time of Green and Royce) idealism had been trimmed back to its Fichtean form—an assemblage of dusty Kantian arguments about the relation between sensation and judgment, combined with intense moral earnestness. But what Fichte had been certain was both demonstrable truth and the beginning of a new era in human history, Green and Royce disconsolately knew to be merely the opinion of a group of professors. By the end of the century the word 'philosophy' had become what it remains today—merely the name, like the words 'classics' and 'psychology', for an academic department where memories of youthful hope are cherished, and wistful yearnings for recapturing past glories survive. We philosophy professors stand to Kant and Fichte as our colleagues in classics stand to Scaliger and Erasmus, or our colleagues in psychology to Bain and Spencer. Philosophy is an autonomous academic discipline with pretensions to be architectonic for culture as a whole not because we can justify either the autonomy or the pretension, but because the German idealists told us that such a discipline was the hope of mankind. But now that idealism is no longer *anybody's* opinion, now that realism-vs.-idealism is something one learns about only in history books, philosophers have lost the conviction that they can tell one about the ultimate nature of reality, or of anything else. They vaguely feel that it is their birthright to preside over the rest of culture, but they cannot figure out how to justify their claim. If I am right in my historical account, philosophers will not regain their old position unless they can once again offer a view about the ultimate nature of reality to compete with that of science. Since idealism is the only interesting suggestion along these lines they have come up with, only if they can resurrect idealism will the rest of culture take their pretensions seriously. The one event seems as unlikely as the other.

III

What survived from the disappearance of metaphysical idealism as a scientific, arguable thesis was, simply, romanticism. In section I, I defined 'romanticism' as the thesis that the one thing needful was to discover not which propositions are true but rather what vocabulary we should use. This may sound both vague and innocuous, but I think that it is the best formula to express the sense of liberation from science which was Hegel's chief legacy to the nineteenth century. Hegel left Kant's ideal of philosophy-as-science a shambles, but he did, as I have said, create a new literary genre, a genre which exhibited the relativity of significance to choice of vocabulary, the bewildering variety of vocabularies from which we can choose, and the intrinsic instability of each. Hegel made unforgettably clear the deep self-certainty given by each achievement of a new vocabulary, each new genre, each new style, each new dialectical synthesis—the sense that now, at last, for the first time, we have grasped things as they truly are. He also made unforgettably clear why such certainty lasts but a moment. He showed how the passion which sweeps through each generation serves the cunning of reason, providing the impulse which drives that generation to self-immolation and transformation. He writes in that tone of belatedness and irony which is characteristic of the literary culture of the present day.

Hegel's romantic description of how thought works is appropriate for post-Hegelian politics and literature and almost entirely inappropriate for science. One can respond to this difference by saying "So much the worse for Hegel," or by saying "So much the worse for science." The choice between those responses is a choice between Snow's "two cultures" (and between "analytic" and "Continental" philosophy, which are, so to speak, the public relations agencies for those two cultures). From Hegel on, intellectuals who wished to transform the world or themselves, who wished for more than science could give, felt entitled simply to *forget* about science. Hegel had put the study of nature in its place—a relatively low one. Hegel had also shown that there can be a kind of rationality without argumentation, a rationality which works outside the bounds of what Kuhn calls a "disciplinary matrix," in an ecstasy of spiritual freedom. Reason cunningly employed Hegel, contrary to his own intentions, to write the charter of our modern literary culture. This is the culture which claims to have taken over and reshaped whatever is worth keeping in science, philosophy, and religion—looking down on all three from a higher standpoint. It claims to be the guardian of the public weal—Coleridge's "clerisy of the nation." This culture stretches from Carlyle to Isiah Berlin, from Matthew Arnold to Lionel Trilling, from Heine to Sartre, from Baudelaire to Nabokov, from Dostoievsky to Doris Lessing, from Emerson to Harold Bloom. Its luxuriant complexity cannot be conveyed simply by conjoining words like 'poetry', 'the novel', and 'literary criticism'. This culture is a phenomenon the Enlightenment could not have anticipated. Kant has no place for it in his threefold division of possible human activities into scientific cognition, moral action, and the free play of the cognitive faculties in aesthetic enjoyment. But it is as if Hegel knew all about this culture before its birth.

I would claim, then, that the principal legacy of metaphysical idealism is the ability of the literary culture to stand apart from science, to assert its spiritual superiority to science, to claim to embody what is most important for human beings. Kant's suggestion that using the vocabulary of *Verstand*, of science, was simply *one* of the good things human beings could do, was a first and absolutely crucial step in making a secular but nonscientific culture respectable. Hegel's inadvertent exemplification of what such a culture could offer—namely, the historical sense of the relativity of principles and vocabularies to a place and time, the romantic sense that everything can be changed by talking in new terms—was the second, no less necessary step. The romanticism which Hegel brought to philosophy reinforced the hope that literature might be the successor subject to philosophy—that what the philosophers had been seeking, the inmost secrets of the spirit, were to be discovered by the new literary genres which were emerging.

There was, however, a third step in the process of establishing the autonomy and supremacy of the literary culture. This was the step taken by Nietzsche and William James. Their contribution was to replace romanticism by pragmatism. Instead of saying that the discovery of vocabularies could bring hidden secrets to light, they said that new ways of speaking could help get us what we want. Instead of hinting that literature might succeed philosophy as discoverer of ultimate reality, they gave up the notion of truth as a correspondence to reality. Nietzsche and James said, in different tones of voice, that philosophy *itself* had only the status which Kant and Fichte had assigned to science—the creation of useful or comforting pictures. Nietzsche and James interpreted metaphysical idealism, and, more generally, the metaphysical urge to say something about "the ultimate nature of reality," in psychological terms. Marx, of course, had already done this, but unlike Marx, James and Nietzsche did not attempt to formulate a new philosophical position from which to look down on idealism. Instead, they self-consciously abandoned the search for an Archimedean point from which to survey culture. They abandoned the notion of philosophy as super-science. They applied Kant's and Hegel's metaphors of making (as opposed to traditional realist metaphors of finding) not only to Kant and Hegel but to *themselves*. As Nietzsche said, they were the first generation not to believe that they had the truth. So they were content to have *no* answer to the question "Where do you stand when you say all these terrible things about other people?" They were content to take the halo off words like 'truth' and 'science' and 'knowledge' and 'reality', rather than offering a view about the nature of the things named by these words.

This replacement of romanticism by pragmatism within philosophy was paralleled by a change in the literary culture's self-conception. The great figures of that culture in our century—the great "modernists," if you like—have tried to show what our lives might be like if we had no hope of what Nietzsche called "metaphysical comfort." The movement I am calling "textualism" stands to pragmatism and to this body of literature as the nineteenth-century attempt to make literature a discoverer of ultimate truth stood to metaphysical idealism and to Romantic poetry. I think we shall best understand the role of textualism within our culture if we see it as an attempt to think through a thorough-going pragmatism, a thorough-going abandonment of the notion of *discovering the truth* which is common to theology and science.

M. H. Abrams, in an essay about what he calls "Newreading" and I am calling "textualism," opposes it to the traditional "humanistic" conception. He states that conception as follows:

> the author actualizes and records in words what he undertakes to signify of human beings and actions about matters of human concern, addressing himself to those readers who are competent to understand what he has written. The reader sets himself to make out what the author has designed and signified, through putting into play a linguistic and literary expertise that he shares with the author. By approximating what the author undertook to signify the reader understands what the language of the work means.[4]

The textualist conception of criticism, however, brushes aside what the author undertook to signify and takes one or the other of two quite different tacks. The first tack is, to quote Edward Said, to treat the text

> as working alone within itself, as containing a privileged, or, if not privileged, then unexamined and a priori, principle of internal coherence; on the other hand, the text is considered as in itself a sufficient cause for certain very precise effects it has on a (presumed) ideal reader.[5]

Alternatively, however, the textualist may brush aside the notion of the text as machine which operates quite independently of its creator, and offer what Bloom calls a "strong misreading." The critic asks neither the author nor the text about their intentions but simply beats the text into a shape which will serve his own purpose. He makes the text refer to whatever is relevant to that purpose. He does this by imposing a vocabulary—a "grid," in Foucault's terminology—on the text which may have nothing to do with any vocabulary used in the text or by its author, and seeing what happens. The model here is not the curious collector of clever gadgets taking them apart to see what makes them work and carefully ignoring any extrinsic end they may have, but the psychoanalyst blithely interpreting a dream or a joke as a symptom of homicidal mania.

It is important for an understanding of textualism to see both the similarities and the differences between these two models of criticism. The chief similarity is that both start from the pragmatist refusal to think of truth as correspondence to reality. The kind of textualist who claims to have gotten the secret of the text, to have broken its code, prides himself on not being distracted by anything which the text might previously have been thought to be about or anything its author says about it. The strong misreader, like Foucault or Bloom, prides himself on the same thing, on being able to get more out of the text than its author or its intended audience could possibly have found there. Both break with the realism illustrated by the passage I have cited from Abrams. But they differ in that the first kind of critic is only a half-hearted pragmatist. He thinks that there really is a secret code and that once it's discovered we shall have gotten the text right. He believes that criticism is discovery rather than creation. The strong misreader doesn't care about the distinction between discovery and creation, finding and making. He doesn't think this is a useful distinction, any more than Nietzsche or James did. He is in it for what he can get out of it, not for the satisfaction of getting something right.

I can restate this contrast in another way which may make somewhat clearer what I have in mind. Abrams's "humanistic" critic thinks that there is a large, overarching, communal vocabulary in which one can describe what various works of literature are about. The first sort of textualist—the weak textualist—thinks that each work has its own vocabulary, its own secret code, which may not be commensurable with that of any other. The second sort of textualist—the strong textualist—has his own vocabulary and doesn't worry about whether anybody shares it. On the account I am offering, it is the strong textualist who is the true heir of Nietzsche and James, and thus of Kant and Hegel. The weak textualist—the decoder—is just one more victim of realism, of the "metaphysics of presence." He thinks that if he stays within the boundaries of a text, takes it apart, and shows how it works, then he will have "escaped the sovereignty of the signifier," broken with the myth of language as mirror of reality, and so on. But in fact he is just doing his best to imitate science—he wants a *method* of criticism, and he wants everybody to agree that he has cracked the code. He wants all the comforts of consensus, even if only the consensus of readers of the literary quarterlies, just as the microbiologist wants the comfort of consensus, if only that of the other three hundred microbiologists who understand his jargon and care about his problem. The strong textualist is trying to live without that comfort. He recognizes what Nietzsche and James recognized, that the idea of *method* presupposes that of a *privileged vocabulary*, the vocabulary which gets to the essence of the object, the one which expresses the properties which it has in itself as opposed to those which we read into it. Nietzsche and James said that the notion of such a vocabulary was a myth—that even in science, not to mention philosophy, we simply cast around for a vocabulary which lets us get what we want.

I can summarize what I've been saying as follows. Metaphysical idealism was a momentary, though important, stage in the emergence of romanticism. The notion that philosophy might replace science as a secular substitute for religion was a momentary, though important, stage in the replacement of science by literature as the presiding cultural discipline. Romanticism was *aufgehoben* in pragmatism, the claim that the significance of new vocabularies was not their ability to decode but their mere utility. Pragmatism is the philosophical counterpart of literary modernism, the kind of literature which prides itself on its autonomy and novelty rather than its truthfulness to experience or its discovery of pre-existing significance. Strong textualism draws the moral of modernist literature and thus creates genuinely modernist criticism.

This summary puts me in a position to return to the somewhat artificial parallel I drew at the beginning of this paper — between the claim that there are only ideas and the claim that there are only texts. The only textualists who (unlike Derrida, its author) take seriously the latter, metaphysical-sounding sort of claim, are the weak ones — the critics who think that they have now found the true method for analyzing literary works because they have now found the fundamental problematic with which these works deal. This sort of claim gets made because such critics have not grasped that, from a full-fledged pragmatist point of view, there is no interesting difference between tables and texts, between protons and poems. To a pragmatist, these are *all* just permanent possibilities for use, and thus for redescription, reinterpretation, manipulation. But the weak textualist thinks, with Dilthey and Gadamer, that there is a great difference between what scientists do and what critics do.[6] He thinks that the fact that the former often agree and the latter usually don't shows something about the natures of their respective subject-matters, or about the special epistemological difficulties encountered by their respective methods. The strong textualist simply asks himself the same question about a text which the engineer or the physicist asks himself about a puzzling physical object: how shall I describe this in order to get it to do what I want? Occasionally a great physicist or a great critic comes along and gives us a new vocabulary which enables us to do a lot of new and marvelous things. Then we may exclaim that we have now found out the true nature of matter, or poetry, or whatever. But Hegel's ghost, embodied in Kuhn's romantic philosophy of science or Bloom's philosophy of romantic poetry, reminds us that vocabularies are as mortal as men. The pragmatist reminds us that a new and useful vocabulary is just *that*, not a sudden unmediated vision of things or texts as they are.

As usual with pithy little formulae, the Derridean claim that "There is nothing outside the text" is right about what it implicitly denies and wrong about what it explicitly asserts. The *only* force of saying that texts do not refer to nontexts is just the old pragmatist chestnut that any specification of a referent is going to be in some vocabulary. Thus one is really comparing two descriptions of a thing rather than a description with the thing-in-itself. This chestnut, in turn, is just an expanded form of Kant's slogan that "Intuitions without concepts are blind," which, in turn, was just a sophisticated re-statement of Berkeley's ingenuous remark that "nothing can be like an idea except an idea." These are all merely misleading ways of say-ing that we shall not see reality plain, unmasked, naked to our gaze. Textualism has nothing to add to this claim except a new misleading image—the image of the world as consisting of everything written in all the vocabularies used so far. The practices of the textualists have nothing to add save some splendid examples of the fact that the au-thor of a text did not know a vocabulary in which his text can use-fully be described. But this insight—that a person's own vocabulary of self-description is not necessarily the one which helps us understand him—does not need any metaphysical or epistemological or semantic back-up. It is the sort of claim which becomes convincing only through the accumulation of examples of the practices it inspires. Strong textualists like Bloom and Foucault are busy providing us with such examples.

I conclude, therefore, that textualism has nothing to add to ro-manticism and pragmatism save instances of what can be achieved once one stops being bothered by realistic questions such as "Is that what the text really *says*?" or "How could one *argue* that that is what the poem is really *about*?" or "How are we to distinguish between what is in the text from what the critic is imposing upon it?" The claim that the world is nothing but texts is simply the same sort of light-hearted extravagance as the claim that it is nothing but matter in motion, or a permanent possibility of sensation, or the sensible material of our duty. Taken in a strong and ironic sense, the claim that everything is texts can be read as saying: "It makes as much sense to say that atoms are simply Democritean texts as to say that Democritus is merely a collection of atoms. That is because both slo-gans are attempts to give one vocabulary a privileged status, and are therefore equally silly." Taken in a weakly literal-minded sense, how-ever, this claim is just one more metaphysical thesis. There are, alas, people nowadays who owlishly inform us "philosophy has *proved*" that language does not refer to anything nonlinguistic, and thus that everything one can talk about is a text. This claim is on a par with the claim that Kant proved that we cannot know about things-in-themselves. Both claims rest on a phony contrast between some sort of nondiscursive unmediated vision of the real and the way we actually talk and think. Both falsely infer from "We can't think without concepts, or talk without words" to "We can't think or talk except about what has been created by our thought or talk."

The *weakest* way to defend the plausible claim that literature has now displaced religion, science, and philosophy as the presiding discipline of our culture is by looking for a philosophical foundation for the practises of contemporary criticism.[7] That would be like defending Galilean science by claiming that it can be found in the Scriptures, or defending transcendental idealism as the latest result of physiological research. It would be acknowledging the authority of a deposed monarch in order to buttress the claims of a usurper. The claims of a usurping discipline to preside over the rest of culture can only be defended by an exhibition of its ability to put the other disciplines in their places. This is what the literary culture has been doing recently, with great success. It is what science did when it displaced religion and what idealist philosophy did when it briefly displaced science. Science did not *demonstrate* that religion was false, nor philosophy that science was merely phenomenal, nor can modernist literature or textualist criticism *demonstrate* that the "metaphysics of presence" is an outdated genre. But each in turn has managed, without argument, to make its point.

IV

In saying that textualism adds nothing save an extra metaphor to the romanticism of Hegel and the pragmatism of James and Nietzsche, I am agreeing with critics of textualism, like Gerald Graff. Graff rightly says that current fashions in literary criticism continue to develop the themes already stated in New Criticism—"modernist assumptions about language, knowledge, and experience"[8] —assumptions he opposes to the older view that literature can "contribute to man's understanding of how things really are, not merely how they appear to our consciousness."[9] He is also right in saying that only rarely is any argument given to support these assumptions. But I think he is wrong in saying that

> from the thesis that language cannot correspond to reality, it is a short
> step to the current revisionist mode of interpretation that specializes in
> reading all literary works as commentaries on their own epistemological
> problematics.[10]

It is in fact a rather long step, and a step backward. The tendency Graff speaks of is real enough, but it is a tendency to think that literature can take the place of philosophy by *mimicking* philosophy —by being, of all things, *epistemological*. Epistemology still looks classy to weak textualists. They think that by viewing a poet as having an epistemology they are paying him a compliment. They even think that in criticizing his theory of knowledge they are being something more than a mere critic—being, in fact, a philosopher. Thus conquering warriors might mistakenly think to impress the populace by wrapping themselves in shabby togas stripped from the local senators. Graff and others who have pointed to the weirdly solemn pretentiousness of much recent textualist criticism are right, I think, in claiming that such critics want to have the supposed prestige of philosophy without the necessity of offering arguments.

Where I chiefly differ from Graff, however, is in his claim that

> writing, to be effective, has to spring from a coherent and convincing philosophy of life—or at least of that part of life with which the writer deals. There seems no way of getting away from the fact that literature must have an ideology—even if this ideology is one that calls all ideologies into question. The very act of denying all "naive" realisms presupposes an objective standpoint.[11]

This seems to me wrong as a statement about effective writing. It would force one to say either that Baudelaire and Nabokov did not write effectively or that their ironism expressed a "coherent and convincing philosophy of life." Neither alternative is attractive. It also seems wrong about what is required to deny the truth of realism. One *can* do that without proposing an "objective" theory about the real nature of reality or knowledge or language. It is just not the case that one need adopt one's opponents' vocabulary or method or style in order to defeat him. Hobbes did not have theological arguments against Dante's world-picture; Kant had only a very bad scientific argument for the phenomenal character of science; Nietzsche and James did not have epistemological arguments for pragmatism. Each of these thinkers presented us with a new form of intellectual life, and asked us to compare its advantages with the old. Strong textualists are currently presenting us with such another new form of life. There is as little point in asking for epistemological arguments in its favor as in pretending that it gives us a new and better way of doing epistemology.

The serious objections to textualism, I think, are not epistemological but moral. Writers such as Lionel Trilling and M. H. Abrams would join Graff in offering such objections. Abrams sympathizes with Bloom in his protests against Derrida's and Foucault's attempt to eliminate the author of a text, and to substitute inhuman intertextuality for human influence. But he is unable to accept Bloom's self-descriptions of his books on Yeats and Stevens as "strong misreadings." He thinks Bloom often gets Yeats and Stevens right, in a good old-fashioned realist sense of "right," and he wants Bloom to admit it. He wants this, I think, because he wants Yeats and Stevens to be more than grist for their successors' mills. He thinks their moral integrity is impugned by Bloom's treatment. Further, he wants literary criticism to be a field in which one can argue, and thus one in which one is *not* free to lay down any grid one pleases in the hope of getting "creative or interesting misreadings."[12]

Though Abrams admits that what he calls "Newreading" can provide "new and exciting things to say about a literary work which has been again and again discussed," he thinks that the "choice between a radical Newreading and the old way of reading is a matter of cultural cost-accounting":

> What we lose is access to the inexhaustible variety of literature as determinably meaningful texts by, for and about human beings, as well as access to the enlightening things that have been written about such texts by the humanists and critics who were our precursors, from Aristotle to Lionel Trilling.[13]

Implicit in this remark is the moral outlook which Abrams shares with Trilling: the view that, in the end, when all the intellectuals have done all their tricks, morality remains widely shared and available to reflection—something capable of being discovered rather than created, because already implicit in the common consciousness of everyone. It is this Kantian conviction, I think, which leads Trilling to protest against one of the most distinctive features of romanticism and of our literary culture, its ability to make what Trilling called "figures" out of writers—a term which he defines as follows:

> figures—that is to say, creative spirits whose work requires an especially conscientious study because in it are to be discerned significances, even mysteries, even powers, which carry it beyond what in a loose and general sense we call literature, beyond even what we think of as very good literature, and bring it to as close an approximation of a sacred wisdom as can be achieved in our culture.[14]

Here Trilling echoes what Kant said about the "metaphysics of the schools"—about learned men who claim to know more of morality and its supposed "foundations" than the ordinary decent citizen. This is the side of Kant which is turned towards Rousseau rather than towards Hegel. It is the side which is democratic rather than elitist, which regards culture as in the service of the people (rather than, as with Hegel, conversely). Trilling and Abrams and Graff do not want there to *be* a sacred wisdom which takes precedence over the common moral consciousness. Therefore they resist the romantic attempt to make a "figure" out of a poet, and also the suggestion that a misreader has no obligation to argue with those who disagree with his reading. Because they want criticism to bring an antecedent morality to light, enlarge upon it and enrich it, they resist the suggestion that there is no common vocabulary in terms of which critics can argue with one another about how well this task has been performed.

This moral objection to textualism is also a moral objection to pragmatism's claim that all vocabularies, even that of our own liberal imagination, are temporary historical resting-places. It is also an objection to the literary culture's isolation from common human concerns. It says that people like Nietzsche, Nabokov, Bloom, and Foucault achieve their effects at a moral cost which is too much to pay. Put in the pragmatist's own preferred cost-accounting terms, it says that the stimulus to the intellectual's private moral imagination provided by his strong misreadings, by his search for sacred wisdom, is purchased at the price of his separation from his fellow-humans.[15]

I think that this moral objection states the really important issue about textualism and about pragmatism. But I have no ready way to dispose of it. I should like to do so by drawing a further distinction among strong textualists—a distinction between, for example, Bloom and Foucault. Bloom is a pragmatist in the manner of James, whereas Foucault is a pragmatist in the manner of Nietzsche. Pragmatism appears in James and Bloom as an identification with the struggles of finite men. In Foucault and Nietzsche it appears as contempt for one's own finitude, as a search for some mighty, inhuman force to which one can yield up one's identity. Bloom's way of dealing with texts preserves our sense of a common human finitude by moving back and forth between the poet and his poem. Foucault's way of dealing with texts is designed to eliminate the author—and indeed the very idea of "man"—altogether. I have no wish to defend Foucault's inhumanism, and every wish to praise Bloom's sense of our common human lot. But I do not know how to back up this preference with argument, or even with a precise account of the relevant differences. To do so would involve a full-scale discussion of the possibility of combining private fulfillment, self-realization, with public morality, a concern for justice.

Notes

1. Maurice Mandelbaum, *History, Man and Reason* (Baltimore: Johns Hopkins University Press, 1971), p. 6.

2. George Pitcher, *Berkeley* (London: Routledge, Kegan Paul, 1977), p. 4.

3. David Hume, *Treatise of Human Nature*, I, ii, 2.

4. M. H. Abrams, "How to Do Things with Texts," *Partisan Review*, 46 (1979).

5. Edward Said, "Roads Taken and Not Taken in Contemporary Criticism," *Contemporary Literature*, 17 (Summer, 1976): 337. In this article Said draws a distinction between Bloom and Foucault (and others such as Bate and Lukacs) on the one hand and textualist critics who exemplify the approach described in the passage I have quoted. This roughly parallels my distinction between strong and weak textualists, but Said puts the difference in terms of "formality vs. materiality," rather than in terms of a half-hearted and a whole-hearted pragmatism.

6. On this point, see my remarks directed at Charles Taylor's Diltheyan views in "A Reply to Dreyfus and Taylor," *The Review of Metaphysics*, 33 (1980): 36-46, and in Essay 11, below.

7. Thus when Geoffrey Hartman says, in the preface to *Deconstruction and Criticism* (New York: The Seabury Press, 1979, p. 6) that it would be fruitful for literary criticism and philosophy to interact, he strikes me as simply being courteous to a defeated foe. But perhaps he may be read simply as saying, quite rightly, that it would be useful if people who had read a lot of philosophy books would join with people who had read a lot of poetry and novels in relating these two streams of texts to one another.

8. Gerald Graff, *Literature Against Itself* (Chicago: University of Chicago Press, 1979), p. 5.

9. *Ibid.*, p. 7.

10. *Ibid.*, p. 9.

11. *Ibid.*, p. 11.

12. Cf. Abrams, "How to . . . ," pp. 584-585.

13. *Ibid.*, p. 588.

14. Lionel Trilling, "Why We Read Jane Austen," in *The Last Decade* (New York: Harcourt, Brace, Jovanovich, 1979), pp. 206-207.

15. I have discussed, inconclusively, the claim that pragmatism is morally dangerous in Essay 9, below.

9

Pragmatism, Relativism, and Irrationalism

Part I: Pragmatism

"Pragmatism" is a vague, ambiguous, and overworked word. Nevertheless, it names the chief glory of our country's intellectual tradition. No other American writers have offered so radical a suggestion for making our future different from our past, as have James and Dewey. At present, however, these two writers are neglected. Many philosophers think that everything important in pragmatism has been preserved and adapted to the needs of analytic philosophy. More specifically, they view pragmatism as having suggested various holistic corrections of the atomistic doctrines of the early logical empiricists. This way of looking at pragmatism is not wrong, as far as it goes. But it ignores what is most important in James and Dewey. Logical empiricism was one variety of standard, academic, neo-Kantian, epistemologically-centered philosophy. The great pragmatists should not be taken as suggesting an holistic variation of this variant, but rather as breaking with the Kantian epistemological tradition altogether. As long as we see James or Dewey as having "theories of truth" or "theories of knowledge" or "theories of morality" we shall get them wrong. We shall ignore their criticisms of the assumption that there ought to *be* theories about such matters. We shall not see how radical their thought was—how deep was their criticism of the attempt, common to Kant, Husserl, Russell, and C. I. Lewis, to make philosophy into a foundational discipline.

One symptom of this incorrect focus is a tendency to overpraise Peirce. Peirce is praised partly because he developed various logical

160

notions and various technical problems (such as the counterfactual conditional) which were taken up by the logical empiricists. But the main reason for Peirce's undeserved apotheosis is that his talk about a general theory of signs looks like an early discovery of the importance of language. For all his genius, however, Peirce never made up his mind what he wanted a general theory of signs *for*, nor what it might look like, nor what its relation to either logic or epistemology was supposed to be. His contribution to pragmatism was merely to have given it a name, and to have stimulated James. Peirce himself remained the most Kantian of thinkers—the most convinced that philosophy gave us an all-embracing ahistorical context in which every other species of discourse could be assigned its proper place and rank. It was just this Kantian assumption that there was such a context, and that epistemology or semantics could discover it, against which James and Dewey reacted. We need to focus on this reaction if we are to recapture a proper sense of their importance.

This reaction is found in other philosophers who are currently more fashionable than James or Dewey—for example, Nietzsche and Heidegger. Unlike Nietzsche and Heidegger, however, the pragmatists did not make the mistake of turning against the community which takes the natural scientist as its moral hero—the community of secular intellectuals which came to self-consciousness in the Enlightenment. James and Dewey rejected neither the Enlightenment's choice of the scientist as moral example, nor the technological civilization which science had created. They wrote, as Nietzsche and Heidegger did not, in a spirit of social hope. They asked us to liberate our new civilization by giving up the notion of "grounding" our culture, our moral lives, our politics, our religious beliefs, upon "philosophical bases." They asked us to give up the neurotic Cartesian quest for certainty which had been one result of Galileo's frightening new cosmology, the quest for "enduring spiritual values" which had been one reaction to Darwin, and the aspiration of academic philosophy to form a tribunal of pure reason which had been the neo-Kantian response to Hegelian historicism. They asked us to think of the Kantian project of grounding thought or culture in a permanent ahistorical matrix as *reactionary*. They viewed Kant's idealization of Newton, and Spencer's of Darwin, as just as silly as Plato's idealization of Pythagoras, and Aquinas' of Aristotle.

Emphasizing this message of social hope and liberation, however, makes James and Dewey sound like prophets rather than thinkers. This would be misleading. They had things to say about truth, knowledge, and morality, even though they did not have *theories* of them, in the sense of sets of answers to the textbook problems. In what follows, I shall offer three brief sloganistic characterizations of what I take to be their central doctrine.

My first characterization of pragmatism is that it is simply anti-essentialism applied to notions like "truth," "knowledge," "language," "morality," and similar objects of philosophical theorizing. Let me illustrate this by James's definition of "the true" as "what is good in the way of belief." This has struck his critics as not to the point, as unphilosophical, as like the suggestion that the essence of aspirin is that it is good for headaches. James's point, however, was that there *is* nothing deeper to be said: truth is not the sort of thing which *has* an essence. More specifically, his point was that it is no use being told that truth is "correspondence to reality." Given a language and a view of what the world is like, one can, to be sure, pair off bits of the language with bits of what one takes the world to be in such a way that the sentences one believes true have internal structures isomorphic to relations between things in the world. When we rap out routine undeliberated reports like "This is water," "That's red," "That's ugly," "That's immoral," our short categorical sentences can easily be thought of as pictures, or as symbols which fit together to make a map. Such reports do indeed pair little bits of language with little bits of the world. Once one gets to negative universal hypotheticals, and the like, such pairing will become messy and *ad hoc*, but perhaps it can be done. James's point was that carrying out this exercise will not enlighten us about why truths are good to believe, or offer any clues as to why or whether our present view of the world is, roughly, the one we should hold. Yet nobody would have asked for a "theory" of truth if they had not wanted answers to these latter questions. Those who want truth to have an essence want knowledge, or rationality, or inquiry, or the relation between thought and its object, to have an essence. Further, they want to be able to use their knowledge of such essences to criticize views they take to be false, and to point the direction of progress toward the discovery of more truths. James thinks these hopes are vain. There are no essences anywhere in the area. There is no wholesale, epistemological way to direct, or criticize, or underwrite, the course of inquiry.

Rather, the pragmatists tell us, it is the vocabulary of practise rather than of theory, of action rather than contemplation, in which one can say something useful about truth. Nobody engages in epistemology or semantics because he wants to know how "This is red" pictures the world. Rather, we want to know in what sense Pasteur's views of disease picture the world accurately and Paracelsus' inaccurately, or what exactly it is that Marx pictured more accurately than Machiavelli. But just here the vocabulary of "picturing" fails us. When we turn from individual sentences to vocabularies and theories, critical terminology naturally shifts from metaphors of isomorphism, symbolism, and mapping to talk of utility, convenience, and likelihood of getting what we want. To say that the parts of properly analyzed true sentences are arranged in a way isomorphic to the parts of the world paired with them sounds plausible if one thinks of a sentence like "Jupiter has moons." It sounds slightly less plausible for "The earth goes round the sun," less still for "There is no such thing as natural motion," and not plausible at all for "The universe is infinite." When we want to praise or blame assertions of the latter sort of sentence, we show how the decision to assert them fits into a whole complex of decisions about what terminology to use, what books to read, what projects to engage in, what life to live. In this respect they resemble such sentences as "Love is the only law" and "History is the story of class struggle." The whole vocabulary of isomorphism, picturing, and mapping is out of place here, as indeed is the notion of being true *of objects*. If we ask what objects these sentences claim to be true of, we get only unhelpful repetitions of the subject terms— "the universe," "the law," "history." Or, even less helpfully, we get talk about "the facts," or "the way the world is." The natural approach to such sentences, Dewey tells us, is not "Do they get it right?", but more like "What would it be like to believe that? What would happen if I did? What would I be committing myself to?" The vocabulary of contemplation, looking, *theoria*, deserts us just when we deal with theory rather than observation, with programming rather than input. When the contemplative mind, isolated from the stimuli of the moment, takes large views, its activity is more like deciding what to *do* than deciding that a representation is accurate. James's dictum about truth says that the vocabulary of practice is uneliminable, that no distinction of kind separates the sciences from the crafts, from moral reflection, or from art.

So a second characterization of pragmatism might go like this: there is no epistemological difference between truth about what ought to be and truth about what is, nor any metaphysical difference between facts and values, nor any methodological difference between morality and science. Even nonpragmatists think Plato was wrong to think of moral philosophy as discovering the essence of goodness, and Mill and Kant wrong in trying to reduce moral choice to rule. But every reason for saying that they were wrong is a reason for thinking the epistemological tradition wrong in looking for the essence of science, and in trying to reduce rationality to rule. For the pragmatists, the pattern of all inquiry—scientific as well as moral—is deliberation concerning the relative attractions of various concrete alternatives. The idea that in science or philosophy we can substitute "method" for deliberation between alternative results of speculation is just wishful thinking. It is like the idea that the morally wise man resolves his dilemmas by consulting his memory of the Idea of the Good, or by looking up the relevant article of the moral law. It is the myth that rationality consists in being constrained by rule. According to this Platonic myth, the life of reason is not the life of Socratic conversation but an illuminated state of consciousness in which one never needs to ask if one has exhausted the possible descriptions of, or explanations for, the situation. One simply arrives at true beliefs by obeying mechanical procedures.

Traditional, Platonic, epistemologically-centered philosophy is the search for such procedures. It is the search for a way in which one can avoid the need for conversation and deliberation and simply tick off the way things are. The idea is to acquire beliefs about interesting and important matters in a way as much like visual perception as possible—by confronting an object and responding to it as programmed. This urge to substitute *theoria* for *phronesis* is what lies behind the attempt to say that "There is no such thing as natural motion" pictures objects in the same way as does "The cat is on the mat." It also lies behind the hope that some arrangement of objects may be found which is pictured by the sentence "Love is better than hate," and the frustration which ensues when it is realized that there may be no such objects. The great fallacy of the tradition, the pragmatists tell us, is to think that the metaphors of vision, correspondence, mapping, picturing, and representation which apply to small, routine assertions will apply to large and debatable ones. This basic error begets the notion that where there are no objects to correspond to we have no hope of rationality, but only taste, passion, and will. When the pragmatist attacks the notion of truth as accuracy of representation he is thus attacking the traditional distinctions between reason and desire, reason and appetite, reason and will. For none of these distinctions make sense unless reason is thought of on the model of vision, unless we persist in what Dewey called "the spectator theory of knowledge."

The pragmatist tells us that once we get rid of this model we see that the Platonic idea of the life of reason is impossible. A life spent representing objects accurately would be spent recording the results of calculations, reasoning through sorites, calling off the observable properties of things, construing cases according to unambiguous criteria, getting things right. Within what Kuhn calls "normal science," or any similar social context, one can, indeed, live such a life. But conformity to *social* norms is not good enough for the Platonist. He wants to be constrained not merely by the disciplines of the day, but by the ahistorical and nonhuman nature of reality itself. This impulse takes two forms—the original Platonic strategy of postulating novel *objects* for treasured propositions to correspond to, and the Kantian strategy of finding *principles* which are definatory of the essence of knowledge, or representation, or morality, or rationality. But this difference is unimportant compared to the common urge to escape the vocabulary and practices of one's own time and find something ahistorical and necessary to cling to. It is the urge to answer questions like "Why believe what I take to be true?" "Why do what I take to be right?" by appealing to something *more* than the ordinary, retail, detailed, concrete reasons which have brought one to one's present view. This urge is common to nineteenth-century idealists and contemporary scientific realists, to Russell and to Husserl; it is definatory of the Western philosophical tradition, and of the culture for which that tradition speaks. James and Dewey stand with Nietzsche and Heidegger in asking us to abandon that tradition, and that culture.

Let me sum up by offering a third and final characterization of pragmatism: it is the doctrine that there are no constraints on inquiry save conversational ones—no wholesale constraints derived from the nature of the objects, or of the mind, or of language, but only those retail constraints provided by the remarks of our fellow-inquirers. The way in which the properly-programmed speaker cannot help believing that the patch before him is red has *no* analogy for the more interesting and controversial beliefs which provoke epistemological reflection. The pragmatist tells us that it is useless to hope that objects will constrain us to believe the truth about them, if only they are approached with an unclouded mental eye, or a rigorous method, or a perspicuous language. He wants us to give up the notion that God, or evolution, or some other underwriter of our present world-picture, has programmed us as machines for accurate verbal picturing, and that philosophy brings self-knowledge by letting us read our own program. The only sense in which we are constrained to truth is that, as Peirce suggested, we can make no sense of the notion that the view which can survive all objections might be false. But objections—conversational constraints—cannot be anticipated. There is no method for knowing *when* one has reached the truth, or when one is closer to it than before.

I prefer this third way of characterizing pragmatism because it seems to me to focus on a fundamental choice which confronts the reflective mind: that between accepting the contingent character of starting-points, and attempting to evade this contingency. To accept the contingency of starting-points is to accept our inheritance from, and our conversation with, our fellow-humans as our only source of guidance. To attempt to evade this contingency is to hope to become a properly-programmed machine. This was the hope which Plato thought might be fulfilled at the top of the divided line, when we passed beyond hypotheses. Christians have hoped it might be attained by becoming attuned to the voice of God in the heart, and Cartesians that it might be fulfilled by emptying the mind and seeking the indubitable. Since Kant, philosophers have hoped that it might be fulfilled by finding the a priori structure of any possible inquiry, or language, or form of social life. If we give up this hope, we shall lose what Nietzsche called "metaphysical comfort," but we may gain a renewed sense of community. Our identification with our community —our society, our political tradition, our intellectual heritage—is heightened when we see this community as *ours* rather than *nature's, shaped* rather than *found,* one among many which men have made. In the end, the pragmatists tell us, what matters is our loyalty to other human beings clinging together against the dark, not our hope of getting things right. James, in arguing against realists and idealists that "the trail of the human serpent is over all," was reminding us that our glory is in our participation in fallible and transitory human projects, not in our obedience to permanent nonhuman constraints.

Part II: Relativism

"Relativism" is the view that every belief on a certain topic, or perhaps about *any* topic, is as good as every other. No one holds this view. Except for the occasional cooperative freshman, one cannot find anybody who says that two incompatible opinions on an important topic are equally good. The philosophers who get *called* "relativists" are those who say that the grounds for choosing between such opinions are less algorithmic than had been thought. Thus one may be attacked as a relativist for holding that familiarity of terminology is a criterion of theory-choice in physical science, or that coherence with the institutions of the surviving parliamentary democracies is a criterion in social philosophy. When such criteria are invoked, critics say that the resulting philosophical position assumes an unjustified primacy for "our conceptual framework," or our purposes, or our institutions. The position in question is criticized for not having done what philosophers are employed to do: explain why our framework, or culture, or interests, or language, or whatever, is at last on the right track—in touch with physical reality, or the moral law, or the real numbers, or some other sort of object patiently waiting about to be copied. So the real issue is not between people who think one view as good as another and people who do not. It is between those who think our culture, or purpose, or intuitions cannot be supported except conversationally, and people who still hope for other sorts of support.

If there *were* any relativists, they would, of course, be easy to refute. One would merely use some variant of the self-referential arguments Socrates used against Protagoras. But such neat little dialectical strategies only work against lightly-sketched fictional characters. The relativist who says that we can break ties among serious and incompatible candidates for belief only by "nonrational" or "noncognitive" considerations is just one of the Platonist or Kantian philosopher's imaginary playmates, inhabiting the same realm of fantasy as the solipsist, the skeptic, and the moral nihilist. Disillusioned, or whimsical, Platonists and Kantians occasionally play at being one or another of these characters. But when they do they are never offering relativism or skepticism or nihilism as a serious suggestion about how we might do things differently. These positions are adopted to make *philosophical* points—that is, moves in a game played with fictitious opponents, rather than fellow-participants in a common project.

The association of pragmatism with relativism is a result of a confusion between the pragmatist's attitude toward *philosophical* theories with his attitude towards *real* theories. James and Dewey are, to be sure, metaphilosophical relativists, in a certain limited sense. Namely: they think there is no way to choose, and no point in choosing, between incompatible philosophical theories of the typical Platonic or Kantian type. Such theories are attempts to ground some element of our practices on something external to these practices. Pragmatists think that any such philosophical grounding is, apart from elegance of execution, pretty much as good or as bad as the practice it purports to ground. They regard the project of grounding as a wheel that plays no part in the mechanism. In this, I think, they are quite right. No sooner does one discover the categories of the pure understanding for a Newtonian age than somebody draws up another list that would do nicely for an Aristotelian or an Einsteinian one. No sooner does one draw up a categorical imperative for Christians than somebody draws up one which works for cannibals. No sooner does one develop an evolutionary epistemology which explains why our science is so good than somebody writes a science-fiction story about bug-eyed and monstrous evolutionary epistemologists praising bug-eyed and monstrous scientists for the survival value of their monstrous theories. The reason this game is so easy to play is that none of these philosophical theories have to do much hard work. The real work has been done by the scientists who developed the explanatory theories by patience and genius, or the societies which developed the moralities and institutions in struggle and pain. All the Platonic or Kantian philosopher does is to take the finished first-level product, jack it up a few levels of abstraction, invent a metaphysical or epistemological or semantical vocabulary into which to translate it, and announce that he has *grounded* it.

"Relativism" only seems to refer to a disturbing view, worthy of being refuted, if it concerns *real* theories, not just philosophical theories. Nobody really cares if there are incompatible alternative formulations of a categorical imperative, or incompatible sets of categories of the pure understanding. We *do* care about alternative, concrete, detailed cosmologies, or alternative concrete, detailed proposals for political change. When such an alternative is proposed, we debate it, not in terms of categories or principles but in terms of the various concrete advantages and disadvantages it has. The reason relativism is talked about so much among Platonic and Kantian philosophers is that they think being relativistic about philosophical theories—attempts to "ground" first-level theories—leads to being relativistic about the first-level theories themselves. If anyone really believed that the worth of a theory depends upon the worth of its philosophical grounding, then indeed they would be dubious about physics, or democracy, until relativism in respect to philosophical theories had been overcome. Fortunately, almost nobody believes anything of the sort.

What people do believe is that it would be good to hook up our views about democracy, mathematics, physics, God, and everything else, into a coherent story about how everything hangs together. Getting such a synoptic view often does require us to change radically our views on particular subjects. But this holistic process of readjustment is just muddling through on a large scale. It has nothing to do with the Platonic-Kantian notion of grounding. That notion involves finding constraints, demonstrating necessities, finding immutable principles to which to subordinate oneself. When it turns out that suggested constraints, necessities, and principles are as plentiful as blackberries, nothing changes except the attitude of the rest of culture towards the philosophers. Since the time of Kant, it has become more and more apparent to nonphilosophers that a really professional philosopher can supply a philosophical foundation for just about anything. This is one reason why philosophers have, in the course of our century, become increasingly isolated from the rest of culture. Our proposals to guarantee this and clarify that have come to strike our fellow-intellectuals as merely comic.

Part III: Irrationalism

My discussion of relativism may seem to have ducked the real issues. Perhaps nobody is a relativist. Perhaps "relativism" is *not* the right name for what so many philosophers find so offensive in pragmatism. But surely there *is* an important issue around somewhere. There is indeed an issue, but it is not easily stated, nor easily made amenable to argument. I shall try to bring it into focus by developing it in two different contexts, one microcosmic and the other macrocosmic. The microcosmic issue concerns philosophy in one of its most parochial senses—namely, the activities of the American Philosophical Association. Our Association has traditionally been agitated by the question of whether we should be free-wheeling and edifying, or argumentative and professional. For my purposes, this boils down to an issue about whether we can be pragmatists and still be professionals. The macrocosmic issue concerns philosophy in the widest sense—the attempt to make everything hang together. This is the issue between Socrates on the one hand and the tyrants on the other—the issue between lovers of conversation and lovers of self-deceptive rhetoric. For my purposes, it is the issue about whether we can be pragmatists without betraying Socrates, without falling into irrationalism.

I discuss the unimportant microcosmic issue about professionalism first because it is sometimes confused with the important issue about irrationalism, and because it helps focus that latter issue. The question of whether philosophy professors should edify agitated our Association in its early decades. James thought they should, and was dubious about the growing professionalization of the discipline. Arthur Lovejoy, the great opponent of pragmatism, saw professionalization as an unmixed blessing. Echoing what was being said simultaneously by Russell in England and by Husserl in Germany, Lovejoy urged the sixteenth annual meeting of the APA to aim at making philosophy into a science. He wanted the APA to organize its program into well-structured controversies on sharply defined problems, so that at the end of each convention it would be agreed who had won.[1] Lovejoy insisted that philosophy could either be edifying and visionary *or* could produce "objective, verifiable, and clearly communicable truths," but not both. James would have agreed. He too thought that one could *not* be both a pragmatist and a professional. James, however, saw professionalization as a failure of nerve rather than as a triumph of rationality. He thought that the activity of making things hang together was *not* likely to produce "objective, verifiable, and clearly communicable truths," and that this did not greatly matter.

Lovejoy, of course, won this battle. If one shares his conviction that philosophers should be as much like scientists as possible, then one will be pleased at the outcome. If one does not, one will contemplate the APA in its seventy-sixth year mindful of Goethe's maxim that one should be careful what one wishes for when one is young, for one will get it when one is old. Which attitude one takes will depend upon whether one sees the problems we discuss today as permanent problems for human thought, continuous with those discussed by Plato, Kant, and Lovejoy—or as modern attempts to breathe life into dead issues. On the Lovejoyan account, the gap between philosophers and the rest of high culture is of the same sort as the gap between physicists and laymen. The gap is not created by the artificiality of the problems being discussed, but by the development of technical and precise ways of dealing with real problems. If one shares the pragmatists' anti-essentialism, however, one will tend to see the problems about which philosophers are now offering "objective, verifiable, and clearly communicable" solutions as historical relics, left over from the Enlightenment's misguided search for the hidden essences of knowledge and morality. This is the point of view adopted by many of our fellow-intellectuals, who see us philosophy professors as caught in a time-warp, trying to live the Enlightenment over again.

I have reminded you of the parochial issue about professionalization not in order to persuade you to one side or the other, but rather to exhibit the source of the anti-pragmatist's passion. This is his conviction that conversation necessarily aims at agreement and at rational consensus, that we converse in order to make further conversation unnecessary. The anti-pragmatist believes that conversation only makes sense if something like the Platonic theory of Recollection is right—if we all have natural starting-points of thought somewhere within us, and will recognize the vocabulary in which they are best formulated once we hear it. For only if something like that is true will conversation have a natural goal. The Enlightenment hoped to find such a vocabulary—nature's own vocabulary, so to speak. Lovejoy —who described himself as an "unredeemed *Aufklärer*"—wanted to continue the project. Only if we had agreement on such a vocabulary, indeed, could conversation be reduced to argumentation—to the search for "objective, verifiable, and clearly communicable" solutions to problems. So the anti-pragmatist sees the pragmatist's scorn for professionalism as scorn for consensus, for the Christian and democratic idea that every human has the seeds of truth within. The pragmatist's attitude seems to him elitist and dilettantish, reminiscent of Alcibiades rather than of Socrates.

Issues about relativism and about professionalization are awkward attempts to formulate this opposition. The real and passionate opposition is over the question of whether loyalty to our fellow-humans presupposes that there is something permanent and unhistorical which explains *why* we should continue to converse in the manner of Socrates, something which guarantees convergence to agreement. Because the anti-pragmatist believes that without such an essence and such a guarantee the Socratic life makes no sense, he sees the pragmatist as a cynic. Thus the microcosmic issue about how philosophy professors should converse leads us quickly to the macrocosmic issue: whether one can be a pragmatist without being an irrationalist, without abandoning one's loyalty to Socrates.

Questions about irrationalism have become acute in our century because the sullen resentment which sins against Socrates, which withdraws from conversation and community, has recently become articulate. Our European intellectual tradition is now abused as "merely conceptual" or "merely ontic" or as "committed to abstractions." Irrationalists propose such rubbishy pseudo-epistemological notions as "intuition" or "an inarticulate sense of tradition" or "thinking with the blood" or "expressing the will of the oppressed classes." Our tyrants and bandits are more hateful than those of earlier times because, invoking such self-deceptive rhetoric, they pose as intellectuals. Our tyrants write philosophy in the morning and torture in the afternoon; our bandits alternately read Hölderlin and bomb people into bloody scraps. So our culture clings, more than ever, to the hope of the Enlightenment, the hope that drove Kant to make philosophy formal and rigorous and professional. We hope that by formulating the *right* conceptions of reason, of science, of thought, of knowledge, of morality, the conceptions which express their *essence,* we shall have a shield against irrationalist resentment and hatred.

Pragmatists tell us that this hope is vain. On their view, the Socratic virtues—willingness to talk, to listen to other people, to weigh the consequences of our actions upon other people—are *simply* moral virtues. They cannot be inculcated nor fortified by theoretical research into essence. Irrationalists who tell us to think with our blood cannot be rebutted by better accounts of the nature of thought, or knowledge, or logic. The pragmatists tell us that the conversation which it is our moral duty to continue is *merely* our project, the European intellectual's form of life. It has no metaphysical nor epistemological guarantee of sucess. Further (and this is the crucial point) *we do not know what "success" would mean except simply "continuance."* We are not conversing because we have a goal, but because Socratic conversation is an activity which is its *own* end. The antipragmatist who insists that agreement is its goal is like the basketball player who thinks that the reason for playing the game is to make baskets. He mistakes an essential moment in the course of an activity for the end of the activity. Worse yet, he is like a basketball fan who argues that all men by nature desire to play basketball, or that the nature of things is such that balls can go through hoops.

For the traditional, Platonic or Kantian philosopher, on the other hand, the possibility of *grounding* the European form of life—of showing it to be more than European, more than a contingent human project—seems the central task of philosophy. He wants to show that sinning against Socrates is sinning against our nature, not just against our community. So he sees the pragmatist as an irrationalist. The charge that pragmatism is "relativistic" is simply his first unthinking expression of disgust at a teaching which seems cynical about our deepest hopes. If the traditional philosopher gets beyond such epithets, however, he raises a question which the pragmatist must face up to: the *practical* question of whether the notion of "conversation" *can* substitute for that of "reason." "Reason," as the term is used in the Platonic and Kantian traditions, is interlocked with the notions of truth as correspondence, of knowledge as discovery of essence, of morality as obedience to principle, all the notions which the pragmatist tries to deconstruct. For better or worse, the Platonic and Kantian vocabularies are the ones in which Europe has described and praised the Socratic virtues. It is not clear that we know how to describe these virtues without those vocabularies. So the deep suspicion which the pragmatist inspires is that, like Alcibiades, he is essentially frivolous—that he is commending uncontroversial common goods while refusing to participate in the only activity which can preserve those goods.

He seems to be sacrificing our common European project to the delights of purely negative criticism.

The issue about irrationalism can be sharpened by noting that when the pragmatist says "All that can be done to explicate 'truth', 'knowledge', 'morality', 'virtue' is to refer us back to the concrete details of the culture in which these terms grew up and developed," the defender of the Enlightenment takes him to be saying "Truth and virtue are simply what a community agrees that they are." When the pragmatist says "We have to take truth and virtue as whatever emerges from the conversation of Europe," the traditional philosopher wants to know what is so special about Europe. Isn't the pragmatist saying, like the irrationalist, that *we* are in a privileged situation simply by being *us*? Further, isn't there something terribly dangerous about the notion that truth can only be characterized as "the outcome of doing more of what we are doing now"? What if the "we" is the Orwellian state? When tyrants employ Lenin's blood-curdling sense of "objective" to describe their lies as "objectively true," what is to prevent them from citing Peirce in Lenin's defense?[2]

The pragmatist's first line of defense against this criticism has been created by Habermas, who says that such a definition of truth works only for the outcome of *undistorted* conversation, and that the Orwellian state is the paradigm of distortion. But this is *only* a first line, for we need to know more about what counts as "undistorted." Here Habermas goes transcendental and offers principles. The pragmatist, however, must remain ethnocentric and offer examples. He can only say: "undistorted" means employing *our* criteria of relevance, where *we* are the people who have read and pondered Plato, Newton, Kant, Marx, Darwin, Freud, Dewey, etc. Milton's "free and open encounter," in which truth is bound to prevail, must itself be described in terms of examples rather than principles—it is to be more like the Athenian market-place than the council-chamber of the Great King, more like the twentieth century than the twelfth, more like the Prussian Academy in 1925 than in 1935. The pragmatist must avoid saying, with Peirce, that truth is *fated* to win. He must even avoid saying that truth *will* win. He can only say, with Hegel, that truth and justice lie in the direction marked by the successive stages of European thought. This is not because he knows some "necessary truths" and cites these examples as a result of this knowledge. It is simply that the pragmatist knows no better way to explain his convictions than to remind his interlocutor of the position they both are in, the contingent starting points they both share, the floating, ungrounded conversations of which they are both members. This means that the pragmatist cannot answer the question "What is so special about Europe?" save by saying "Do you have anything non-European to suggest which meets *our* European purposes better?" He cannot answer the question "What is so good about the Socratic virtues, about Miltonic free encounters, about undistorted communication?" save by saying "What else would better fulfill the purposes *we* share with Socrates, Milton, and Habermas?"

To decide whether this obviously circular response is enough is to decide whether Hegel or Plato had the proper picture of the progress of thought. Pragmatists follow Hegel in saying that "philosophy is its time grasped in thought." Anti-pragmatists follow Plato in striving for an escape from conversation to something atemporal which lies in the background of all possible conversations. I do not think one can decide between Hegel and Plato save by meditating on the past efforts of the philosophical tradition to escape from time and history. One can see these efforts as worthwhile, getting better, worth continuing. Or one can see them as doomed and perverse. I do not know what would count as a noncircular metaphysical or epistemological or semantical argument for seeing them in either way. So I think that the decision has to be made simply by reading the history of philosophy and drawing a moral.

Nothing that I have said, therefore, is an argument in favor of pragmatism. At best, I have merely answered various superficial criticisms which have been made of it. Nor have I dealt with the central issue about irrationalism. I have not answered the deep criticism of pragmatism which I mentioned a few minutes ago: the criticism that the Socratic virtues cannot, as a practical matter, be defended save by Platonic means, that without some sort of metaphysical comfort nobody will be able *not* to sin against Socrates. William James himself was not sure whether this criticism could be answered. Exercising his own right to believe, James wrote: "If this life be not a real fight in which something is eternally gained for the universe by success, it is no better than a game of private theatricals from which we may withdraw at will." "It *feels*," he said, "like a fight."

For us, footnotes to Plato that we are, it *does* feel that way. But if James's own pragmatism were taken seriously, if pragmatism became central to our culture and our self-image, then it would no longer feel that way. We do not know how it *would* feel. We do not even know whether, given such a change in tone, the conversation of Europe might not falter and die away. We just do not know. James and Dewey offered us no guarantees. They simply pointed to the situation we stand in, now that both the Age of Faith and the Enlightenment seem beyond recovery. They grasped our time in thought. We did not change the course of the conversation in the way they suggested we might. Perhaps we are still unable to do so; perhaps we never shall be able to. But we can nevertheless honor James and Dewey for having offered what very few philosophers have succeeded in giving us: a hint of how our lives might be changed.

Notes

1. See A. O. Lovejoy, "On Some Conditions of Progress in Philosophical Inquiry," *The Philosophical Review*, XXVI (1917): 123-163 (especially the concluding pages). I owe the reference to Lovejoy's paper to Daniel J. Wilson's illuminating "Professionalization and Organized Discussion in the American Philosophical Association, 1900-1922," *Journal of the History of Philosophy*, XVII (1979): 53-69.

2. I am indebted to Michael Williams for making me see that pragmatists have to answer this question.

10

Cavell on Skepticism

Cavell's *The Claim of Reason*[1] consists of two books in one—the first (Parts I-III) written some twenty years back, and the second (Part IV) composed quite recently.[2] Most (Parts I-II) of the first book is about epistemology, and this is the book with which I want to take issue. So I shall spend most of my time on it, saying only a little, towards the end, about the second book. This is unfortunate, since I admire the second book as much as I disagree with the first. But one always has more to say in disagreement than in agreement.

Parts I-II suggest that the material studied in the standard introductory courses in epistemology (Descartes' table, Berkeley's tree, Moore's hand, and the like) helps us see something important about the human situation, about human finitude. It takes us from epistemology to romance. It promises to relieve us philosophy professors from the shame we have felt ever since we began to suspect that our introductory courses in epistemology merely kicked up a cloud of dust around our students—so that they might be grateful to us for leading them out of it into the light. Austin, Bouwsma, Wittgenstein, Wisdom, and Ryle all suggested that we just shrug off the claims which Berkeley and Descartes and Moore made on us—that we teach epistemology as the history of some bad ideas. Now Cavell tells us that, unless we take these claims very seriously indeed, we shan't get the full benefit of what Wittgenstein and Austin (in particular) can do for us. We mustn't, he tells us, shrug off skepticism too easily, for then we may miss "the truth of skepticism": "that the human creature's basis in the world as a whole, its relation to the world as such, is not

176

that of knowing, anyway not what we think of as knowing" (p. 241).

What Cavell wants us not to miss is, to be sure, as important as he thinks it. But does he *have* to drag us back through Berkeley and Descartes to get us to see it? Why aren't "Rousseau and Thoreau and Kierkegaard and Tolstoy and Wittgenstein" (to cite one of Cavell's lists of heroes) enough? Why "the external world" *again*?

Cavell sometimes seems to argue as follows:

Wittgenstein is as important as Rousseau or Thoreau or Kierkegaard or Tolstoy, for getting us to see these things

Wittgenstein spent a lot of time discussing problems raised by people who claimed to doubt the external world

So we had better take such doubts seriously.

This seems to me like arguing that we should take Napoleon seriously because of the amount of time Tolstoy spent on studying him in *War and Peace*. Frederick the Great would have served Tolstoy's purposes almost as well, especially if he had been an Austrian rather than a Russian. Analogously, I think we should view skepticism about the external world as just a handy, local, "English" example of a much more general phenomenon: what Cavell calls "the attempt to convert the human condition, the condition of humanity, into an intellectual difficulty" (p. 493). Had Wittgenstein stayed in Central Europe, he would have met philosophy professors who worried more about the transcendental standpoint and less about skepticism. But he would probably have written pretty much the same books, and directed our attention to the same things.[3]

Wittgenstein, however, is not Cavell's only hero. Shrugging off the problem of the external world *would* matter to a reading of Austin, Moore, or C. I. Lewis. Perhaps we just wouldn't read them any more. These writers, unlike Wittgenstein, are *just* philosophy professors. One may feel grateful to Austin for freeing one from Moore's worries about unsensed sensibilia, or Lewis' about terminating judgments, but this is the perfunctory gratitude due a doctor who cures a minor ailment, brought on by a colleague's malpractice. It is not the sort of gratitude one feels towards the romantic hero, or the psychoanalyst, who saves one from monsters. Cavell, however, does seem to view Austin as a romantic hero. He even views Lewis and Moore as something more than professors. Thus he speaks of the "genuineness of philosophical inspiration in the teaching of C. I. Lewis." One of his epigraphs is a tribute by I. A. Richards to Moore's "intensity." He dedicates *The Claim of Reason* in part to Austin and in part to Thompson Clarke who, Cavell says, showed him that "the dictates of ordinary language . . . were as supportive as they were destructive of the enterprise of traditional epistemology" (p. xii). More generally, Cavell says that one of his motives is to

> keep lines open to the events within American philosophical life that we can call the reception of ordinary language philosophy (sometimes called then Oxford philosophy, and represented here primarily by some work of J. L. Austin's) together with that of Wittgenstein's *Investigations*, as if certain paths for philosophy, opened by those events, are always in danger of falling into obscurity (p. xiv).

For, he says,

> it can seem that the reception of Wittgenstein and of Austin has yet to have its public or historical effect on this [our American] philosophical culture. I do not say that this is a bad thing. Wittgenstein's writing is not of a character that lends itself to professionalization . . . and if Austin wished for professionalization, it was not to be as philosophy. Nor do I say that this lack of a certain reception is surprising. *Philosophical Investigations*, like the major modernist works of the past century at least, is, logically speaking, esoteric. That is, such works seek to split their audiences into insiders and outsiders (and split each member of it). . . . If I say that the basis of the present publication is that Wittgenstein is still to be received, I mean to suggest that his work, and of course not his alone, is essentially and always *to be* received, as thoughts must be that would refuse professionalization. (p. xvi)

But if one is not concerned about being professional, why worry about "American philosophical life"? The latter phrase can only refer to current trends in fashionable philosophy departments. Among intellectuals generally, Wittgenstein is in fact being read and used more and more. It is only within certain philosophy departments that he, and "Oxford philosophy," are *vieux jeu*. Such parochial matters should not concern Cavell, nor lead him to conclude that "certain paths for philosophy, opened by these events, are always in danger of falling into obscurity." Cavell says he wants to "understand philosophy not as a set of problems but as a set of texts," and believes that "the contribution of a philosopher . . . to the subject of philosophy is not to be understood as a contribution to, or of, a set of *given* problems" (pp. 3-4). So one would have expected him to conclude that Wittgenstein would be better served by *forgetting* "events within American philosophical life" than by recapturing them.

Cavell's ambiguous attitude toward the "events" of which he speaks is part of an equally ambiguous attitude towards academic philosophy's place in culture. Sometimes he uses "philosophy" in a large sense in which it means "the criticism a culture produces of it-self" (p. 175) or "the education of grownups" (p. 125). Sometimes he uses it in a narrow "professional" sense in which it is plausible to say that epistemological skepticism is central to philosophy, and in which fashions in philosophy departments matter to philosophy. He plays back and forth between these two senses in such passages as the following, which treat "philosophy" and "skepticism" as near synonyms:

> But the philosopher has to *make* a problem for us, show us in what sense it might so much as *be* a problem. And though intellectual advance often depends upon someone's ability to do just that, the conclusion the philosopher takes us to goes beyond anything we should expect from investigations which seem to proceed as his does.
>
> To some philosophers that fact has itself, I think, proved the power and subtlety of philosophy; while to others it has only demonstrated its intellectual frivolity. If one has felt both of these ways about skepticism, then one may come to sense that this very conflict itself may be displaying, or concealing, some critical fact about the mind, and one which neither side has been able, or willing, to articulate. (p. 159)
>
> . . . the methods of ordinary language, far from trivializing the impulse to philosophy (as many of its detractors, not, perhaps, without some reason, have found it to do) show how complex and serious an ambition the criticism of philosophy, which must inevitably remain internal to philosophizing itself, ought to be. (p. 166)

In the latter passage, "the impulse to philosophy" is implicitly identified with the impulse to raise the sort of problems (of epistemological skepticism) in which the "ordinary language philosophers" specialized. Nobody, after all, has thought that the criticism of culture was frivolous. But they have thought that philosophers were frivolously neglecting the duty to offer such criticism by getting hung up on "the external world."

Perhaps I can make this complaint clearer by distinguishing between two intellectual phenomena which I think Cavell wrongly conflates:

(a) The "professional" philosopher's skepticism created by what Reid called "the theory of ideas" (the theory which analyzes perception in terms of immediately, certainly known givens).

(b) The Kantian, Romantic worry about whether the words we use have any relation to the way the world actually is in itself.

These two phenomena have all sorts of historical connections, but they are dialectically independent. Suppose one pooh-poohs the

theory of ideas in good Austinian fashion. Unlike Austin, one may
still feel something like panic at the thought that there is no way to
hold the world in one hand and our descriptions of it in the other
and compare the two—to get, as Cavell says, "outside language-
games."

Both (a) and (b) seem distinct from a third phenomenon (c), described by Cavell as

> that experience I have called "seeing ourselves outside the world as a
> whole," looking in at it, as we now look at some objects from a position
> among others. This experience I have found to be fundamental in classical
> epistemology (and, indeed, moral philosophy). It sometimes presents
> itself to me as a sense of powerlessness to know the world, or to act upon
> it; I think it is also working in the existentialist's (or, say, Santayana's)
> sense of the precariousness and arbitrariness of existence, the utter con-
> tingency in the fact that things are as they are. . . .
>
> All of existence is squeezed into the philosopher's tomato when he rolls
> it toward his overwhelming question. . . . (p. 236)

The tomato in question is the one about which H. H. Price, in the
opening pages of his *Perception*, said, "there is much that I can
doubt." The differences in tone between that work, Fichte's *Voca-
tion of Man, and Nausea* might normally be accounted for by saying
that Price was presupposing (a), whereas Fichte was expressing (b),
and Sartre (c). Price doesn't find his questions overwhelming, nor do
most writers on the subjects he discusses, most of the writers in what
Cavell calls "the English tradition" (p. xiii). Cavell, however, lumps
these writers together with Kant, and (a) together with (b), in such
passages as the following:

> Locke avoided skepticism only apparently, through distraction and good
> English sense; Berkeley through God; Descartes through God and a special
> faculty of intellectual "perception"; Kant, denying such a faculty, avoided
> it through world-creating categories; Hume, to the extent that he did,
> through "natural belief"; Moore, through furious common sense. And all
> who have followed the argument respond to it as a discovery about our
> world, one catastrophic in its implications, overturning what we all, until
> now, believed as completely as we believed anything. (pp. 222-223)

The "argument" in question is the usual textbook, Pricean argument, in which we are driven to admit that we don't see a whole
tomato, but only . . . Cavell is either being obscurely ironic, or is
just wrong, in saying that "all who have followed the argument
respond to it as a catastrophic discovery." Most of them, including
Locke and Hume, thought of the skeptical consequences of the

theory of ideas in the same way as the developers of a revolutionary scientific theory think of the "anomalies" (in Kuhn's sense) which the theory generates. They view them as annoying and unfortunate, but by no means catastrophic, and providing employment for epigoni. (If Cavell means by "apparently" and "to the extent that," that Locke and Hume *should*, by rights, have been overwhelmed, then he is not making the point he wants to make.) The only people who go all existential about the invisibility of the rest of the tomato are lecturers on epistemology who relieve the classroom tedium by hype. When such lecturers encounter an unstable freshman who actually does feel the tomato to have catastrophic implications, they hasten to join his more robust classmates in assuring him that it is all "just philosophy."

One would have thought that, once we were lucky enough to get writers like Wittgenstein and Nietzsche who resist professionalization, we might get some criticism of philosophy which *did not* remain internal to philosophy. (As Montaigne, Spinoza, and Feuerbach gave us criticism of religion which was *not* internal.) But Cavell switches with insouciance from the narrow and professional identification of "philosophy" with epistemology to a large sense in which one cannot escape philosophy by criticizing it, simply because any criticism of culture is to be called "philosophy." To resolve this ambiguity, Cavell would have to convince us that skepticism in the narrow sense, the sense used in ritual interchanges between philosophy professors (Green and Bain, Bradley and Moore, Austin and Ayer), is important for an understanding of skepticism in some deep and romantic sense. He would have to show us that "skepticism" is a good name for the impulse which leads grownups to try to educate themselves, and cultures to try to criticize themselves. Then he would have to connect this broad sense with the narrow, "technical" sense. My main complaint about his book is that Cavell doesn't argue for such a connection, but takes it for granted. He doesn't help us see people like Moore and Austin as important thinkers. Rather, he answers the transcendental *quaestio juris*—how *could* they, appearances perhaps to the contrary, be important?—while begging the *quaestio facti*. He is "professional," it seems to me, in just the sense that he criticizes others for being so. He *takes for granted* that the "philosophical problems" with which we infect the freshman by assigning Descartes and Berkeley are something the freshman really needs—not just so that he can understand history, but so that he can be in touch with himself, with his own humanity.

In an attempt to establish connections between (a), (b), and (c), Cavell connects a particular notion of knowledge which he takes to be characteristic of "the Cartesian project" with the attempt to escape from human finitude which he takes to be "the cause of skepticism." He says that

> the project of assessing the validity of knowledge as a whole, as that is prosecuted by the Cartesian tradition, is based upon a particular concept of knowledge (and thus leads to a particular *problem* of knowledge), viz., the concept I have characterized, with little sense of satisfaction, as a concept of knowledge as revelatory of the world's existence; and I contrasted that with a concept of knowledge such as Austin's, a concept of knowledge as the identification or recognition of things. (p. 224)

This contrast seems to me real and important, but not to serve Cavell's purposes. It is the contrast between knowledge as what Kant told us we couldn't have—knowledge of things as they are in themselves, formulated in those things' *own* language, rather than ours—and knowledge as justified true belief, where "justification" is the ordinary sort given by the language-game we in fact play. Kant made epistemology Romantic, and thereby made room for moral faith. The theory of ideas as Reid knew it, before it went transcendental, was not romantic. It was just an incidental spin-off of the Galileo-Newton world-picture, one which did not pan out well.

By contrast, Cavell *can* connect (b) with (c), Kant with Sartre. He can view the Kantian hope for an impossible kind of knowledge, a knowledge unmediated by our language-games, our patterns of justification, our ideas or words—knowledge "revelatory of the world's [not just *our* world's] existence"—as produced by the Sartrean sense that only such an impossible sort of knowledge would overcome our terror at the sheer contingency of things. But I do not see how he can connect Pricean puzzles about getting from perceptions to nonperceptions with either Kantian longing or Sartrean terror.

Cavell seems to think he has made this latter connection by noting that, in his phrase, epistemological skepticism has to be about a "generic object"—not a goldfinch but "the physical object as such," not one's sister but "any passing humanoid form." To questions about whether it's a goldfinch or a goldcrest, whether one's sister is disappointed or pleased, there are commonsensical answers, and commonsensical justifications of these answers. To set the freshman up for epistemology, we have to generalize our way out of common sense. This is a very nice point, but it does not do the job Cavell wants it to do—it does not take us across the Channel from Berkeley to Kant, from (a) to (b), from perceptual error to romance. All it shows is that we can only get the freshman from the silly stuff about tomatoes to the heavy stuff about things-in-themselves by dropping the "problem of perception," skipping sense-data, and inculcating a contrast between "for us" and "in itself" which problems about perception do *not* illustrate. As long as we stick to breaking the tomato up into *sensibilia*, there will be, as Austin said, "the bit where you say it and the bit where you take it back," the bit where you deconstruct the tomato and the bit where you reconstruct it. It is only when we drop the Lockean question about whether the redness is "out there" or "in us" and get to the romantic Kantian question, "Is there anything beyond the coherence of our judgments to which we can be faithful?", that the student is hooked. There is no logical connection between the "in the mind/outside the mind" contrast and the "for us" vs. "in itself" contrast.[4] "For us" means, roughly, "inside our language-games, our conventions, our form of life, our standards of legitimation." "In the mind" is an uncashed and probably uncashable metaphor, as Reid saw very clearly. Kant's phenomenal world is not Price's tomato on a grand scale. It is a change of subject, a way of expounding (b) rather than (a). Cavell's point that skepticism only makes sense for generic objects shows just what he doesn't want to show—that one can leave Ayer and Price in the care of Austin and Ryle, and hasten on to the serious thinkers across the water.

Cavell says (in unfortunately professionalized terms) that he is interested in

> a tradition, anyway an idea, of philosophizing opposed to the tradition in English, as that tradition is represented in the best English-speaking departments of philosophy.

But, he says,

> I have made no effort to sophisticate my early, tentative amateur efforts to link the English and the Continental traditions, because I want them to show that to realign these traditions, after their long mutual shunning, at any rate to write witnessing the loss in that separation, has been a formative aspiration of mine from the earliest of the work I refer to here. (p. xiii)

Nevertheless, the strategy of these efforts is clear. Cavell's way of linking the traditions is the reverse of that used by most bridge-builders who start from our side. Usually we Anglo-Americans try to deromanticize the Continental tradition by showing that it has some good arguments. Cavell tries to romanticize our own tradition by showing that it does not. As he says, the so-called "discovery" that "the object is gone, unknowable by the senses alone" (p. 222) is a stage effect, produced by intruding "an invention, a production of dialectic, a historical-philosophical construction called the senses" (p. 224). To show that this invention is not just a suitable subject for Rube Goldberg or Ronald Searle (which is how Austin thought of it), he has got to show that the motives for its fabrication are the same as, or at least as interesting as, the motives for various bits of Continental apparatus.

I take it that Cavell's strategy is to find these motives in (c)—the Sartrean sense of contingency—and to construe the attempt, described by Heidegger and Sartre, to escape our humanity, our finitude, as an attempt to evade this sense. He wants to construe "ordinary language philosophy" as an effort "to reclaim the human self from its denial and neglect by modern philosophy" (p. 154) and he thinks of the history of this topic as suitably titled "Philosophy and the Rejection of the Human" (p. 207). I think that Cavell is dead right in analyzing the Cartesian project as an expression of this need to transcend our condition, but I think that he oversophisticates his point. It seems a sufficient diagnosis of Cartesianism to say (with Gilson, Burtt, Maritain, Randall, Malcolm, and others) that Cartesianism asks for impossible certainty, that its methodological solipsism is an impossible demand to do it all by oneself. This Luciferian attempt to cut oneself off from God, or one's fellow-humans, by using only one's natural light has usually been taken as sufficient motive for inventing what Cavell calls "absolute simples . . . outside language-games" (clear and distinct ideas, sense-data, indubitable first principles, primitive terms, and so on) (p. 226).

Cavell, however, thinks that "the quest for certainty" is an inadequate diagnosis of the Cartesian project. He criticizes the Deweyan dismissal of this project as "not taking the problem of the existence of objects seriously" and says that "it is too late to tell a philosopher to forego the quest for certainty when it is the sheer existence of objects—of anything at all—that seems to be at stake" (pp. 224-225). Perhaps he just means that anybody who has somehow managed to connect textbook skepticism about the external world with the experience of "seeing oneself outside the world as a whole" will not be responsive to the usual Gilson-Dewey-Malcolm treatment of the Cartesian illness. This is doubtless true; but it seems like saying that somebody who is wholeheartedly psychotic, rather than merely neurotically confused, will not be helped by psychoanalysis. What we need to understand is how it is *possible* to get this far out, how one *could* connect (a) with (c), how anybody *could* think that textbook "English" epistemology is intimately connected with a sense of the contingency of everything. My complaint about Cavell's treatment of skepticism may be summed up by saying that his book never makes this possibility clear for someone for whom it is not yet an actuality. It is fairly easy to connect (b) with (c): the realization that the world is available to us only under a description hooks up with the realization that it exists without a self-description, that it has no language of its own which we might one day learn. Its existence "makes no sense" because sense is relative to descriptions and existence is not. But, just as I do not know how to hook up (a) with (b), I do not know how to hook up (a) with (c) either. Thus (c) seems to me not to serve as a useful link between (a) and (b).

So much for my complaints, which have centered around Cavell's discussion of "external world" skepticism in Parts I and II. I hope, however, that dissatisfaction with the argument of these parts will not prevent readers from forging ahead through Parts III and IV. In Part III Cavell drops the topic of skepticism and the attempt to re-capture the importance of "ordinary language philosophy." This part consists of four short essays on what is wrong with what various people have said about the nature of moral philosophy—Stevenson, Rawls (in his early "Two Concepts of Rules"), and Prior. These essays remind us that moral reflection cannot be identified with appeals to principle, that morality is not a name for whatever influences choice, that

> morality must leave itself open to repudiation; it provides *one* possibility of settling conflict. . . . Other ways of settling or encompassing conflict are provided by politics, religion, love and forgiveness, rebellion, and with-drawal. Morality is a valuable way because the others are so often inaccessible or brutal; but it is not everything. . . . (p. 269)

Part III, all by itself, is one of the best books on moral philosophy which has appeared in recent years. It ranks with Iris Murdoch's *Sovereignty of Good* as a criticism of the notion that moral philosophy must be a search for yet more "absolute simples"—self-evident principles, basic values. Like Murdoch, Cavell criticizes the Bentham-Kant-Sidgwick notion that rational action is action on principle, and the corollary that moral reflection is the attempt to discover the rules by which each of us, simply as a human being, is committed to living. He says:

> No rule or principle could function in a moral context the way regulatory or defining rules function in games. It is as essential to the form of life called morality that rules so conceived be absent as it is essential to the form of life we call playing a game that they be present. . . .
>   . . . a suggestion emerges about why philosophers appeal to rules in

theorizing about morality, and about how rules are then conceived. The appeal is an attempt to explain why such an action as promising is *binding* upon us. But if you *need* an explanation for that, if there is a sense that something more than personal commitment is necessary, then the appeal to rules comes too late. For rules are themselves binding only subject to our commitment. (p. 307)

He thus helps us see the quest for "foundations of moral obligation" as parallel to the Cartesian quest for "foundations of knowledge." Both are attempts to get outside language-games, to find some "natural" way of getting in touch with reality or goodness which is independent of the actual people among whom we live, who talk in a certain way. Both help us avoid acknowledging that we are mortals, who think and talk as we do because we have read the books we have read, talked with the people we have talked with. They encourage us to think that philosophy will do for us what we once thought religion might do—take us right outside language, history, and finitude and put us in the presence of the atemporal. They lead the philosopher to think himself so little dependent upon his community that what he says will "work on people at random, like a ray" (p. 326).

Cavell's comments on the form of life of Anglo-Saxon moral philosophers are much more external, and thus much clearer and more useful, than his comments in Parts I and II on that of Anglo-Saxon epistemologists. In the case of the moral philosophers, he sees why they want to do what they do, diagnoses it quickly and surely, and then lets go of it. In the case of epistemologists, he insists on regarding their plight as a sickness which somehow we are all bound to suffer, as a necessary stage in reaching intellectual maturity. His insistence on the pathos and ubiquity of epistemology leads him, I have argued above, to confuse temporary, historically conditioned little frenzies (the seventeenth-century theory of ideas, ordinary language philosophy) with aspects of the human condition. In Part III, by contrast, he no longer avoids history. He briskly and brilliantly explains (pp. 259ff.) the connection between Galilean models of scientific explanation and the philosophical claim that science is "rational" in a way that moral reflection is not. He concludes:

> If you begin by being struck with the peculiarity of ethical arguments as perhaps unsettleable, and struck with how different other questions are, then you will pick examples from science which illustrate its capacity for agreement, and then you will have the idea, or illusion, that you know that, and why, science is rational and morality not. (p. 263)

Applying lessons learned from Kuhn's *Structure of Scientific Revolutions*, Cavell in these pages does a great deal to help rid us of the distinctions between "science" and "nonscience," "objective" and "subjective," "fact" and "value," "reason" and "emotion," which have been the warp of intellectual life in recent centuries.

Part IV is rather perversely called "Skepticism and the Problem of Others," but is coextensive with Chapter XIII, which is more helpfully titled "Between Acknowledgement and Avoidance." This material is, Cavell tells us, more recent than anything else he has written. In particular, as noted above, it was written some twenty or twenty-five years after some of the material in Parts I-III. In this later manner — that of "Leopards in Connecticut" and "The Avoidance of Love" — he comes into his own. He speaks with a much stronger voice. Now he is free of worry about rival philosophers, or about what makes epistemology, or skepticism, or philosophy, special and deep. He just reflects on the fact that there are such things.

In this part Cavell is concerned with a "problem of other minds" which does not even pretend to hook up with the "professional problem of how, given that the logical construction of the Other's body uses up the sensory qualia I receive, I have a right to construct a mind for him as well. Wittgenstein taught us that this problem results from thinking that one first describes oneself to oneself in ostensively-learned Mental, the Lockean inner language of the ideas themselves. So one might expect Cavell to repeat that if we drop Locke and the theory of ideas we shall no longer speculate about private languages, the possible inner emptiness of the Other, and so on. Instead, Cavell shrugs off all that and goes straight to a deep reading of such speculations:

> The wish underlying this fantasy [of a private language] covers a wish that underlies skepticism, a wish for the connection between my claims of knowledge and the objects upon which the claims are to fall to occur without my intervention, apart from my agreements. As the wish stands, it is unappeasable. In the case of knowing myself, such self-defeat would be doubly exquisite: I must disappear in order that search for myself be successful. . . . (pp. 351-352)

This reading uproots the "problem of other minds" from the soil in which it is usually taken to have sprouted — empiricism and phenomenalism — and transplants it across the Channel. It is now the sort of problem you have after reading the *Phenomenology of Spirit*, or the *Critique of Practical Reason*, or *Being and Nothingness*. This is a good thing to do if you want to find something interesting to say about Other Minds. It ignores the question of whether the "professional," "English," epistemological question has anything to do with romantic Kantian questions, whether (a) has anything to do with (b).

One of the advantages of the later over the earlier Cavell—of Part IV over Parts I-II—is that he *does* ignore this question. For now he is no longer concerned about hooking up with what the "professionals" do. This permits him, at last, to explain what he was hinting at in earlier passages about "reclaiming the human self" and modern philosophy's "rejection of the human." What he has in mind is summed up in such passages as the following:

> The skeptic insinuates that there are possibilities to which the claim of certainty shuts its eyes; or: whose eyes the claim of certainty shuts. It is the voice, or an imitation of the voice, of intellectual conscience. Wittgenstein replies, "They are shut." It is the voice of human conscience. . . . In the face of the skeptic's picture of intellectual limitedness, Wittgenstein proposes a picture of human finitude. (p. 431)

Where else can we find out about human finitude? Presumably in novels, plays, and works of "Continental" philosophy rather than in epistemology courses, or in the sort of reflection on science in which "English" philosophy specializes:

> science fiction cannot house tragedy because in it human limitations can from the beginning be by-passed. This idea helps me explain my difference in intuition from those philosophers who take it that a scientific speculation, or fiction, is sufficient to suggest skepticism; for example, the speculation that for all I know I may be a brain in a vat. (p. 457)

The human self which philosophy has been avoiding is the one described in all the vocabularies which are of no use for predicting and controlling people—the vocabularies which are useless for science, and for philosophy when it is conceived as quasi-science. "Literature" tells us, as do Hegel and Sartre, that there is no universal religious, or scientific, or philosophical vocabulary to use in talking about, or dealing with, our fellow-humans, but that we cannot help thinking that there must be one:

> Tragedy and comedy are all but filled with this possibility—that one among the endless true descriptions of me tells who I am. (p. 388)

Pre-Kantian, pre-Romantic philosophy was filled with assurance that that possibility had been actualized. The self-knowledge which was prevented by this kind of philosophy (a kind which survives in Anglo-Saxon philosophy departments, though it is pretty much extinct elsewhere) is the knowledge that

> with respect to the external world, an initial sanity requires recognizing that I cannot live my skepticism, whereas with respect to others a final sanity requires recognizing that I can. I do. (p. 451)

This makes "final sanity" consist in getting out from under the impulse which led to "professional" philosophy, in escaping the temptation "to convert the human condition, the condition of humanity, into an intellectual difficulty" (p. 493). In one of the best remarks in Part IV —a part which is studded with splendid sentences—Cavell says

> Not finitude, but the denial of finitude, is the mark of tragedy. This denial of finitude has also been taken as the mark of sin. It was to free humanity of that libel of sinfulness that Blake and Nietzsche undertook, as it were, to deny the distinction between the finite and the infinite in thinking of the human. (p. 455)

I doubt that the aim of "modern" writing has been better stated than in this final phrase.

I hope that my account of the various parts of *The Claim of Reason* has made clear that its second half (Parts III and IV) makes it an important book, and also why a prospective reader should not be daunted by Part I, nor by Cavell's (occasionally) heavy-handed style. One way of describing its importance is to say that it helps us realize what Wittgenstein did for us. Unlike Austin and Ryle, he did not *just* help us shrug off the theory of ideas. He also raised the question of the *moral* worth of our epistemology courses, of our discipline, of our form of life. We philosophy professors are lucky that one of the great writers of the century came among us, and left behind a description of our habits which we might never have formulated for ourselves. Wittgenstein suffered from, and constantly complained about, the company he had to keep in the course of this endeavor. But he persisted, and produced writings which even the determined efforts of a host of commentators will not be able to construe as offering "philosophical theories" or "solutions to philosophical problems." Cavell is one of the few interpreters Wittgenstein has so far had who (at least in Part IV of his book) is free from the temptation so to construe him.[5] He is also one of the few who puts him in suitable company—that of Rousseau and Thoreau, Kierkegaard and Tolstoy, Blake and Nietzsche, the friends of finitude, the friends of man.[6]

Notes

1. Stanley Cavell, *The Claim of Reason: Wittgenstein, Skepticism, Morality and Tragedy* (Oxford: Clarendon Press, 1979). Parenthetical page references are to this book.

2. Part III is a reworking of material from Cavell's twenty-year-old dissertation (as were, to some extent, Parts I and II).

3. See Jacques Bouveresse's treatment of Wittgenstein as "the anti-Husserl" in *Le Mythe de l'Intériorité* (Paris: Editions Minuit, 1978).

4. Recently, however, philosophers have once again started to run these two contrasts together. For example, Bernard Williams, in his *Descartes: The Project of Pure Enquiry*, tries to rehabilitate Descartes' project through a notion of "the absolute conception of reality," a notion which Williams thinks involved in our intuition about the nature of knowledge, and which raises the skeptical question of whether knowledge is possible. This notion, as Williams formulates it, is ambiguous between a "determinate picture of what the world is like independent of thought" (Williams, p. 65) (the sort of thing which Kant told us we wouldn't have) and a description of the world "using concepts which are not peculiarly ours, and not peculiarly relative to our experience" (*ibid.*, p. 244). The latter phrase is Williams' attempt (unsuccessful, in my view) to update Locke's notion of "resembling objects." Another example is Thomas Nagel's use of the "subjective vs. objective" distinction to cover both the difference between a "personal" and an "impersonal" account of, e.g., the morally relevant features of a situation *and* the difference between the linguistically-inarticulable phenomenological character of an experience and a characterization of the experience in ordinary public terms. (Cf. Nagel's *Mortal Questions* [Cambridge: Cambridge University Press, 1978], chap. 14: "Subjective-Objective.") Both Williams and Nagel, on my view, misleadingly yoke together the contrast between the veridical (the "objective" as the "intersubjective") and the nonveridical (the "subjective" as the "merely apparent") with the quite different contrast between the communicable (what our concepts catch) and the incommunicable (what they may, or must, fail to catch).

5. Another of these happy few is James C. Edwards. See his forthcoming *Ethics Without Philosophy: Wittgenstein and the Moral Life* (Gainesville: University Presses of Florida, 1982). Cavell's and Edwards' books, taken together, suggest that Wittgenstein commentary has recently turned a corner.

6. I am grateful to John Cooper for helpful comment on the first draft of this essay.

11

Method, Social Science, and Social Hope

I. Science Without Method

Galileo and his followers discovered, and subsequent centuries have amply confirmed, that you get much better predictions by thinking of things as masses of particles blindly bumping each other than by thinking of them as Aristotle thought of them—animistically, teleologically, and anthropomorphically. They also discovered that you get a better handle on the universe by thinking of it as infinite and cold and comfortless than by thinking of it as finite, homey, planned, and relevant to human concerns. Finally, they discovered that if you view planets or missiles or corpuscles as point-masses, you can get nice simple predictive laws by looking for nice simple mathematical ratios. These discoveries are the basis of modern technological civilization. We can hardly be too grateful for them. But they do not, *pace* Descartes and Kant, point any epistemological moral. They do not tell us anything about the nature of science or rationality. In particular, they did not result from the use of, nor do they exemplify, something called "the scientific method."

The tradition we call "modern philosophy" asked itself "How is it that science has had so much success? What is the secret of this success?" The various bad answers to these bad questions have been variations on a single charming but uncashable metaphor: viz., the New Science discovered the language which nature itself uses. When Galileo said that the Book of Nature was written in the language of mathematics, he meant that his new reductionistic, mathematical vocabulary didn't just *happen* to work, but that it worked *because* that was the way things *really were*. He meant that the vocabulary worked because it fitted the universe as a key fits a lock. Ever since, philosophers have been trying, and failing, to give sense to these notions of "working *because*," and "things as they *really are*."

Descartes explicated these notions in terms of the natural clarity and distinctness of Galilean ideas—ideas which, for some reason, had been foolishly overlooked by Aristotle. Locke, struck by the indistinctness of this notion of "clarity," thought he might do better with a program of reducing complex ideas to simple. To make this program relevant to current science, he used an *ad hoc* distinction between ideas which resemble their objects and those which do not. This distinction was so dubious as to lead us, via Berkeley and Hume, to Kant's rather desperate suggestion that the key only worked because we had, behind our own backs, constructed the lock it was to fit. In retrospect, we have come to see Kant's suggestion as giving the game away. For his transcendental idealism opened the back door to all the teleological, animistic, Aristotelian notions which the intellectuals had repressed for fear of being old-fashioned. The speculative idealists who succeeded Kant dropped the notion of finding nature's secrets. They substituted the notion of making worlds by creating vocabularies, a notion echoed in our century by maverick philosophers of science like Cassirer and Goodman.

In an effort to avoid these so-called "excesses of German idealism," a host of philosophers—roughly classifiable as "positivist"—have spent the last hundred years trying to use notions like "objectivity," "rigor," and "method" to isolate science from nonscience. They have done this because they thought that the idea that we can explain scientific success in terms of discovering Nature's Own Language must, *somehow*, be right—even if the metaphor could *not* be cashed, even if neither realism nor idealism could explain just what the imagined "correspondence" between nature's language and current scientific jargon could consist in. Very few thinkers have suggested that maybe science doesn't *have* a secret of success—that there is *no* metaphysical or epistemological or transcendental explanation of why Galileo's vocabulary has worked so well so far, any more than there is an explanation of why the vocabulary of liberal democracy has worked so well so far. Very few have been willing to abjure the notions that "the mind" or "reason" has a nature of its own, that discovery of this nature will give us a "method," and that following that method will enable us to penetrate beneath the appearances and see nature "in its own terms."[1]

The importance of Kuhn seems to me to be that, like Dewey, he is one of these few. Kuhn and Dewey suggest we give up the notion of science traveling towards an end called "correspondence with reality" and instead say *merely* that a given vocabulary works better than another for a given purpose. If we accept their suggestion, we shall not be inclined to ask "What method do scientists use?" Or, more precisely, we shall say that within what Kuhn calls "normal science" — puzzle-solving — they use the same banal and obvious methods all of us use in every human activity. They check off examples against criteria; they fudge the counter-examples enough to avoid the need for new models; they try out various guesses, formulated within the current jargon, in the hope of coming up with something which will cover the unfudgeable cases. We shall not think there is or could be an epistemologically pregnant answer to the question "What did Galileo do right that Aristotle did wrong?", any more than we should expect such an answer to the questions "What did Plato do right that Xenophon did wrong?" or "What did Mirabeau do right that Louis XVI did wrong?" We shall just say that Galileo had a good idea, and Aristotle a less good idea; Galileo was using some terminology which helped, and Aristotle wasn't. Galileo's terminology was the *only* "secret" he had — he didn't pick that terminology because it was "clear" or "natural," or "simple," or in line with the categories of the pure understanding. He just lucked out.

The moral which seventeenth-century philosophers *should* have drawn from Galileo's success was a Whewellian and Kuhnian one: viz., that scientific breakthroughs are not so much a matter of deciding which of various alternative hypotheses are true, but of finding the right jargon in which to frame hypotheses in the first place. But, instead, as I have said, they drew the moral that the new vocabulary was the one nature had always *wanted* to be described in. I think they drew this moral for two reasons. First, they thought that the fact that Galileo's vocabulary was devoid of metaphysical comfort, moral significance, and human interest was a reason why it worked. They vaguely thought that it was *because* the Galilean scientist was able to face up to the frightening abysses of infinite space that he was being so successful. They identified his distance from common sense and from religious feeling — his distance from decisions about how men should live — as part of the secret of his success. So, they said, the more metaphysically comfortless and morally insignificant our vocabulary, the likelier we are to be "in touch with reality" or to be "scientific," or to describe reality as it wants to be described and thereby get it under control. Second, they thought the only way to eliminate "subjective" notions—those expressible in *our* vocabulary but not in nature's—was to eschew terms which could not be definitionally linked to those in Galileo's and Newton's vocabularies, terms denoting "primary qualities."

These intertwined mistakes—the notion that a term is more likely to "refer to the real" if it is morally insignificant and if it occurs in true, predictively useful generalizations—give substance to the idea of "scientific method" as (in Bernard Williams' phrase)[2] the search for "an absolute conception of reality." This is reality conceived as somehow represented by representations which are not merely ours but its own, as it looks to itself, as it would describe itself if it could. Williams, and others who take Cartesianism seriously, not only think this notion is unconfused but regard it as one of our intuitions about the nature of knowledge. On my account, by contrast, it is merely one of our intuitions about what counts as being philosophical. It is the Cartesian form of the archetypal philosophical fantasy—first spun by Plato—of cutting through all description, all representation, to a state of consciousness which, *per impossibile*, combines the best features of inarticulate confrontation with the best features of linguistic formulation. This fantasy of discovering, and somehow *knowing* that one has discovered, Nature's Own Vocabulary *seemed* to become more concrete when Galileo and Newton formulated a comprehensive set of predictively useful universal generalizations, written in suitably "cold," "inhuman," mathematical terms. From their time to the present, the notions of "rationality," "method," and "science" have been bound up with the search for such generalizations.

Without this model to go on, the notion of "a scientific method," in its modern sense, could not have been taken seriously. The term "method" would have retained the sense it had in the period prior to the New Science, for people like Ramus and Bacon. In that sense, to have a method was simply to have a good comprehensive list of topics or headings—to have, so to speak, an efficient filing system. In its post-Cartesian philosophical sense, however, it does not mean simply ordering one's thoughts, but *filtering* them in order to eliminate "subjective" or "noncognitive" or "confused" elements, leaving only the thoughts which are Nature's Own. This distinction between the parts of one's mind which do and don't correspond to reality is, in the epistemological tradition, confused with the distinction between rational and irrational ways of doing science. If "scientific method" means merely being rational in some given area of inquiry, then it has a perfectly reasonable "Kuhnian" sense—it means obeying the normal conventions of your discipline, not fudging the data *too* much, not letting your hopes and fears influence your conclusions unless those hopes and fears are shared by all those who are in the same line of work, being open to refutation by experience, not blocking the road of inquiry. In this sense, "method" and "rationality" are names for a suitable balance between respect for the opinions of one's fellows and respect for the stubbornness of sensation. But epistemologically-centered philosophy has wanted notions of "method" and "rationality" which signify more than good epistemic manners, notions which describe the way in which the mind is naturally fitted to learn Nature's Own Language.

If one believes, as I do, that the traditional ideas of "an absolute ('objective') conception of reality" and of "scientific method" are neither clear nor useful, then one will see the interlocked questions "What should be the method of the social sciences?" and "What are the criteria of an objective moral theory?" as badly posed. In the remainder of this paper, I want to say in detail why I think these are bad questions, and to recommend a Deweyan approach to both social science and morality, one which emphasizes the utility of narratives and vocabularies rather than the objectivity of laws and theories.

II. "Value-Free" Social Science and "Hermeneutic" Social Science

There has recently been a reaction against the idea that students of man and society will be "scientific" only if they remain faithful to the Galilean model—if they find "value-neutral," purely descriptive terms in which to state their predictive generalizations, leaving evaluation to "policy-makers." This has led to a revival of Dilthey's notion that to understand human beings "scientifically" we must apply non-Galilean, "hermeneutic" methods. From the point of view I wish to suggest, the whole idea of "being scientific" or of choosing between "methods" is confused. Consequently, the question about whether social scientists should seek value-neutrality along Galilean lines, or rather should try for something more cozy, Aristotelian, and "softer" —a distinctive "method of the human sciences"—seems to me misguided.

One reason this quarrel has developed is that it has become obvious that *whatever* terms are used to describe human beings *become* "evaluative" terms. The suggestion that we segregate the "evaluative" terms in a language and use their absence as one criterion for the "scientific" character of a discipline or a theory cannot be carried out. For there is no way to prevent anybody using *any* term "evaluatively."

If you ask somebody whether he is using "repression" or "primitive" or "working class" normatively or descriptively, he might be able to answer in the case of a given statement, made on a given occasion. But if you ask him whether he uses the term only when he is describing, only when he is engaging in moral reflection, or both, the answer is almost always going to be "both." Further—and this is the crucial point—unless the answer *is* "both," it is just not the sort of term which will do us much good in social science. Predictions will do "policy-making" no good if they are not phrased in the terms in which policy can be formulated.

Suppose we picture the "value-free" social scientist walking up to the divide between "fact" and "value" and handing his predictions to the policy-makers who live on the other side. They will not be of much use unless they contain some of the terms which the policy-makers use among themselves. What the policy-makers would like, presumably, are rich juicy predictions like "If basic industry is socialized, the standard of living will [or won't] decline," "If literacy is more widespread, more [or fewer] honest people will be elected to office," and so on. They would like hypothetical sentences whose consequents are phrased in terms which might occur in morally urgent recommendations. When they get predictions phrased in the sterile jargon of "quantified" social sciences ("maximizes satisfaction," "increases conflict," etc.), they either tune out, or, more dangerously, begin to use the jargon in moral deliberation. The desire for a new, "interpretive" social science seems to me best understood as a reaction against the temptation to formulate social policies in terms so thin as barely to count as "moral" at all—terms which never stray far from definitional links with "pleasure," "pain," and "power."

The issue between those who hanker after "objective," "value-free," "truly scientific" social science and those who think this should be replaced with something more hermeneutical is misdescribed as a quarrel about "method." A quarrel about method requires a common goal, and disagreement about the means for reaching it. But the two sides to this quarrel are not disagreeing about how to get more accurate predictions of what will happen if certain policies are adopted. Neither side is very good at making such predictions, and if anybody ever did find a way of making them both sides would be equally eager to incorporate this strategy in their view. The nature of the quarrel is better, but still misleadingly, seen as one between the competing goals of "explanation" and "understanding." As this contrast has developed in the recent literature, it is a contrast between the sort of jargon which permits Galilean-style generalizations, and

Hempelian specification of confirming and disconfirming instances of such generalizations, and the sort which sacrifices this virtue for the sake of describing in roughly the same vocabulary as one evaluates (a "teleological" vocabulary, crudely speaking).

This contrast is real enough. But it is not an issue to be resolved, only a difference to be lived with. The idea that explanation and understanding are opposed ways of doing social science is as misguided as the notion that microscopic and macroscopic descriptions of organisms are opposed ways of doing biology. There are lots of things you want to do with bacteria and cows for which it is very useful to have biochemical descriptions of them; there are lots of things you want to do with them for which such descriptions would be merely a nuisance. Similarly, there are lots of things you want to do with human beings for which descriptions of them in nonevaluative, "inhuman" terms are very useful; there are others (e.g., thinking of them as your fellow-citizens) in which such descriptions are not. "Explanation" is merely the sort of understanding one looks for when one wants to predict and control. It does not contrast with something else called "understanding" as the abstract contrasts with the concrete, or the artificial with the natural, or the "repressive" with the "liberating." To say that something is better "understood" in one vocabulary than another is always an ellipsis for the claim that a description in the preferred vocabulary is more useful for a certain purpose. If the purpose is prediction, then one will want one sort of vocabulary. If it is evaluation, one may or may not want a different sort of vocabulary. (In the case of evaluating artillery fire, for example, the predictive vocabulary of ballistics will do nicely. In the case of evaluating human character, the vocabulary of stimulus and response is beside the point.)

To sum up this point: there are two distinct requirements for the vocabulary of the social sciences:

(1) It should contain descriptions of situations which facilitate their prediction and control

(2) It should contain descriptions which help one decide what to do.

Value-free social science assumed that a thin "behavioristic" vocabulary met the first requirement. This assumption has not panned out very well; the last fifty years of research in the social sciences have not notably increased our predictive abilities. But even if it *had* succeeded in offering predictions, this would not *necessarily* have helped fulfill the second requirement. It would not necessarily have been useful in deciding what to do. The debate between friends of value-freedom and friends of hermeneutics has often taken for granted that neither requirement can be satisfied unless the other is also. Friends of hermeneutics have protested that Behaviorese was inappropriate for "understanding" people—meaning that it could not catch what they were "really" doing. But this is a misleading way of saying it is not a good vocabulary for moral reflection. We just don't want to be the sort of policy-makers who use those terms for deciding what to do to our fellow-humans. Conversely, friends of value-freedom, insisting that as soon as social science finds its Galileo (who is somehow known in advance to be a behaviorist) the first requirement will be satisfied, have argued that it is our duty to start making policy decisions in suitably thin terms—so that our "ethics" may be "objective" and "scientifically based." For only in that way will we be able to make maximal use of all those splendid predictions which will shortly be coming our way. Both sides make the same mistake in thinking that there is some intrinsic connection between the two requirements. It is a mistake to think that when we know how to deal justly and honorably with a person or a society we *thereby* know how to predict and control him or her or it, and a mistake to think that ability to predict and control is *necessarily* an aid to such dealing.

To be told that only a certain vocabulary is *suited* to human beings or human societies, that only *that* vocabulary permits us to "understand" them, is the seventeenth-century myth of Nature's Own Vocabulary all over again. If, with Dewey, one sees vocabularies as instruments for coping with things rather than representations of their intrinsic natures, then one will not think that there is an intrinsic connection, nor an intrinsic *lack* of connection, between "explanation" and "understanding"—between being able to predict and control people of a certain sort and being able to sympathize and associate with them, to view them as fellow-citizens. One will not think that there are two "methods"—one for explaining somebody's behavior and another for understanding his nature.

III. Epistemic and Moral Privilege

The current movement to make the social sciences "hermeneutical" rather than Galilean makes a reasonable, Deweyan point if it is taken as saying: narratives as well as laws, redescriptions as well as predictions, serve a useful purpose in helping us deal with the problems of society. In this sense, the movement is a useful protest against the fetishism of old-fashioned, "behaviorist" social scientists who worry about whether they are being "scientific." But this protest goes too far when it waxes philosophical and begins to draw a principled distinction between man and nature, announcing that the ontological difference dictates a methodological difference. Thus, for example, when it is said that "interpretation begins from the postulate that the web of meaning constitutes human existence,"[3] this suggests that fossils (for example) might get constituted *without* a web of meanings. But once the relevant sense of "constitution" is distinguished from the physical sense (in which houses are "constituted out of" bricks), the claim that "X constitutes Y" reduces to the claim that you can't know anything about Y without knowing a lot about X. To say that human beings wouldn't be human, would be merely animal, unless they talked a lot is true enough. If you can't figure out the relation between a person, the noises he makes, and other persons, then you won't know much about him. But one could equally well say that fossils wouldn't be fossils, would be merely rocks, if we couldn't grasp their relations to lots of other fossils. Fossils are constituted *as* fossils by a web of relationships to other fossils and to the speech of the paleontologists who describe such relationships. If you can't grasp some of these relationships, the fossil will remain, to you, a mere rock. *Anything* is, for purposes of being inquired into, "constituted" by a web of meanings.

To put this another way: if we think of the fossil record as a text, then we can say that paleontology, in its early stages, followed "interpretive" methods. That is, it cast around for some way of making sense of what had happened by looking for a vocabulary in which a puzzling object could be related to other, more familiar objects, so as to become intelligible. Before the discipline became "normalized," nobody had any clear idea of what sort of thing might be relevant to predicting where similar fossils might be found. To say that "Paleontology is now a science" means something like "Nobody now has any doubts about what sorts of questions you are supposed to ask, and what sort of hypotheses you can advance, when confronted with a puzzling fossil." On my view, being "interpretive" or "hermeneutical" is not having a special method but simply casting about for a vocabulary which might help. When Galileo came up with his mathematicized vocabulary, he was successfully concluding an inquiry which was, in the only sense I can give the term, hermeneutical. The same goes for Darwin. I do not see any interesting differences between what they were doing and what biblical exegetes, literary critics, or historians of culture do. So I think that it would do no harm to adopt the term "hermeneutics" for the sort of by-guess-and-by-God hunt for new terminology which characterizes the initial stages of any new line of inquiry.

But although this would do no harm, it also would do no particular good. It is no more useful to think of people or fossils on the model of texts than to think of texts on the model of people or of fossils. It only appears more useful if we think that there is something *special* about texts—e.g., that they are "intentional" or "intelligible only holistically." But I do not think—*pace*, e.g., Searle's notion of "intrinsic intentionality"—that "possessing intentionality" means more than "suitable to be described anthropomorphically, as if it were a language-user."[4] The relation, on my view, between actions and movements, noises and assertions, is that each is the other described in an alternative jargon. Nor do I see that explanation of fossils is less holistic than explanation of texts—in both cases one needs to bring the object into relation with many other different sorts of objects in order to tell a coherent narrative which will incorporate the initial object.

Given this attitude, it behooves me to offer an explanation of why some people *do* think that texts are very different from fossils. I have suggested elsewhere, in arguing against Charles Taylor,[5] that such people make the mistaken assumption that somebody's *own* vocabulary is always the best vocabulary for understanding what he is doing, that his own explanation of what's going on is the one we want. This mistake seems to me a special case of the confused notion that science tries to learn the vocabulary which the universe uses to explain itself to itself. In both cases, we are thinking of our explanandum as if it were our epistemic equal or superior. But this is not always correct in the case of our fellow-humans, and it is merely a relic of pre-Galilean anthropomorphism in the case of nature. There are, after all, cases in which the other person's, or culture's, explanation of what it's up to is so primitive, or so nutty, that we brush it aside. The only general hermeneutical rule is that it's always wise to ask what the subject *thinks* it's up to before formulating our own hypotheses. But this is an effort at saving time, not a search for the "true meaning" of the behavior. If the explanandum can come up with a good vocabulary for explaining its own behavior, this saves us the trouble of casting about for one ourselves. From this point of view, the only difference between an inscription and a fossil is that we can imagine coming across another inscription which is a gloss on the first. By contrast, we shall describe the relation between the first fossil and the one next door, even though perhaps equally illuminating, in a nonintentional vocabulary.

In addition to the mistake of thinking that a subject's own vocabulary is always relevant to explaining him, philosophers who make a sharp distinction between man and nature are, like the positivists, bewitched by the notion that the irreducibility of one vocabulary to another implies something ontological. Yet the discovery that we can or cannot reduce a language containing terms like "is about," "is true of," "refers to," etc., or one which contains "believes" or "intends," to a language which is extensional and "empiricist" would show us nothing at all about how to predict, or deal with, language-users or intenders. Defenders of Dilthey make a simple inversion of the mistake made, e.g., by Quine, who thinks there can be no "fact of the matter" about intentional states of affairs because different such states can be attributed without making a difference to the elementary particles. Quine thinks that, if a sentence can't be paraphrased in the sort of vocabulary which Locke and Boyle would have liked, it doesn't stand for anything real. Diltheyans who exaggerate the differences between the *Geistes-* and the *Naturwissenschaften* think that the fact that it can't be paraphrased is a hint about a distinctive metaphysical or epistemic status, or the need for a distinctive methodological strategy. But surely all that such irreducibility shows is that one particular vocabulary (Locke's and Boyle's) is not going to be helpful for doing certain things with certain explananda (e.g., people and cultures). This shows as little, to use Hilary Putnam's analogy, as the fact that if you want to know why a square peg doesn't fit into a round hole you had better *not* describe the peg in terms of the positions of its constituent elementary particles.

The reason definitional irreducibility acquires this illusionary importance, it seems to me, is that it *is* important to make a *moral* distinction between the brutes and ourselves. So, looking about for relevantly distinct behavior, we have traditionally picked our ability to *know*. In previous centuries, we made the mistake of hypostatizing cognitive behavior as the possession of "mind" or "consciousness" or "ideas" and then insisting on the irreducibility of mental representations to their physiological correlates. When this became *vieux jeu*, we switched from mental representations to linguistic representations. We switched from Mind to Language as the name of a quasi-substance or quasi-power which made us morally different. So recent defenders of human dignity have been busy proving the irreducibility of the semantic instead of the irreducibility of the psychical. But all the Ryle-Wittgenstein sorts of arguments against the ghost in the machine work equally well against the ghost between the lines—the notion that having been penned by a human hand imparts a special something, textuality, to inscriptions, something which fossils can never have.

As long as we think of knowledge as representing reality rather than coping with it, mind or language will continue to seem numinous. "Materialism" or "behaviorism," and the Galilean style, may continue to seem morally dubious. We shall be struck with this notion of "representing" or "corresponding to" reality as long as we think that there is some analogy between calling things by their "right"—i.e., their conventional—names and finding the "right"—i.e., Nature's Own —way of describing them. But if we could abandon this metaphor, and the vocabulary of representation which goes with it—as Kuhn and Dewey suggest we might—then we would not find language or mind mysterious, nor "materialism" or "behaviorism" particularly dangerous. If the line I am taking is correct, we need to think of our distinctive moral status as just *that*, rather than as "grounded" on our possession of mind, language, culture, feeling, intentionality, textuality, or anything else. All these numinous notions are just expressions of our awareness that we are members of a moral community, phrased in one or another pseudo-explanatory jargon. This awareness is something which cannot be further "grounded"—it is simply taking a certain point of view on our fellow-humans. The question of whether it is an "objective" point of view is not to any point.

This can be made a bit more concrete as follows. I said that, *pace* Taylor, it was a mistake to think of somebody's own account of his behavior or culture as epistemically privileged. He might have a good account of what he's doing or he might not. But it is *not* a mistake to think of it as morally privileged. We have a duty to listen to his account, not because he has privileged access to his own motives but because he is a human being like ourselves. Taylor's claim that we need to look for *internal* explanations of people or cultures or texts takes civility as a methodological strategy. But civility is not a method, it is simply a virtue. The reason why we invite the moronic psychopath to address the court before being sentenced is not that we hope for better explanations than expert psychiatric testimony has offered. We do so because he is, after all, one of us. By asking for his own account in his own words, we hope to decrease our chances of acting badly. What we hope for from social scientists is that they will act as interpreters for those with whom we are not sure how to talk. This is the same thing we hope for from our poets and dramatists and novelists.

Just as I argued in the previous section of this paper that it is a mistake to think that there is a principled distinction between explanation and understanding, or between two methods, one appropriate for nature and the other for man, I have been arguing in this section that the notion that we know *a priori* that nature and man are distinct sorts of objects is a mistake. It is a confusion between ontology and morals. There are lots of useful vocabularies which ignore the non-human/human or thing/person distinctions. There is at least one vocabulary—the moral—and possibly many more, for which these distinctions are basic. Human beings are no more "really" described in the latter sort of vocabulary than in the former. Objects are not "more objectively" described in any vocabulary than in any other. Vocabularies are useful or useless, good or bad, helpful or misleading, sensitive or coarse, and so on; but they are not "more objective" or "less objective" nor more or less "scientific."

IV. Ungrounded Hope: Dewey vs. Foucault

The burden of my argument so far has been that if we get rid of traditional notions of "objectivity" and "scientific method" we shall be able to see the social sciences as continuous with literature—as interpreting other people to us, and thus enlarging and deepening our sense of community. We shall see the anthropologists and historians as having made it possible for us—educated, leisured policy-makers of the West—to see any exotic specimen of humanity as also "one of us." We shall see the sociologists as having done the same for the poor (and various other sorts of nearby outsiders), and the psychologists as having done the same for the eccentric and the insane. This is not all that the social sciences have done, but it is perhaps the most important thing. If we emphasize this side of their achievement, then we shall not object to their sharing a narrative and anecdotal style with the novelist and the journalist. We shall not worry about how this style is related to the "Galilean" style which "quantified behavioral science" has tried to emulate. We shall not think either style particulary appropriate or inappropriate to the study of man. For we shall not think that "the study of man" or "the human sciences" have a nature, any more than we think that man does. When the notion of knowledge as representation goes, then the notion of inquiry as split into discrete sectors with discrete subject matters goes. The lines between novels, newspaper articles, and sociological research get blurred. The lines between subject matters are drawn by reference to current practical concerns, rather than putative ontological status.

Once this pragmatist line is adopted, however, there are still two ways to go. One can emphasize, as Dewey did, the moral importance of the social sciences—their role in widening and deepening our sense of community and of the possibilities open to this community. Or one can emphasize, as Michel Foucault does, the way in which the social sciences have served as instruments of "the disciplinary society," the connection between knowledge and power rather than that between knowledge and human solidarity. Much present-day concern about the status and the role of the social sciences comes out of the realization that in addition to broadening the sympathies of the educated classes, the social sciences have also helped them manipulate all the other classes (not to mention, so to speak, helping them manipulate themselves). Foucault's is the best account of this dark side of the social sciences. Admirers of Habermas and of Foucault join in thinking of the "interpretive turn" in the social sciences as a turn against their use as "instruments of domination," as tools for what Dewey called "social engineering." This has resulted in a confusing quasi-politicization of what was already a factitious "methodological" issue. In this final section, I want to argue that one should not attribute undue importance to the "Galilean-vs.-hermeneutic" or "explanation-vs.-understanding" contrasts by seeing them as parallel with the contrast between "domination" and "emancipation." We should see Dewey and Foucault as differing not over a theoretical issue, but over what we may hope.

Dewey and Foucault make exactly the same criticism of the tradition. They agree, right down the line, about the need to abandon traditional notions of rationality, objectivity, method, and truth. They are both, so to speak, "beyond method." They agree that rationality is what history and society make it—that there is no overarching ahistorical structure (the Nature of Man, the laws of human behavior, the Moral Law, the Nature of Society) to be discovered. They share the Whewellian and Kuhnian notion of Galilean Science—as exemplifying the power of new vocabularies rather than offering the secret of scientific success. But Dewey emphasizes that this move "beyond method" gives mankind an opportunity to grow up, to be free to make itself, rather than seeking direction from some imagined outside source (one of the ahistorical structures mentioned above). His experimentalism asks us to see knowledge-claims as proposals about what actions to try out next:

> The elaborate systems of science are born not of reason but of impulses at first slight and flickering; impulses to handle, to move about, to hunt, to uncover, to mix things separated and divide things combined, to talk and to listen. Method is their effectual organization into continuous dispositions of inquiry, development, and testing. . . . Reason, the rational attitude, is the resulting disposition. . . .[6]

Foucault also moves beyond the traditional ideals of method and rationality as antecedent constraints upon inquiry, but he views this move as the Nietzschean realization that all knowledge-claims are moves in a power-game. "We are subject to the production of truth through power, and we cannot exercise power except through the production of truth."[7]

Here we have two philosophers saying the same thing but putting a different spin on it. The same phenomenon is found in their respective predecessors. James and Nietzsche (as Arthur Danto has pointed out[8]) developed the same criticisms of traditional notions of truth, and the same "pragmatic" (or "perspectivalist") alternative. James jovially says that "ideas become true just insofar as they help us to get into satisfactory relation with other parts of our experience,"[9] and Dewey follows this up when he says that "rationality is the attainment of a working harmony among diverse desires."[10] Nietzsche says that "the criterion of truth resides in the enhancement of the feeling of power"[11] and that

> [the] mistake of philosophy is that, instead of seeing logic and the categories of reasons as means for fixing up the world for utilitarian ends . . . one thinks that they give one a criterion of truth about *reality*.[12]

Foucault follows this up by saying that "we should not imagine that the world presents us with a legible face . . . [we] must conceive discourse as a violence that we do to things."[13] The arguments which James and Dewey on the one hand, and Nietzsche and Foucault on the other, present for these identical views are as similar as the tone of each is different. Neither pair has any arguments except the usual "idealist" ones, familiar since Kant, against the notion of knowledge as correspondence to nonrepresentations (rather than coherence among representations). These are the arguments in whose direction I gestured in the first section of this paper, when I said that all attempts to cash Galileo's metaphor of Nature's Own Language had failed. Since the cash-value of a philosophical conclusion is the pattern of argument around it, I do not think that we are going to find any *theoretical* differences which divide these two pairs of philosophers from each other.

Is the difference then *merely* one of tone—an ingenuous Anglo-Saxon pose as opposed to a self-dramatizing Continental one? The difference could be better put in terms of something like "moral outlook." One is reminded of the famous passage in Wittgenstein:

> If good or bad willing changes the world, it can only change the limits of the world, not the facts; not the things that can be expressed in language.

> In brief, the world must thereby become quite another. It must so to speak wax or wane as a whole. The world of the happy is quite another than that of the unhappy.[14]

But again, "good and bad willing," "happy and unhappy" are not right for the opposition we are trying to describe. "Hopeful" and "hopeless" are a bit better. Ian Hacking winds up a discussion of Foucault by saying:

> "What is man?" asked Kant. "Nothing," says Foucault. "For what then may we hope?" asks Kant. Does Foucault give the same *nothing* in reply? To think so is to misunderstand Foucault's reply to the question about Man. Foucault said that the concept Man is a fraud, not that you and I are as nothing. Likewise the concept Hope is all wrong. The hopes attributed to Marx and Rousseau are perhaps part of that very concept Man, and they are a sorry basis for optimism. Optimism, pessimism, nihilism and the like are all concepts that make sense only within the idea of a transcendental or enduring subject. Foucault is not in the least incoherent about all this. If we're not satisfied, it should not be because he is pessimistic. It is because he has given no surrogate for whatever it is that springs eternal in the human breast.[15]

What Foucault doesn't give us is what Dewey wanted to give us—a kind of hope which doesn't *need* reinforcement from "the idea of a transcendental or enduring subject." Dewey offered ways of using words like "truth," "rationality," "progress," "freedom," "democracy," "culture," "art," and the like which presupposed neither the ability to use the familiar vocabulary of what Foucault calls "the classic age," nor that of the nineteenth-century French intellectuals (the vocabulary of "man and his doubles").

Foucault sees no middle ground, in thinking about the social sciences, between the "classic" Galilean conception of "behavioral sciences" and the French notion of *"sciences de l'homme."* It was just such a middle ground that Dewey proposed, and which inspired the social sciences in America before the failure of nerve which turned them "behavioral." More generally, the recent reaction in favor of hermeneutical social sciences which I discussed earlier has taken for granted that if we don't want something like Parsons, we have to take something like Foucault; i.e., that overcoming the deficiencies of Weberian *Zweckrationalität* requires going all the way, repudiating the "will to truth." What Dewey suggested was that we keep the will to truth and the optimism that goes with it, but free them from the behaviorist notion that Behaviorese is Nature's Own Language *and* from the notion of man as "transcendental or enduring subject." For, in Dewey's hands, the will to truth is not the urge to dominate but the urge to create, to "attain working harmony among diverse desires."

This may sound too pat, too good to be true. I suggest that the reason we find it so is that we are convinced that liberalism requires the notion of a common human nature, or a common set of moral principles which binds us all, or some other descendent of the Christian notion of the Brotherhood of Man. So we have come to see liberal social hope—such as Dewey's—as inherently self-deceptive and philosophically naive. We think that, once we have freed ourselves from the various illusions which Nietzsche diagnosed, we *must* find ourselves all alone, without the sense of community which liberalism requires. Perhaps, as Hacking says, Nietzsche and Foucault are not saying that you and I are as nothing, but they do seem to hint that you and I together, as *we*, aren't much—that human solidarity goes when God and his doubles go. Man as Hegel thought of him, as the Incarnation of the Idea, doubtless does have to go. The proletariat as the Redeemed Form of Man has to go, too. But there seems no particular reason why, after dumping Marx, we have to keep on repeating all the nasty things about bourgeois liberalism which he taught us to say. There is no inferential connection between the disappearance of the transcendental subject—of "man" as something having a nature which society can repress or understand—and the disappearance of human solidarity. Bourgeois liberalism seems to me the best example of this solidarity we have yet achieved, and Deweyan pragmatism the best articulation of it.[16]

The burden of my argument here is that we should see Dewey as having already gone the route Foucault is traveling, and as having arrived at the point Foucault is still trying to reach—the point at which we can make philosophical and historical ("genealogical") reflection useful to those, in Foucault's phrase, "whose fight is located in the fine meshes of the webs of power."[17] Dewey spent his life trying to lend a hand in these little fights, and in the course of doing so he worked out the vocabulary and rhetoric of American "pluralism." This rhetoric made the first generation of American social scientists think of themselves as apostles of a new form of social life. Foucault does not, as far as I can see, do more than update Dewey by warning that the social scientists have often been, and are always likely to be, co-opted by the bad guys. Reading Foucault reinforces the disillusion which American intellectuals have suffered during the last few decades of watching the "behavioralized" social sciences team up with the state.

The reason why it may appear that Foucault has something new and distinctive to add to Dewey is that he is riding the crest of a powerful but vaguely-defined movement which I have elsewhere[17] described as "textualism"—the movement which suggests, as Foucault puts it at the end of *The Order of Things*, that "Man is in the process of perishing as the being of language continues to shine ever brighter upon our horizon."[18] Another reason is that Foucault is attempting to transform political discourse by seeing "power" as not intrinsically repressive—because, roughly, there is no naturally good self to repress. But Dewey, it seems to me, had already grasped both points. Foucault's vision of discourse as a network of power-relations isn't very different from Dewey's vision of it as instrumental, as one element in the arsenal of tools people use for gratifying, synthesizing, and harmonizing their desires. Dewey had learned from Hegel what Foucault learns from Nietzsche—that there is nothing much to "man" except one more animal, until culture, the meshes of power, begin to shape him into something else. For Dewey too there is nothing Rousseauian to be "repressed"; "repression" and "liberation" are just names for the sides of the structures of power we like and the sides we don't like. Once "power" is freed from its connotation of "repression," then Foucault's "structures of power" will not seem much different from Dewey's "structures of culture." "Power" and "culture" are equipollent indications of the social forces which make us more than animals—and which, when the bad guys take over, can turn us into something worse and more miserable than animals.

These remarks are not meant to downgrade Foucault—who seems to me one of the most interesting philosophers alive—but just to insist that we go slow about assuming that the discovery of things like "discourse," "textuality," "speech-acts," and the like have radically changed the philosophical scene. The current vogue of "hermeneutics" is going to end soon, and badly, if we advertise these new notions as more than they are—namely, one more jargon which tries to get out from under some of the mistakes of the past. Dewey had his own jargon—popular at the time, but now a bit musty—for the same purpose. But the difference in jargon should not obscure the common aim. This is the attempt to free mankind from Nietzsche's "longest lie," the notion that outside the haphazard and perilous experiments we perform there lies something (God, Science, Knowledge, Rationality, or Truth) which will, if only we perform the correct rituals, step in to save us. Although Foucault and Dewey are trying to do the same thing, Dewey seems to me to have done it better, simply because his vocabulary allows room for unjustifiable hope, and an ungroundable but vital sense of human solidarity.

Notes

1. I expand on these points in "A Reply to Dreyfus and Taylor," *Review of Metaphysics*, XXIV (1980): 39-46, and in the ensuing discussion, pp. 47-55.

2. Cf. Bernard Williams, *Descartes: The Project of Pure Enquiry* (London and New York: Penguin Books, 1978), pp. 64ff.

3. Paul Rabinow and William M. Sullivan, "The Interpreting Turn: Emergence of an Approach" in *Interpretive Social Science*, ed. Rabinow and Sullivan (Berkeley: University of California Press, 1979), p. 5.

4. See the discussion of Searle's "Minds, Brains and Programs," in *The Behavioral and Brain Sciences*, 3 (1980): 417-457, esp. my "Searle and the Secret Powers of the Brain" at pp. 445-446 and Searle's "Intrinsic Intentionality" at pp. 450-456.

5. See the material cited in n. 1, above.

6. John Dewey, *Human Nature and Conduct* (New York: Modern Library, 1930), p. 196.

7. Michel Foucault, *Power/Knowledge* (Brighton: Harvester Books, 1980), p. 93.

8. Arthur Danto, *Nietzsche as Philosopher* (New York: Macmillan, 1965), chap. 3.

9. William James, *Pragmatism* (New York: Longmans Green, 1947), p. 58.

10. Dewey, *op. cit.*, p. 196.

11. Friedrich Nietzsche, *The Will to Power*, trans. Kaufmann (New York: Random House, 1967), p. 290.

12. Nietzsche, *Werke*, ed. Schlechta, III, p. 318.

13. Foucault, *The Archaeology of Knowledge* (New York: Harper and Row, 1972), p. 229.

14. Ludwig Wittgenstein, *Tractatus Logico-Philosophicus* 6.42.

15. Ian Hacking, review of Foucault's *Power/Knowledge*, in *New York Review of Books*, April 1981.

16. Dewey seems to me the twentieth-century counterpart of John Stuart Mill, whose attempt to synthesize Coleridge with Bentham is paralleled by Dewey's attempt to synthesize Hegel with Mill himself. In a brilliant critique of liberalism, John Dunn describes Mill as attempting to combine the "two possible radical intellectual strategies open to those who aspire to rescue liberalism as a coherent political option":

> One is to shrink liberalism to a more or less pragmatic and sociological doctrine about the relations between types of political and social order and the enjoyment of political liberties. The version of liberalism which embraces this option is usually today termed "pluralism," a conception . . . which is still in effect the official intellectual ideology of American society. The second possible radical strategy is simply to repudiate the claims of sociology, to take an epistemological position of such stark scepticism that the somewhat over-rated causal status of sociology can safely be viewed with limited scorn. (*Western Political Values in the Face of the Future* [Cambridge: Cambridge University Press, 1979], pp. 47-48)

Dunn thinks Mill's attempt to "integrate intellectual traditions so deeply and explicitly inimical to one another" failed, and that modern pluralism fails also:

> Modern pluralism is thus at least sufficiently sociologically self-aware not to blanch from the insight that a liberal polity is the political form of bourgeois capitalist society. But the price which it has paid, so far pretty willingly, for this self-awareness, is the surrender of any plausible overall intellectual frame, uniting epistemology, psychology and political theory, which explains and celebrates the force of such political commitment. (*Ibid.*, p. 49).

My view is that such an overall intellectual frame was exactly what Dewey gave us, and that he did so precisely by carrying out Mill's combination of strategies. (For some links between Rawls [who is Dunn's favorite example of modern pluralism] and Dewey, see Rawls's Dewey Lectures, "Kantian Constructivism in Moral Theory," *Journal of Philosophy* LXXVII (1980): 515-572. Note esp. p. 542, on a conception of justice which swings free of religious, philosophical or moral doctrines," and *Weltanschauungen* generally. See also p. 519 for Rawls's repudiation of an "epistemological problem," and his doctrine of "moral facts" as "constructed.") Dunn seems to me right in saying that liberalism has little useful to say about contemporary global politics, but wrong in pinning the blame for this on its lack of a philosophical synthesis of the old, Kantian, unpragmatic sort. On my view, we should be more willing than we are to celebrate bourgeois capitalist society as the best polity actualized so far, while regretting that it is irrelevant to most of the problems of most of the population of the planet.

17. See Essay 9, above.

18. Foucault, *The Order of Things* (New York: Random House, 1973), p. 386.

12

Philosophy in America Today

1. Analytic Philosophy and the Tradition

Revolutionary movements within an intellectual discipline require a revisionist history of that discipline. Reichenbach performed this service for analytic philosophy in his *Rise of Scientific Philosophy*. That book, published in 1951, presents the view of history which explains Quine's quip that people go into philosophy for one of two reasons: some are interested in the history of philosophy, and some in philosophy. Quine's wisecrack assumes, and Reichenbach's book argues, that the proper concern of philosophy is to solve a set of identifiable problems, problems arising out of the activity and results of the natural sciences. Reichenbach describes his book as follows:

> It maintains that philosophic speculation is a passing stage, occurring when philosophic problems are raised at a time which does not possess the logical means to solve them. It claims that there is, and always has been, a scientific approach to philosophy. And it wishes to show that from this ground has sprung a scientific philosophy which, in the science of our time, has found the tools to solve those problems that in earlier times have been the subject of guesswork only. To put it briefly: this book is written with the intention of showing that philosophy has proceeded from speculation to science.[1]

Reichenbach's history could no longer be written in the terms in which he wrote it, since he took for granted all the positivist doctrines which, in the intervening thirty years, have been dismantled by Wittgenstein, Quine, Sellars, and Kuhn. But most post-positivistic analytic philosophers would still agree that philosophy has, in relatively recent times, "proceeded from speculation to science." They would accept the view that one can define philosophy in terms of a set of identifiable, enduring problems, which were dealt with in awkward and unsophisticated ways in earlier periods, and are now being dealt with in a precision and rigor hitherto unknown. There may be disagreement about which of these problems are to be solved and which dissolved or simply set aside. There may also be disagreement about whether, as Reichenbach thought, the tools are provided by science or whether, instead, they must be forged by the philosophers themselves. But these disagreements are minor compared to the broad agreement on the sort of historical story which is to be told.

Reichenbach's construction of a sweeping historical drama required him to be selective in his choice of incident. If one wants to interpret philosophy as an attempt to understand the nature of natural science, as flourishing when natural science has flourished, and as capable of being brought to a satisfactory conclusion now that the sciences have become "mature," one must take "the problems of philosophy" to be those which were formulated clearly, for the first time, in the seventeenth and eighteenth centuries—the period in which the phenomenon of the New Science was the chief object of philosophers' attention. These were primarily problems about the nature and possibility of scientific knowledge, epistemological problems. Having identified philosophy with these problems, one can explain the Greek and mediaeval failure to formulate them clearly by reference to the primitive state of science before 1600, while brushing aside as unphilosophical and ideological the Greek concern with politics and poetry and the Christian concern with God. This will enable one to see Kant as, in Reichenbach's phrase, "the climax of speculative philosophy," and to skip lightly over the nineteenth and early twentieth centuries (a habit which still prevails among analytic philosophers—who see the interval between Kant and Frege as an unfortunate period of confusion).

Reichenbach thought it a serious misunderstanding of Kant to think of Hegel as his successor; rather, he said, "Hegel's system is the poor construction of a fanatic who has seen one empirical truth and attempts to make it a logical law within the most unscientific of all logics" (p. 72). On Reichenbach's view, Marx abandoned empiricism and embraced Hegelianism for unfortunate "psychological reasons" (p. 71). The nineteenth century is to be seen not as the beginning of a search for meaning in history but as the period in which natural scientists, rather than philosophy professors, proceeded to solve the questions which Descartes, Hume, and Kant had posed. Reichenbach condemns the sort of textbook which, in the chapter on the nineteenth century, mentions Fichte, Schelling, Hegel, Schopenhauer, Spencer, and Bergson, and records their systems as though they were philosophical creations homogeneous with the systems of earlier periods. Instead, Reichenbach says, we should see that

> the philosophy of the systems ends with Kant, and it is a misunderstanding of the history of philosophy to discuss the later systems on a level with those of Kant or Plato. Those older systems were expressive of the science of their time and gave pseudo-answers when no better answers were available. The philosophical systems of the nineteenth century were constructed at a time when a better philosophy was in the making; they are the work of men who did not see the philosophic discoveries immanent in the science of their time and who developed, under the name of philosophy, systems of naive generalizations and analogies. . . . Considered historically, these systems would be better compared to the dead end of a river that after flowing through fertile lands finally dries out in the desert. (pp. 121-122)

This account of the history of philosophy makes a lot of sense even if one has been convinced by Kuhn that science is not as methodical as we once thought, and by Quine that the "philosophic discoveries" Reichenbach admired were mostly dogmas. One can drop the dogmas and still preserve most of Reichenbach's history. One can still cleave to the view that philosophy began as natural science's account of itself, that attempts to claim knowledge outside of the natural sciences are to be measured against the procedures used within them, and that philosophy has recently become scientific and rigorous. I think that these views are held by the vast majority of analytic philosophers, and I do not wish to argue against a contextual definition of "philosophy" in these terms. It is as good a definition as we are likely to get *if* we want "philosophy" to be the name of a discipline, a set of research programs, an autonomous sector of culture. Reichenbach was right in saying that certain seventeenth- and eighteenth-century problems—Kant's problems, roughly speaking—which arose out of the attempt to give a scientific account of science itself, have often been thought of as *the* philosophical problems. He was also right, I think, in dismissing lots of philosophical programs as attempts to claim the status of "science" without imitating its procedures or respecting its results.

I myself would join Reichenbach in dismissing classical Husserlian phenomenology, Bergson, Whitehead, the Dewey of *Experience and*

Nature, the James of *Radical Empiricism*, neo-Thomist epistemolog- ical realism, and a variety of other late nineteenth- and early twen- tieth-century systems. Bergson and Whitehead, and the bad ("meta- physical") parts of Dewey and James, seem to me merely weakened versions of idealism—attempts to answer "unscientifically" formu- lated epistemological questions about the "relation of subject and object" by "naive generalizations and analogies" which emphasize "feeling" rather than "cognition." Phenomenology and neo-Thomism also seem diagnosable and dismissable along Reichenbachian lines. Both movements tried in vain to isolate a *Fach* for themselves, distinct from science and its self-clarification, by giving sense to the notion of distinctively "philosophical," super-scientific knowledge.[2]

So I think that positivism in general, and Reichenbach in particu- lar, served American philosophy well by making a clear distinction between philosophy as an explanation of, or an expansion of, scien- tific knowledge, and philosophy as something else. But I want to raise two questions about the relation between analytic philosophy and the tradition:

(1) Can a Reichenbachian account of the past give us a story about the present and the future which describes a significant cultural function for philosophy to perform, a continuing task?

(2) What about "philosophy as something else"—for example, the work of philosophers who do not *claim* to be giving anything like "solu- tions to philosophic problems" or "super-scientific knowledge"—the "Continental" competition, writers like Heidegger, Foucault, and their nineteenth-century precursors? What do we lose by reading them out of philosophy?

In what follows, I shall try to answer both questions.

2. Analytic Philosophy a Generation after Its Triumph

About the time of Reichenbach's book, in the early fifties, analytic philosophy began to take over American philosophy departments. The great emigrés—Carnap, Hempel, Feigl, Reichenbach, Bergmann, Tarski—began to be treated with the respect they deserved. Their disciples began to be appointed to, and to dominate, the most prestig- ious departments. Departments which did not go along with this trend began to lose their prestige. By 1960, a new set of philosophical para- digms was in place. A new sort of graduate education in philosophy was entrenched—one in which Dewey and Whitehead, heroes of the previous generation, were no longer read, in which the history of philosophy was decisively downgraded, and in which the study of logic assumed an importance previously given to the study of languages. Thanks to the postwar baby boom, the sixties and early seventies also happened to be the period in which the majority of living American Ph.D.'s in philosophy were educated. As a result, most of today's teachers of philosophy in American colleges and universities assimilated some version of Reichenbach's picture of the history of philosophy in graduate school. They were brought up to believe themselves the lucky participants in the beginnings of a new philosophical age—an Age of Analysis, in which things would finally be done properly. They were often led to despise the sort of person who was interested in the history of philosophy, or more generally in the history of thought, rather than in solving philosophical problems. With Reichenbach, they assumed that

> the philosopher of the old school is usually a man trained in literature and history, who has never learned the precision methods of the mathematical sciences or experienced the happiness of demonstrating a law of nature by a verification of all its consequences. (p. 308)

According to the hopes of the logical positivists, the advent of this new generation should have given rise to an unprecedented era of cooperation, teamwork, agreement on results attained. Solid building blocks should have been added to the edifice of knowledge. This did not happen. Indeed, it now, in 1981, seems far more improbable a forecast of the future of philosophy than it did in 1951, when Reichenbach wrote. In 1951, a graduate student who (like myself) was in the process of learning about, or being converted to, analytic philosophy, could still believe that there were a finite number of distinct, specifiable philosophical problems to be resolved—problems which any serious analytic philosopher would agree to be *the* outstanding problems. For example, there was the problem of the counterfactual conditional, the problem of whether an "emotive" analysis of ethical terms was satisfactory, Quine's problem about the nature of analyticity, and a few more. These were problems which fitted nicely into the vocabulary of the positivists. They could easily be seen as the final, proper formulation of problems which had been seen, as in a glass darkly, by Leibniz, Hume, and Kant. Further, there was agreement on what a solution to a philosophical problem looked like—e.g., Russell on definite descriptions, Frege on meaning and reference, Tarski on truth. In those days, when my generation was young, all the conditions for a Kuhnian "normal," problem-solving discipline were fulfilled.

To recite this list of problems and paradigms is to evoke memories of a simple, brighter, vanished world. In the interlocking "central" areas of analytic philosophy—epistemology, philosophy of language, and metaphysics—there are now as many paradigms as there are major philosophy departments. What counts as a serious problem for a UCLA Ph.D. need not count as one for a Chicago or a Cornell Ph.D., and conversely. Any problem that enjoys a simultaneous vogue in ten of the hundred or so "analytic" philosophy departments in America is doing exceptionally well. The field these days is a jungle of competing research programs, programs which seem to have a shorter and shorter half-life as the years go by. The fifteen years after Reichenbach wrote witnessed the rise and fall of "Oxford philosophy." In the fifteen years since "West Coast Semantics" swept eastward and effected a *translatio imperii* from Oxford to the UCLA-Princeton-Harvard axis, we have had several brief shining moments in which the future of philosophy, or at least of philosophy of language, seemed clearly marked out. But each of these illuminations has suffered eclipse. There is no more consensus about the problems and methods of philosophy in America today than there was in Germany in 1920. At that time most philosophers were, perhaps, more or less "neo-Kantian," but the dominant mode of academic life was that each *Ordinarius* had his system, and produced students who thought of problems within that system as "the leading problems of philosophy." That is pretty much the mode of life in American philosophy departments today. Most philosophers are more or less "analytic," but there is no agreed-upon interuniversity paradigm of philosophical work, nor any agreed-upon list of "central problems." The best hope for an American philosopher is Andy Warhol's promise that we shall *all* be superstars, for approximately fifteen minutes apiece.

The situation in moral and social philosophy, admittedly, is not the same as in the so-called "central" areas of philosophy. Here we have Rawls's *Theory of Justice* as a genuine interuniversity paradigm, a book whose importance and permanence are deservedly recognized on all sides. But analytic philosophy cannot draw any comfort from this fact when it looks for a self-description which preserves and updates Reichenbach's. *A Theory of Justice* simply bypasses the metaethical issues which, in Reichenbach's eyes, were the sole connection between philosophy and normative judgments. (Cf. Reichenbach, chap. 17.) It is a book which descends straight from Kant, Mill, and Sidgwick. The same book could have been written if logical positivism had never existed. It is not a triumph of "analytic" philosophizing. It is simply the best update of liberal social thought which we have. It happens to have been written by a professor of philosophy, but if Rawls had studied jurisprudence or political science rather than philosophy it is not clear that he would have been led to write anything very different, nor even to argue in a different style.

Just as one would be hard put to it to say what the nature of "philosophy" is such that Marx, Kierkegaard, and Frege are all great nineteenth-century *philosophers*, so it is hard to define "philosophy" so as to make clear why, e.g., Kuhn, Kripke, and Rawls are three important contemporary *philosophers* (as opposed to some bland generic term like "thinkers" or "intellectuals"), not to speak of why they are all "analytic" philosophers. This is not, to be sure, a serious problem. One should not, I think, try to construct definitions of "philosophy" which will mark it off, ahistorically, from other academic disciplines. But it is important to see that Reichenbach thought we *should*, and that analytic philosophy grew up with a self-image which depended upon its being possible to do so. Reichenbach told us that what made philosophy philosophy was a list of problems which could now be clearly seen—problems about the nature and possibility of scientific knowledge, and of its relations to the rest of culture. Analytic philosophers have continued to believe that *some* problems are distinctly *philosophical* problems. But they are no longer able either to accept Reichenbach's list or to construct principles for drawing up a new list. Instead, they have simply let the list be constructed anew every few years. One of the reasons people come to the divisional meetings of the APA is to find out what the fashionable new problems are—what the "good people in the field" are talking about nowadays. For it has now become enough to constitute a problem as "philosophical" that a well-known professor of philosophy has written an interesting paper posing it. The institutional tail is wagging the scientific dog. We no longer have a story to tell about the relation between our problems and those of the past, one which shows how much more clearly we understand them than, say, Leibniz or Hume did. Instead, we have a thriving enterprise which looks back only a few decades, and finds its principal justification in the sheer intelligence of the people who are part of it.

In saying that "analytic philosophy" now has only a stylistic and sociological unity, I am not suggesting that analytic philosophy is a bad thing, or is in bad shape. The analytic style is, I think, a *good* style. The *ésprit de corps* among analytic philosophers is healthy and useful. All I am saying is that analytic philosophy has become, whether it likes it or not, the same sort of discipline as we find in the other "humanities" departments—departments where pretensions to "rigor" and to "scientific" status are less evident. The normal form of life in

the humanities is the same as that in the arts and in belles-lettres: a
genius does something new and interesting and persuasive, and his or
her admirers begin to form a school or movement. Thus, for example,
the *Annales* sort of historiography is currently fashionable in many
American history departments, deconstructive criticism in many departments of comparative literature, and "possible world semantics"
in many philosophy departments. To say that these movements are
fashionable is to say that Fernand Braudel, or Jacques Derrida, or
Richard Montague, has done some remarkable work and has many
readers and imitators. It would be a mistake to try to do more than
this—to try to explain, in the manner of Reichenbach, that Montague
has at last succeeded in clearly stating, or in solving, some long-stand-
ing "problem of scientific philosophy," or some of "the outstanding
problems of analytic philosophy." Any genealogy we construct to
back up such a claim is going to be wildly implausible and gerryman-
dered, as would one which tried to show that Derrida is the true heir
of Dr. Johnson, or Braudel of Ranke.

Rather, we should relax and say, with our colleagues in history and
literature, that we in the humanities differ from natural scientists
precisely in *not* knowing in advance what our problems are, and in
not *needing* to provide criteria of identity which will tell us whether
our problems are the same as those of our predecessors. To adopt this
relaxed attitude is to *let* the institutional tail wag the pseudo-scientific
dog. It is to admit that our geniuses invent problems and programs
de novo, rather than being presented with them by the subject-matter
itself, or by the "current state of research." The same point can be
made by saying that it is a mark of humanistic culture *not* to try to
reduce the new to the old, nor to insist upon a canonical list of problems or methods, nor upon a canonical vocabulary in which problems
are to be stated. This Gadamerian point can be put in Kuhnian terms
by saying that the essential thing is not to be "scientific" but to have
a disciplinary matrix for ongoing work which maintains a reasonable
balance between "standards" and openness, or in Habermasian terms
by saying that what matters is that conversation be continuous and
undistorted.

3. Analytic Philosophy, "Philosophical Ability," and Conceptual Clarification

The relaxed attitude I am recommending suggests that we should not
worry about whether analytic philosophy has retained the "scientific"
status which Reichenbach claimed for logical positivism, nor should

we worry about whether what we, or somebody else, is doing is "really philosophy." We should let a hundred flowers bloom, admire them while they last, and leave botanizing to the intellectual historians of the next century. But this attitude does not chime with that of most analytic philosophers. They are not willing to give up the Reichenbachian attempt to get philosophy out of the "humanities" and into the "sciences." They would insist that we analytic philosophers have a certain special distinction which marks us off from the "humanists." This distinction is not our concern with an enumerable list of problems, as Reichenbach thought it was, but rather our possession of a special intellectual virtue, a virtue shared with mathematicians and physicists, but not with the average professor of literature or history. On this view, merit in philosophy is not so much a matter of having actually solved some of the "problems of philosophy" (since it is tacitly admitted that what counts as a "problem" is pretty much up for grabs), but rather a matter of sheer intelligence, sheer problem-solving ability. The suggestion is that there is a certain range of talent, or cast of mind, or something of the sort, of which philosophers typically have a lot.

If one asks for more detail on what this intellectual virtue called "philosophical ability" consists in, the answer would presumably go something like this: the able philosopher should be able to spot flaws in any argument he hears. Further, he should be able to do this on topics outside of those usually discussed in philosophy courses as well as on "specifically philosophical" issues. As a corollary, he should be able to construct as good an argument as *can* be constructed for *any* view, no matter how wrong-headed. The ideal of philosophical ability is to see the entire universe of possible assertions in all their inferential relationships to one another, and thus to be able to construct, or criticize, any argument.

I think it is true that analytic philosophers typically do have a lot of this sort of ability. But, in any case, it is a gradually self-validating self-description. One will not be encouraged to go to a prestigious American graduate philosophy department if one does not have this particular intellectual virtue. Even if one loves to study Plato, Augustine, Spinoza, Kant, Hegel, etc., but lacks this skill at argumentation, one will not be encouraged to pursue a career in philosophy. One will wind up studying, instead, in a comparative literature department, or a politics department, or a history department. The result is gradually to strengthen the analytic philosophers' image of themselves as, not specialists in a certain area of scientific inquiry, but rather a *corps d'élite* united by talent rather than a list of shared problems and prior results—the *Inspecteurs des Finances* of the academy, so to speak. It thus becomes less and less important for analytic philosophy to have a coherent metaphilosophical account of itself, or to have answers to the question "What counts as a 'specifically *philosophical*' problem?" It becomes less important to find links between the issues discussed by Kuhn, Kripke, and Rawls. It also becomes less important for analytic philosophy to have what Reichenbach gave positivism—an account of its relation to the past. For it is common skills rather than common problems or a common genealogy that matters.

This means that the claim, "Philosophy has now become scientific rather than speculative," has come to mean something very different for contemporary analytic philosophy than it meant for Reichenbach. "Scientific" now means something like "argumentative." The contrast between the old and the new is no longer a contrast between an immature prescientific and a mature scientific stage of discussion of a common set of problems, but a contrast between styles—the "scientific" style and the "literary" style. The former style asks that premises be explicitly spelled out rather than guessed at, that terms be introduced by definitions rather than by allusion. The latter style may involve argumentation, but that is not essential; what is essential is telling a new story, suggesting a new language-game, in the hope of a new form of intellectual life.

If what I have said in the previous section is right, then this shift in identifying criterion from subject to style is natural and predictable. If a discipline has no well-defined subject matter, and no inter-university paradigms of achievement, then it will have to have *stylistic* paradigms. This, I think, is what has happened to analytic philosophy as it moved from its positivistic to its post-positivistic stage, in the course of the last thirty years. But, once again, I do not take this to be a denigrating remark. It is not a suggestion that philosophers are doing something they shouldn't be doing. Believing, as I do, that philosophy is not the sort of thing that *has* an historical essence or mission, I am *not* saying that the analytic movement has somehow wandered off the true path. "Philosophy," in the narrow and professional sense, is just whatever we philosophy professors do. Having a common style, and a niche in the normal table of organization of academic departments, is quite enough to make our discipline as identifiable and respectable as any other. Indeed, where the style is the kind of argumentative skill I have described, it is enough to make it socially valuable. A nation can count itself lucky to have several thousand relatively leisured and relatively unspecialized intellectuals who are exceptionally good at putting together arguments and pulling them apart. Such a group is a precious cultural resource. As we keep saying on our grant applications, the nation would do well to have analytic philosophers advise on public projects. We shall kibitz at least as well as any other professional group, and perhaps rather better than most.

However, there is *something* dubious about the current self-image of analytic philosophy. I can perhaps bring it out by saying that we are in bad faith insofar as we tend to take credit for being wise as well as clever. We are not entitled to this double dollop of self-esteem. Philosophy professors were traditionally thought of as wise because they were believed to have read and experienced much, traveled far in the realms of thought, pondered the great problems which have always troubled the human spirit. This image was more or less plausible as long as the study of philosophy centered around the study of the history of philosophy (as it did before 1950 in American philosophy departments, and still does in, e.g., France and Germany). The positivist revolution, however, changed the image of the philosopher from scholar to scientist. It suggested that the best philosophy student would not be the sort who might have gone into intellectual history, but rather the sort who might have gone into mathematics or physics. In the course of the transition to post-positivistic analytic philosophy, the image of the scientist has been replaced by another, though it is not quite clear what. Perhaps the most appropriate model for the analytic philosopher is now the *lawyer*, rather than either the scholar or the scientist. The ability to construct a good brief, or conduct a devastating cross-examination, or find relevant precedents, is pretty much the ability which analytic philosophers think of as "distinctively philosophical." It is sufficient to be a good lawyer or to be a good analytic philosopher that you be able to see at a glance the inferential relationships between all the members of a bewilderingly large set of propositions.

The reason why philosophers still are inclined to credit themselves with wisdom is that contemporary analytic philosophy inherits from the logical positivism of thirty years ago the pretension to possess a secure matrix of heuristic concepts—categories which permit it to classify, comprehend, and criticize the rest of culture. But it does not. There has been no successor to the positivist scheme which even attempts a similar comprehensiveness, much less a consensus on such a scheme among post-positivistic analytic philosophers. But the rhetoric we often use in grant-getting, and the condescension we often exhibit to professors of other subjects, still takes for granted that we have a mastery of "conceptual questions." They carry the suggestion

222 Philosophy in America Today

that in addition to our well-known argumentative ability we have a special, privileged knowledge about concepts which gives us a privileged position. But we have no such knowledge, no such higher standpoint. We have dismantled Reichenbach's heuristic scaffolding, and his list of "the problems of scientific philosophy" along with it. We have not substituted anything for it, and we should not try to do so. If there is one thing we have learned about concepts in recent decades it is that to have a concept is to be able to use a word, that to have a mastery of concepts is to be able to use a language, and that languages are created rather than discovered. We should renounce the idea that we have access to some superconcepts which are the concepts of no particular historical epoch, no particular profession, no particular portion of culture, but which somehow necessarily inhere in all subordinate concepts, and can be used to "analyze" the latter. We would thus give up the old dream, shared by Plato and by Reichenbach, from which Wittgenstein woke us—the dream of philosophy as *scientia scientiarum*, as knowledge about the nature of scientific knowledge, as a result of successful inquiry into the nature of all possible inquiry.

Let me try to make this last point more concrete in a brief excursus on "applied philosophy," an area in which talk of "conceptual issues" is unhappily common. If we give up the rhetoric of the sage, we shall no longer say that whereas a physician faced with a medico-moral dilemma may *use* the concept of "person" or "best interest," we, the philosophers, can *analyze* it for her, *clarify* it. The most we can do is explain the way in which various people we have read (Mill, Hume, Spinoza, Kant, Hegel) used the term, and the kind of things they said employing it. This may add something, perhaps even something useful, to the way in which the doctor uses the term henceforth, and so to the decision she will make. But it does not tell her what she really meant, what presuppositions she made, what was really in question. It just does what any other increase in humanistic culture does—it gives a sense of some new alternatives, new contexts, new languages. We are not doing something different in kind from what the professor of literature or history would or could do in the same situation. We are just enlarging a linguistic and argumentative repertoire, and thus an imagination. Beyond this traditional humanist task, we can do only what lawyers do—provide an argument for whatever our client has decided to do, make the chosen cause appear the better.

We fool ourselves on this point, I think, because we frequently encounter physicians, or psychologists, or historians, or literary critics, or simply ordinary citizens, parroting words, or slogans, which originated with, or were analyzed by, one or another of the great dead philosophers. So we tend to assume that we philosophers know what is going on, in a way in which these people who don't know the genealogy of the terms, or phrases, cannot. This is a *non sequitur*. If a physician is torn between respect for the dignity of her patient and the need to minimize his pain, she is not confused on matters which the philosopher, able to discourse on the advantages and disadvantages of teleological and utilitarian ethics, is clear about. Being articulate is a virtue, but it is not the same as eliminating confusion, the attainment of clarity. One can become more articulate about one's alternatives by employing a web of words which are woven by a novelist, a literary historian, a social historian, or a theologian, as well. But in none of these cases, any more than in the case of a moral philosopher's web, is ability to say more a discovery of what one really meant all along, really presupposed all the time. One of the things Wittgenstein taught us, a lesson which helps us distance ourselves from Reichenbach, is that finding plausible premises from which an assertion can be inferred is not finding what the assertor "really had in mind." Another of the things he taught us was that learning to tell a story about what one is doing is not necessarily, or even usually, a discovery of one's original problem or motive or intention. Constructing an argument, in the scientific style, or a story, in the literary style, are both good things to do. But they are not discoveries of an antecedent reality which has been waiting to be unearthed by "analysis" or "reflection." Everything that has happened within analytic philosophy in the last thirty years has helped us see the differences between such constructions and the sort of scientific discovery to which Reichenbach wished to assimilate philosophical inquiry.

4. The "Analytic"-"Continental" Split

So far I have said that analytic philosophy has been forced, by its own internal anti-positivist dialectic, to move away from an image of itself as a science which achieves results and toward an image in which it is simply the free—and, one might almost say, "speculative"—exercise of argumentative skill. "Speculative" here means "unconstrained by any prior set of distinctions or lists of problems." Reichenbach *redivivus* would presumably be appalled by this lack of constraint—by the confusion of tongues, the proliferation of problems and programs, in contemporary American philosophy. But he would admire the style, the insistence on argument, the dialectical acuity. He would approve of the widespread distrust among philosophers of those who, as he put it, were "trained in literature and history, who have never learned the precision methods of the mathematical sciences." He would agree with a distinguished analytic philosopher who urged that "intellectual hygiene" requires one not to read the books of Derrida and Foucault. This attitude, however, has created practical problems in American academic life, problems epitomized in the question, "Who is going to teach Hegel?" I now want to turn to these problems.

Reichenbach's answer to this question was, "If possible, nobody." This answer makes perfectly good sense if one takes Hegel to be trying and failing to do the sort of thing which Locke, Leibniz, Hume, and Kant wanted to do—namely, understand the nature, possibility, and extent of the achievements of the natural sciences. He certainly did not do that very well. It also makes sense if one emphasizes the *Logic* and Hegel's rhetoric about "system" and *"Wissenschaft."* But these are not the parts of Hegel's work which mattered to Marx or, more generally, to the historical and political thought of the nineteenth century. What mattered were precisely those parts which turned away from the knowledge of nature, from the phenomenon of the New Science, to the historicist self-understanding and self-determination of human beings: the *Phenomenology*, the *Philosophy of Right*, and the *Philosophy of History*. With these works Hegel began a sequence of overlapping stories about the course of human history, a sequence which includes Marx, Nietzsche, late Heidegger, and Foucault. These stories are not "philosophical systems." They do not attempt to provide solutions to problems about subject and object, nor to any of the problems which Reichenbach believed nineteenth-century natural science had settled. But this genre of writing embodies, I think, the chief alternative to Reichenbach's answer to the question: what can philosophy be in the age of modern science?

The question, "Who shall now teach Hegel?" is shorthand for the question, "Who is going to teach this genre—all the so-called 'Continental' philosophers?" The obvious answer to this question is, "Whoever cares to study them." This is also the right answer, but we can only accept it wholeheartedly if we clear away a set of factitious questions. One such question is, "Are these Continental philosophers really *philosophers*?" Analytic philosophers, because they identify philosophical ability with argumentative skill and notice that there isn't anything they would consider an *argument* in a carload of Heidegger or Foucault, suggest that these must be people who tried to be philosophers and failed, incompetent philosophers. This is as silly as saying that Plato was an incompetent sophist, or that a hedgehog is an incompetent fox. Hegel knew what he thought about philosophers who imitated the method and style of the mathematicians. He thought *they* were incompetent. These reciprocal charges of incompetence do nobody any good. We should just drop the question of what philosophy really is, or who really counts as a philosopher.

Ours is neither the first, nor will it be the last, period in which the intellectuals whose self-descriptions included the word "philosophy" divided into separate swarms and battled over territory. In late nineteenth-century America what we now call "philosophy" hived off from what we now call "Christian apologetics," to the accompaniment of reciprocal charges of "not being really a philosopher at all." Similar sorts of things happened when what we now call "empirical psychology" was beginning to set up in business on its own. Nowadays we see struggles between philosophy and mathematics departments to decide whose budget will bear the expense of the one mathematical logician the university can afford. Such disputes over money and power produce a lot of *ad hoc* rhetoric about "the nature of the discipline," rhetoric which an experienced dean will automatically tune out. Such disputes only become dangerous when one side or the other wants to say that the material taught by the other side shouldn't be taught *at all*.

Sadly enough, this sort of thing does get said. I have heard analytic philosophers get furious at comparative literature departments for trespassing on philosophical turf by teaching Nietzsche and Derrida, and doubly furious at the suggestion that they might teach it themselves. Conversely, I have heard fans of Continental philosophy be obnoxious about the "mere logic-chopping" with which their analytic colleagues waste students' time and dehydrate their minds. Like reciprocal charges of incompetence, this sort of rhetoric is pointless. It is also dangerous, for it can actually result in colleges and universities not having people on the faculty who can explain certain books to interested students. Yet the only way in which institutions of liberal learning can justify their existence is to be places in which students can find practically any book in the library—Gadamer or Kripke, Searle or Derrida—and then find somebody to talk with about it. When all the jockeying to decide which department's budget will bear the freight is over, we have to make sure that the result has not been to limit the possibilities open to the students.

It follows from what I've been saying that we should not fuss about "building bridges" between analytic and Continental philosophy. Such a project would make sense if, as is sometimes said, the two sides were

226 Philosophy in America Today

attacking common problems with different "methods." But, in the first place, there are no such common problems: looking for an historical story to tell does not encounter the same sort of problems as are discussed in the "analytic" philosophical journals. In the second place, the notion of "methods" finds no clear application on either side. The notion of "powerful analytic tools" which Reichenbach invoked no longer has any relevance to what analytic philosophers actually do. The tools in question were merely the positivist distinctions of Reichenbach's day. Such new tools as we have acquired are merely the more or less transitory distinctions of later days. The thrust of post-Husserlian "Continental" philosophy has also been *against* "method." Husserl's quest for a phenomenological method was, like Reichenbach's logical positivism, an expression of the urge for "the secure path of a science." But Husserl was a brief and futile interruption of the Hegel-Marx-Nietzsche-Heidegger-Foucault sequence which I am taking as paradigmatically "Continental," and which Husserl condemned as "historicist." What distinguishes Nietzsche, Heidegger, and Foucault from Hegel and Marx is precisely the increasing wholeheartedness with which they *give up* the notions of "system," "method," and "science," their increasing willingness to blur the lines between disciplines, their refusal to insist that philosophy be an autonomous *Fach*.

If we put aside wistful talk of bridge-building and joining forces, we can see the analytic-Continental split as both permanent and harmless. We should not see it as tearing philosophy apart. There is no single entity called "philosophy" which once was whole and now is sundered. "Philosophy" is not the name of a natural kind, but just the name of one of the pigeonholes into which humanistic culture is divided for administrative and bibliographical purposes. A Reichenbachian account of what counts as "scientific philosophy," like a Heideggerian account of what counts as being "ontological" rather than merely "ontic," is merely a device for directing attention to the range of topics one wants to discuss. If we get away from such gerrymandering, to a neutral sense of the term "philosophy" in which it is not a particular research program or style, then we shall have something as bland as Sellars's definition: "seing how things, in the largest sense of the term, hang together, in the largest sense of the term." But this neutral sense has little to do with philosophy in any "professional" sense of "philosophy." Since both post-positivistic analytic philosophy and post-phenomenological Continental philosophy abjure the Reichenbachian notion of a permanent neutral conceptual matrix within which all thought and language must fit, they should join in abdicating the role of sage, of final authority on the meaningfulness or the rationality of assertions or actions. Having joined in this renunciation, they can agree to differ on whether finding interesting new problems about which to argue, or telling sweeping historical stories, is the more profitable residual enterprise.

5. The Hidden Agenda

I can summarize the story I have been telling as follows:

1. Analytic philosophy started off as a way of moving from speculation to science—from philosophy as an historically based discipline to philosophy as a discipline centering around "logical analysis."

2. The notion of "logical analysis" turned upon itself, and committed slow suicide, in Wittgensteinian, "ordinary language," Quinean, Kuhnian, and Sellarsian criticisms of the purportedly "scientific" vocabulary which Reichenbach, e.g., had taken for granted.

3. Analytic philosophy was thus left without a genealogy, a sense of mission, or a metaphilosophy. Training in philosophy turned into a sort of "casebook" procedure, of the sort found in law schools. Students' wits were sharpened by reading preprints of articles by currently fashionable figures, and finding objections to them. The students so trained began to think of themselves neither as continuing a tradition nor as participating in the solution of the "outstanding problems" at the frontiers of a science. Rather, they took their self-image from a style and quality of argumentation. They became quasi-lawyers rather than quasi-scientists—hoping an interesting new case would turn up.

4. This development hardened the split between "analytic" and "Continental" philosophy by moving the study of Hegel, Nietzsche, Heidegger, etc., out of philosophy departments. In American universities, this tradition is now discussed in various other departments—e.g., those of history, politics, and comparative literature.

5. The result is to leave American philosophy departments stranded somewhere between the humanities (their ancestral home), the natural sciences (the territory into which they once hoped to move, but were never fully accepted), and the social sciences (toward which they are now putting out feelers). The older sort of philosophy professor—who might have been an historian or literary critic almost as well—is dying out. The newer sort would like to think of himself as a free-ranging analytic intellect, able to bring "philosophical expertise" to bear on anything that comes up, but also as having a home territory about which he commands special knowledge. This is, however, a

difficult image to sustain. The increasingly short half-lives of philosophical problems and programs makes the home territory shifting ground. The rest of the academy has (reasonably enough) become puzzled about what "philosophical expertise" might be.

My story has been one of struggles between kinds of professors, professors with different aptitudes and consequently with different paradigms and interests. It is a story of academic politics—not much more, in the long run, than a matter of what sort of professors come under which departmental budget. Problems created by academic politics can be solved by more academic politics. One may expect that, by the end of the century, philosophy in America will have gotten over the ambiguities which have marked the last thirty years, and will begin to develop, once again, a clear self-image. One possibility is that this image will be of a *new* discipline, one not much more than fifty years old, and which (unless analytic philosophy has, in the meantime, triumphed in the Continental universities) does not try to link up with, or even to argue with, what is practiced under the heading of "philosophy" in other parts of the world.

However, my treatment of the topic has left something out. Quarrels between professors are never entirely disconnected from larger quarrels. There was a hidden agenda behind the split between old-fashioned "humanistic" philosophy (of the Dewey-Whitehead sort) and the positivists, and a similar agenda lies behind the current split between devotees of "analytic" and of "Continental" philosophy. The heavy breathing on both sides about the immorality or stupidity of the opposition signals passions which academic power struggles cannot fully explain.

Although philosophy is not something which once was whole and now is sundered, something else is—namely, the secular intellectual's conception of himself. Up until Kant, the secular intellectual saw the knowledge gained by the advancing natural sciences as the point of his life. Through the nineteenth century, men like Huxley and Clifford and Peirce still saw respect for scientific truth as the highest human virtue, the moral equivalent of the Christian's love and fear of God. These nineteenth-century figures were Reichenbach's heroes. But the nineteenth century also saw the rise of a *new* sort of secular intellectual, one who had lost faith in science with the same thoroughness as the Enlightenment had lost faith in God. Carlyle and Henry Adams are examples of this new kind of intellectual, the kind whose consciousness is dominated by a sense of the contingency of history, the contingency of the vocabulary which he himself is using, the sense that nature and scientific truth are largely beside the point and that history is up for grabs. This sort of intellectual is secular with a vengeance, for he sees the religion "of science" or "of humanity" as just as self-deceptive as the old-time religion. His thought tends toward Nietzsche's view of science as merely a prolongation of theology, of both as forms of "the longest lie." The attitude of such intellectuals toward "scientific" or "linguistic" philosophy is summed up in Nietzsche's wisecrack: "I fear that we shall be unable to get rid of God, since we still believe in grammar."

This split between two sorts of intellectual has become deeper in our own century. It is, indeed, no mere matter of academic politics. It is the split imprecisely sketched by Snow's contrast between the "scientific culture" and the "literary culture." It is the antagonism which begins to become explicit when analytic philosophers mutter about the "irrationalism" which rages in literature departments and when Continental philosophers become shrill about the lack of "human significance" in the works of the analysts. It is the difference between the intellectual who believes that something like the "application of scientific method" is the best hope of human freedom and the intellectual who, with Foucault and Heidegger, sees this notion of "scientific method" as the mask behind which lurks the cruelty and despair of a nihilistic age. It comes out when analytic philosophers remark that Carnap emigrated while Heidegger joined the Nazi Party, or that Russell saw through Stalinism and Sartre did not, or that Rawls shares the ordinary civilized hope for the rule of law and Foucault does not. It helps explain why Kripke and Kuhn and Rawls are all somehow working the same side of the street, even though their interests hardly overlap, while Heidegger and Foucault and Derrida are working the other, even though they discuss wildly different topics.

One can call this a *political* split because both sides think of themselves as looking out for the interests of the global *polis*, as the leaders who must make articulate to their fellow-citizens the dangers of the time. Further, this division into the "scientific" and the "unscientific" intellectuals is related in all sorts of ways to all sorts of issues which are "political" in narrower and more familiar senses. Rather than pursue these issues, however, I simply want to suggest that we keep pragmatic tolerance going as long as we can—that both sides see the other as honest, if misguided, colleagues, doing their best to bring light to a dark time. In particular, we should remind ourselves that although there *are* relations between academic politics and real politics, they are not tight enough to justify carrying the passions of the latter over into the former.

Notes

1. Hans Reichenbach, *The Rise of Scientific Philosophy* (Berkeley: University of California Press, 1951). All further references to Reichenbach are to pages or chapters of this book, and will be inserted in the text.

2. See chap. 18 for Reichenbach's insistence that the renunciation of attempts at a synthetic a priori is the mark of scientific philosophy, and his diagnosis of philosophers who wish to incorporate the results of scientific philosophy "into an introductory chapter of science and claim that there exists an independent philosophy, which has no concern with scientific research and has direct access to truth" (p. 305).

3. See Janice Moulton, "A Paradigm of Philosophy: The Adversary Method" in *Discovering Reality*, ed. S. Harding and M. Hintikka, 1983. This is a very good account of the juristic way in which analytic philosophers have tended to think of their discipline. Moulton rightly remarks that "Within the Adversary Paradigm we understand earlier philosophers as if they were addressing adversaries instead of trying to build a foundation for scientific reasoning and to explain human nature. Philosophers who cannot be recast into an adversarial mold are likely to be ignored. But our reinterpretations may be misinterpretations, and our choice of great philosophers may be based not so much on what they said as on how we think they said it." In saying that, "In general the inability to win a public debate is not a good reason for giving up a belief," Moulton is taking a position which accords with Robert Nozick's. (See the "Introduction" to Nozick's *Philosophical Explanations* [Cambridge, Mass.: Harvard University Press, 1981].) Moulton and Nozick are evidence of a certain discomfort with the analytic philosopher's usual way of life, and perhaps of the beginnings of something new.

Index

Index

Richard Rorty is Kenan Professor of Humanities at the University of Virginia. He has taught at Wellesley and, from 1961 to 1982, at Princeton University, where he was Stuart Professor of Philosophy. Rorty is the author of *Philosophy and the Mirror of Nature* and editor of *The Linguistic Turn: Recent Essays in Philosophical Method.* In 1979 he served as president of the Eastern Division, American Philosophical Association.